JEFF LEMIRE: CONVERSATIONS

**Conversations with Comic Artists** M. Thomas Inge, General Editor

# Jeff Lemire: Conversations

Edited by Dale Jacobs

University Press of Mississippi • Jackson

The University Press of Mississippi is the scholarly publishing agency of
the Mississippi Institutions of Higher Learning: Alcorn State University,
Delta State University, Jackson State University, Mississippi State University,
Mississippi University for Women, Mississippi Valley State University,
University of Mississippi, and University of Southern Mississippi.

www.upress.state.ms.us

The University Press of Mississippi is a member of the Association of University Presses.

First printing 2022
∞

Harback ISBN 978-1-4968-3909-1
Trade paperback ISBN 978-1-4968-3910-7
Epub single ISBN 978-1-4968-3911-4
Epub institutional ISBN 978-1-4968-3912-1
PDF single ISBN 978-1-4968-3913-8
PDF institutional ISBN 978-1-4968-3914-5

British Library Cataloging-in-Publication Data available

# Major Works by Jeff Lemire

(as both writer and artist unless otherwise noted)

*Ashtray* #1–2 (2003)

*Lost Dogs* (2005)

*Tales from the Farm* (subsequently known as *Essex County Vol. 1: Tales from the Farm*) (2007)

*Essex County Vol. 2: Ghost Stories* (2007)

*Essex County Vol. 3: The Country Nurse* (2008)

*The Complete Essex County* (2009)

*The Nobody* (2009)

*Sweet Tooth* #1–40 (2009–2013)

*Adventure Comics* #516–21 (2010–11), writer on Atom backup feature

*Superboy* vol. 5, #1–11 (2010–11), writer

*Flashpoint: Frankenstein and the Creatures of the Unknown* #1–3 (2011), writer

*Frankenstein: Agent of S.H.A.D.E.* #1–9 (2011–12), writer

*Animal Man* vol. 2, #1–29 (2011–14), writer

*National Comics: Eternity* (2012), writer

*The Underwater Welder* (2012)

*Justice League Dark* #7–23 (2012–13), writer

*Constantine* #1–6 (2013), writer

*Trillium* (2013–14)

*Green Arrow* vol. 5, #17–34 (2013–14), writer

*Teen Titans: Earth One* (2014), writer

*Justice League United* #0–10 (2014–15), writer

*The New 52: Futures End* #0–48 (2014–15), one of several writers

*The Valiant* #1–4 (2014–15), writer

*All-New Hawkeye* vol. 1, #1–5 (2015), writer

*All-New Hawkeye* vol. 2, #1–6 (2015–16), writer

*Bloodshot Reborn* #0–18, Annual #1 (2015–16), writer

*Plutona* #1–5 (2015–16), writer

*Extraordinary X-Men* #1–20 (2015–17), writer

*Descender* #1–32 (2015–18), writer

*Death of X* #1–4 (2016), writer

*Secret Path* (2016), artist

*Bloodshot U.S.A.* #1–4 (2016–17), writer

*Old Man Logan* vol. 2, #1–24 (2016–17), writer

*Moon Knight* vol. 8, #1–14 (2016–17), writer

*Thanos* vol. 2, #1–11 (2016–17), writer
*A.D.: After Death* #1–3 (2016–17), artist
*Black Hammer* #1–13 (2016–17), writer
*Roughneck* (2017)
*Royal City* #1–14 (2017–18)
*Bloodshot Salvation* #1–12 (2017–18), writer
*Sherlock Frankenstein and the Legion of Evil* #1–4 (2017–18), writer
*The Sentry* #1–5 (2018), writer
*Doctor Star and the Kingdom of Lost Tomorrows* #1–4 (2018), writer
*Black Hammer: Age of Doom* #1–12 (2018–19), writer
*The Quantum Age* #1–6 (2018–19), writer
*Gideon Falls* #1-ongoing (2018–present), writer
*Frogcatchers* (2019)
*Black Hammer/Justice League: Hammer of Justice* #1–5 (2019), writer
*Inferior Five* #1–4 (2019–20), writer
*Joker: Killer Smile* (2019–20), writer
*Skulldigger and Skeleton Boy* #1–6 (2019–20), writer
*Ascender* #1-ongoing (2019–present), writer
*Family Tree* #1-ongoing (2019–present), writer
*The Question: The Deaths of Vic Sage* (2020), writer
*Sweet Tooth: The Return* #1–6 (2020–21)

# CONTENTS

# INTRODUCTION

In a 2019 interview with the webzine *DC in the 80s*, Jeff Lemire discusses the comics he read as a child growing up in Essex County, Ontario: his early exposure to reprints of Silver Age DC material, how influential *Crisis on Infinite Earths* and DC's *Who's Who* were on him as a developing comics fan, his first reading of *Watchmen* and *The Dark Knight Returns*, and his transition to reading the first wave of Vertigo titles when he was sixteen. In other interviews, he describes discovering independent comics when he moved to Toronto, days of browsing comics at the Beguiling, and coming to understand what was possible in the medium of comics, lessons he would take to heart as he began to establish himself as a cartoonist.

Discussions of how a cartoonist was introduced to the medium of comics are not at all unusual. Questions of one's history with comics and the influences that can be seen in one's work filter into countless interviews. Many cartoonists deflect from such questions, while others indulge the interview briefly before attempting to steer the questions in another direction. But Lemire seems to bask in these discussions, going so far as to say, at the end of his interview with *DC in the 80s*, "This is the most fun I've ever had with an interview." His love for DC comics as he was growing up comes up over and over in these interviews; before he was ever a comics professional, he was a fan.

What can be traced in these interviews is the story of the movement from comics fan to comics professional. The story of the maturation of a professional cartoonist and writer, and the growing confidence that accompanies that maturation. The story of a working professional in the comics industry finding a balance between his work for Marvel and DC and his creator-owned, independent work, before finally moving on from work-for-hire to focus on his own creations.

These overlapping stories begin after he left film school and turned his attention seriously to comics in 2001. In a 2013 interview with Tom Spurgeon, Lemire recounts these early days of becoming a cartoonist: "I was pretty much in a vacuum; I had no idea how the industry worked: just distributing your stuff in the Diamond catalog, I had no idea how that worked. No concept at that. Doing the Xeric Grant really made me research that, and figure that side of things out." At the time, Lemire was drawing during the day and working as a cook at night, barely able to pay the rent. As he tells Spurgeon, "I would never have been able to afford printing things or getting something together without [the Xeric grant]. That was a really huge step for me." The grant allowed him to self-publish *Lost Dogs* in 2005, a project in which Lemire's nascent creative vision began to take shape. Even as early as the 2007 Top Shelf publication of *Tales from the Farm*, about which Lemire talks extensively in these interviews, the growing confidence in his evocative use of line and his ability to convey emotion through the narrative medium of comics are both apparent.

Loneliness, outsiders, and small towns—themes that have become hallmarks of much of Lemire's work, especially the comics both written and drawn by him—can all be seen in his early books, such as *Essex County* and *The Nobody*, while ideas of fatherhood begin to appear with the publication of *The Underwater Welder*. In the interviews collected here, Lemire often returns to these themes, answering questions from a number of interviewers about how and why he continually engages with these ideas in his work, circling around the ways in which they appear not only in his more realistic work—including in more recent work such as *Roughneck* and *Royal City*—but also in genre work, such as *Sweet Tooth*. In a 2010 interview with David Harper, Lemire forcefully makes the point: "*Sweet Tooth* is just as personal to me as *Essex* was. The surface elements are slightly more artificial. I'm filtering my themes and ideas through a genre now, and using that to amplify certain things, but in the end those sci-fi and horror elements are just metaphors, just like hockey was in *Essex*." This idea that *Sweet Tooth* is just as personal as his other solo work is one to which Lemire returns over and over in these early interviews, just as he continually reasserts his use of genre (including superheroes, various kinds of science fiction, and horror) as a metaphorical means for dealing with the themes important to him, not only in his solo creative work, but also in his collaborative work-for-hire and creator-owned work.

As well, interviewers return again and again to the way hockey appears in much of Lemire's work as a solo cartoonist. In talking about his use of hockey with JP Fallavollita in 2009, Lemire says, "I also think it is a very big part of the Canadian identity, so I used it as a central metaphor in [*Essex County*]." A few years later, in response to a question from Spurgeon about *Essex County*'s inclusion in Canada Reads, Lemire expands on the importance of his Canadian identity: "It is very much in the tradition of Canadian literature, I think, people like Margaret Laurence. It's firmly set in my Canadian experience. I take a lot of pride in being Canadian and being a Canadian storyteller." When Spurgeon presses him about whether there is a Canadian style of cartooning that also encompasses a formal approach to the medium, Lemire answers, "I don't think there's a 'Canadian style.' [*laughter*] I think it's more in the subject matter and how the stories have a connection to the landscape—the land itself is almost a character in my work. It's more that than a formal approach." No matter how many other projects Lemire takes on as he becomes more and more successful in both work-for-hire and creator-owned collaborations, throughout these interviews we see Lemire's commitment to the unique vision that he cultivates through his solo creator-owned work.

In the earliest interview in the volume, conducted by Val D'Orazio in 2007, Lemire says, "I would absolutely love to draw and write a mainstream comic for Marvel or DC." By 2010, having published the graphic novels *Essex County* with Top Shelf and *The Nobody* with Vertigo and already nearly a year into his monthly title, *Sweet Tooth*, Lemire hints to David Harper that he has upcoming work at Marvel and DC. After a short stint writing a backup Atom feature for *Adventure Comics*, Lemire was assigned *Superboy*, a title in which he explored Superboy's relationship with Smallville, an approach he discusses in his 2011 interview with Ed Gross and that certainly fits in with thematic concerns seen in titles such as *Essex County*, *The Nobody*, and, to some extent, *Sweet Tooth*.

By the time of his 2012 interview with Kyle Lemmon, entitled "The Beauty of Collaboration," it is clear that Lemire has become much more comfortable with the collaborative process and with working within the structure of a large company. Responding to a question from Lemmon about *The Atom* and *Superboy*, Lemire says, "[I]t was an adjustment for all of *The Atom*, and the first half of the *Superboy* run. That was the first time I was writing for another artist. Up until that point I'd been doing comics for quite a while, but had always drawn my own stuff. It was a very different experience for me. It was also the first time working with characters that I didn't completely know or control. There were a lot of factors during that first year. I was sort of learning as I went along." In another 2012 interview (with Oliver Sacks), Lemire expands on these ideas, noting, "I'm so used to working on my own stuff that when I started writing *Superboy*, I was a little too specific in my art direction. I kept wanting to maintain too much control over the artists. As a result, it came out a bit stiffer than if I'd let the artists breathe and do their own thing. So when I went on to *Animal Man* and *Frankenstein*, I really kept myself away from the visual aspect of it. I just focused on character and plot and let them completely control the visual side." In these and other interviews, Lemire points to the importance of *Animal Man* and his work with Travel Foreman as a turning point for him as a writer. What he learned on those initial collaborative efforts can be traced through not only Lemire's work for DC and Marvel, but in the many creator-owned collaborations that would follow.

In 2014, Lemire created Equinox as part of his work for DC on *Justice League United*. In an interview that year with Waaseyaa'Sin Christine Sy for *Maissoneuve*, Lemire discusses his burgeoning interest in and awareness of Indigenous issues in Canada, claiming that he created Equinox as "a good way to create a project that was accessible to young people who are in other communities, just to start to scratch the surface of other cultures that are out there and hopefully create something that's a positive representation." When asked by Sy "if the storyline reflects the realities of Indigenous peoples," Lemire delineates the realities of working for one of the mainstream publishers:

> I'll be perfectly honest; it's very hard for me to get too political in a superhero comic book published by an American publisher. They're interested in me telling an entertaining story, a superhero comic, so there are certain limitations, clearly, in what I can show and I didn't really get into it in depth; it was a matter of choosing my battles. So for me, the battle I knew I could win was in creating this character, and creating a character that was full of life and positive and that would be something hopefully young people would enjoy and can hopefully educate them a little bit about Cree culture. I knew if I could do that, this would be a victory. Going beyond that is a little out of the bounds on this project but it is something I am exploring in other projects currently.

Those projects would come to fruition with the publication in 2015 of *Secret Path*, a project written by Gord Downie and drawn by Lemire, and in 2016 of *Roughneck*. By the time that Lemire was interviewed by Tom Power for CBC's *Q*, the surety of purpose that he had shown in his creation of Equinox had waned considerably, as seen in this exchange with Power:

> **Power:** [S]ome of the more interesting things, conversations, that happened around *Secret Path* were you and Gord talking about how in many ways this wasn't your story to tell. And you had to be very cautious in the way that you told it. *Roughneck* again deals with Indigenous issues. I should say if you're listening to this on the radio not watching it, you're not an Indigenous person, you're a white person

from Southern Ontario. What do you see as your role in speaking about Indigenous issues in your work?

**Lemire:** I don't know that I have a role. And I don't even know if we should have done the books to be honest with you.

**Power:** Do you ever feel that way?

**Lemire:** I always feel that way, yeah. It's not my story to tell. None of these stories are.

**Power:** So what keeps you doing it?

**Lemire:** Because you get it in your head, you fall in love with the story, and you just have to do it for better or for worse. It's not going to let you go, you know. This character of Derek and his sister come to life inside me and just like Chaney, the fictional version of Chaney did. And once they're in there you just got to get it out, so.

**Power:** What a strange feeling that must be to work so hard on something and then release it and then go, "I don't really know if I should be putting this out?"

**Lemire:** Well, yeah it is strange. And it's something new for me because I really don't feel like these are my stories to tell. But at the same time, you look at the impact *Secret Path* has had and the fact that it's going to be in I think every school in Ontario next year and you'll have all these children learning about residential schools who had never heard of them before. Gord and I grew up not learning about them in school at all, which is why we wanted to do it in the first place. And then you look at that and I think, "Well, it was worth it, you know." Maybe it's not my story to tell but it's done some good and also the fact that Chaney's family, the Wenjak sisters, embraced us and endorsed the project and supported everything we did, it makes me feel like it's okay that we did it. If his family's okay with it then I'm okay with it.

There is a profound change in the stance that Lemire takes in these two interviews as he thinks through ideas of representation and cultural appropriation, part of the maturation process that we see throughout these interviews.

By 2015, Lemire was firmly established as a writer for hire, having worked extensively with DC during their New 52 relaunch. Through this rise within the industry, he had continued to produce creator-owned material, including *Sweet Tooth*, *The Underwater Welder*, and *Trillium*. In 2015, Lemire not only signed an exclusive writing deal with Marvel—initially on *All-New Hawkeye* and *Extraordinary X-Men*—but also began to form collaborative partnerships on a number of creator-owned titles. Those partnerships began with two titles published by Image Comics: the miniseries *Plutona*, for which he teamed with Emi Lenox, and the ongoing series *Descender*, a cocreation with Dustin Nguyen. Other collaborations quickly followed: *Black Hammer*, with Dean Ormston, *Secret Path*, with Gord Downie, and *A.D.: After Death*, with Scott Snyder, in 2016; *Gideon Falls*, with Andrea Sorrentino, in 2018; and *Family Tree*, with Phil Hester, in 2019.

In the interviews collected here, Lemire talks extensively about these collaborative relationships in ways that emphasize the stance towards working collaboratively that he developed during his time with Travel Foreman on *Animal Man*. For example, during a 2015 interview that both Lemire and Nguyen did with Karin Kross, Lemire addresses the collaborative relationship: "I write the scripts and he just draws them; we don't even communicate or anything. I just trust him completely. . . . We don't get in each other's way at all; we have complete trust. I think we both have a huge amount of respect for one another in what we do and we just want each other to do that, and it just comes together perfectly." Similar formulations of his working relationships with other collaborators can be seen in interviews that focus on individual books.

The way that Lemire came to collaborate with Dean Ormston on the creation of the Black Hammer Universe stands as a useful example of his career trajectory. When asked by Sarah Elizabeth Camp in 2016 about the forthcoming *Black Hammer* and "writing a superhero narrative that is entirely new," Lemire responds,

> I actually came up with *Black Hammer* back in 2007–2008 as I was finishing my *Essex County* graphic novels. At the time I planned on doing it as my own next graphic novel that I would write and draw. Back then, I was still only doing indie comics and I never anticipated a day when I would actually be working on mainstream superhero comics like I am now. So *Black Hammer* was sort of my way of expressing my love for the superhero genre, but filtering it through my own indie style. Then, as things developed in my career, *Black Hammer* got put on the backburner so I could focus on doing *Sweet Tooth* at Vertigo. And, that also led to me writing a lot of mainstream superhero comics since then. But I never forgot *Black Hammer* and would pull it out and tinker with it once a year or so. But it became obvious that I would never have time to draw it myself, with all the other projects I have lined up to draw now, so I started thinking of doing it with a collaborator.

As Lemire was finishing *The Nobody* for Vertigo, his editor, Bob Schreck, asked him to pitch a monthly series. Lemire proposed *Sweet Tooth*, which he had initially planned as a series of graphic novels. At the time, as Lemire related to Noel Murray in 2011, he did not expect to be doing much more work for DC, either for the Vertigo imprint or in the main superhero line. When *Sweet Tooth* was greenlit within a week, Lemire jumped at the chance to work on the monthly series. By the time he returned to the concept that would become the Black Hammer universe, he was established both in the world of superheroes and in the world of indie comics. By that time, his schedule precluded him from both writing and drawing a monthly book, but since he had productively adjusted to the collaborative process in a variety of situations, he was ready and willing to work with Ormston on a new superhero universe that drew from the history of the genre.

The fact that Lemire is able to have one foot in the work-for-hire world and one in the independent, creator-owned world is a topic that comes up regularly in these interviews. In a 2013 interview with Øyvind Holen, Lemire addresses the reasons that he feels comfortable in both spheres: "I feel that my generation grew up reading both superhero stuff *and* independent comics, and as we developed and emerged as creators the boundaries between genre work and more personal comics went away. I don't know why, but today you see that there is just as much genre stuff in indie comics, being treated in an interesting way as slice-of-life stories and personal stories. At the same time, I feel like more and more independent writers and artists are also doing superhero stuff, everything seems to be blending together and the walls are falling down." It is clearly a question Lemire had often been asked and one that would continue to appear in subsequent interviews.

The questions around how he balances his work with Ormston and other collaborators, and his solo work on creator-owned titles with his work-for-hire writing for Marvel, DC, and Valiant follow two paths: the logistical and the creative. Interviewers want to know, in sheer logistical terms, how Lemire is so productive across his various projects. They want to know how he structures his day and his week. They want to know his secrets to time management. In his answers to these logistical questions, Lemire explains that he separates his home and work life by maintaining a studio several blocks away from the family apartment. He tells several interviewers that he draws Monday to Friday during the day and focuses on scripts in the evenings and on weekends. His answers show the discipline that he brings to his work and the way that this professional work ethic has served and continues to serve him well.

In creative terms, interviewers want to know about what he is able to accomplish in artistic and narrative terms in each of these situations. They want to know what pressures come to bear in both cases and how those pressures affect the work. They want to know how much editorial oversight there is when working with the mainstream companies and how that changes his writing in comparison to the internal creative oversight of his solo and collaborative creator-owned work. Since beginning to write for DC in 2010, Lemire's answers to these questions seemed carefully calibrated, especially when talking to interviewers who were clearly more interested and engaged in the mainstream side of the equation. But by 2017, Lemire is no longer so sanguine about work-for-hire and clearly much more interested in his creator-owned projects, as evidenced by this exchange with Andrea Fiamma:

> **Fiamma:** Is it stressing different muscles writing personal works vs. work-for-hire?
>
> **Lemire:** I guess so. I try to approach it the same way; what makes the Marvel stuff successful for me is that I try to bring the same amount of myself to it that I bring to my creator-owned works. I hate to separate them, because you start creating work that feels artificial or forced. But, I mean, by the nature they tend to be a little different, a little more freedom on your work, take the story wherever you want, don't have to get approval every time. I think that freedom gives you a bit of confidence that helps you.
>
> **Fiamma:** Doing superhero stuff gives you the same pleasure?
>
> **Lemire:** To be honest, I grew up reading superhero comics and I love them. I was really excited to write stuff for Marvel and DC for the first few years that I did it, but lately I'm feeling burnout on it, so I think I'm gonna move away from that stuff and just do creator-owned.
>
> And then all the superhero stories that I wanna do, I can kinda do them in *Black Hammer* now, which is my own superhero universe. I'm in a really good spot where I can finally take a break from that stuff. It was fun for a few years, but now it's starting to feel like work and I don't like that.

That balance of mainstream and independent, work-for-hire and creator-owned was coming to an end. In 2019, Lemire told Matt O'Keefe that he didn't see any more work for Marvel or DC in his immediate future.

Having fulfilled his childhood dreams of writing the superheroes he grew up reading in Essex County, Lemire was, by the time of the 2019 interviews, fully invested in his creator-owned work, both collaborative and solo. In the interviews collected here, we see him come to understand the process of collaboration, the balancing act involved in working for different kinds of comics publishers, the responsibilities involved in representing characters outside his own culture, and the possibilities that exist in the comics medium. We see him embrace a variety of genres, using each of them to explore the issues and themes most important to him. And we see a cartoonist and a writer growing in confidence—a working professional coming into his own.

# CHRONOLOGY

1976  Born in Essex County, Ontario.

1995  Begins film school at Ryerson University in Toronto.

2005  Wins a Xeric Grant to aid in the publication of *Lost Dogs*. Graduates from the Advanced Illustration Program at Sheridan College.

2007  Publishes *Tales from the Farm*, the book that would become the first volume of *Essex County*, with Top Shelf. Publishes *Ghost Stories*, the second volume of *Essex County*.

2008  Publishes *The Country Nurse*, the third volume of *Essex County*. Wins a Joe Shuster Award for Outstanding Cartoonist, a Doug Wright Award for Emerging Talent, and an American Library Association Alex Award for the first two volumes of *Essex County*.

2009  Top Shelf issues *The Complete Essex County*. Publishes *The Nobody* with Vertigo and begins serial publication of *Sweet Tooth*, which will continue for forty issues. Begins to map out the ideas that will become *Black Hammer*.

2010  Signs an exclusive writing deal with DC, beginning with The Atom and Superboy.

2011  *Essex County* is selected for Canada Reads, the first graphic novel ever selected. As one of the writers for DC's New 52, begins to write *Animal Man* and *Frankenstein: Agent of S.H.A.D.E.*

2012  Publishes *The Underwater Welder* with Top Shelf. Nominated for Eisner Award for Best Writer.

2013  Begins publication of *Trillium* with Vertigo and begins writing *Green Arrow* for DC.

2014  Creates Equinox, a teenage Cree superhero, for DC Comics during his run on *Justice League United*. Begins to write for Valiant Comics.

2015  Signs an exclusive writing deal with Marvel, beginning with *All-New Hawkeye* and *Extraordinary X-Men*. Begins collaboration (as writer) with Dustin Nguyen on *Descender*, an ongoing series published by Image.

Begins collaboration (as writer) with Emi Lenox on *Plutona*, a five-issue miniseries published by Image.

2016   Begins collaboration (as writer) with Dean Ormston on *Black Hammer*, the launching point for the ongoing Black Hammer Universe, published by Dark Horse. Collaborates (as artist) with Gord Downie on *Secret Path*, a graphic novel published by Simon & Schuster. Collaborates (as artist) with Scott Snyder on *A.D.: After Death*, a three-issue miniseries published by Image. Begins writing *Old Man Logan*, *Moon Knight*, and *Thanos* for Marvel.

2017   Wins an Eisner Award for Best New Series (with Dean Ormston) for *Black Hammer*. Publishes *Roughneck* with Pocket Books. Begins publication of *Royal City* with Image. Publishes (with David Rubin) *Sherlock Frankenstein and the Legion of Evil*, the first of the books in the expanded Black Hammer Universe. Begins working (as writer and showrunner) with First Generation Films and CBC to adapt *Essex County* for television.

2018   Begins collaboration (as writer) with Andrea Sorrentino on *Gideon Falls*, an ongoing series published by Image. In collaboration with various artists, begins publication of *Doctor Star and the Kingdom of Lost Tomorrows* (Max Fiumara), *Black Hammer: Age of Doom* (Dean Ormston), and *The Quantum Age* (Wilfredo Torres), as part of the expanded Black Hammer Universe.

2019   Nominated for Eisner Awards for Best Writer, Best New Series (*Gideon Falls*), Best Continuing Series (*Black Hammer: Age of Doom*), and Single Issue/One-Shot (*Black Hammer: Cthu-Louise*). Publishes *Frogcatchers* with Gallery 13. In collaboration (as writer) with Michael Walsh, publishes *Black Hammer/Justice League: Hammer of Justice* with Dark Horse and DC. Begins collaboration (as writer) with Dustin Nguyen on *Ascender*, the follow-up series to *Descender*, an ongoing series with Image. Begins collaboration (as writer) with Phil Hester on *Family Tree*, an ongoing series with Image.

2020   Begins serial publication of *Sweet Tooth: The Return*, a six-issue miniseries. Filming begins on the Netflix adaptation of *Sweet Tooth*.

JEFF LEMIRE: CONVERSATIONS

# Occasional Interviews:
## *Tales from the Farm*'s Jeff Lemire

VAL D'ORAZIO / 2007

*Occasional Superheroine*, October 9, 2007. Reprinted by permission.

I met Jeff Lemire during the MoCCA festival last summer at the Top Shelf booth and bought a copy of his *Essex County Vol. 1: Tales from the Farm* graphic novel on the spot.

This week, the sequel, *Essex County Vol. 2: Ghost Stories*, is coming out, and to mark the occasion I thought an interview with the Canadian artist might be in order. And don't forget to check out the six-page preview of *Ghost Stories* at the end of the article!

**Val D'Orazio:** What was your first professional comic book gig?

**Jeff Lemire:** Five pages of *Beowulf*, from the now defunct Speakeasy Comics (for which I was never paid!)

**D'Orazio:** There is a very memoir-like feel to *Tales from the Farm*. Is the book at all autobiographical?

**Lemire:** I grew up in the "real" Essex County, on a farm much like the characters in my books. The settings are very much real, but the characters, plots, and themes are mostly fictional.

**D'Orazio:** There seems to be a Jack Kirby-like influence in the design of the character Jimmy—he seems almost reminiscent of Rocky from *Challengers of the Unknown*. Were you a fan of Kirby's work?

**Lemire:** Wow, I never thought about the Kirby-look of Jimmy before. It's funny, at the time I wrote and drew *Tales*, I wasn't really into Kirby. I was always more of a DC Silver Age fan—Kubert, Infantino, and Kane. But recently I have started to look at more Kirby. So, no, at the time Jimmy wasn't directly influenced by the King, but I can totally see it in the big blocky fingers, etc. I guess Kirby's shadow is so big that as a comic artist you're standing in it even when you don't realize you are.

**D'Orazio:** Was the comic book that Lester drew in *Tales from the Farm*, a real book you drew as a child?

**Lemire:** Yeah, I drew that when I was eight or nine years old. I found it around the time I was working on *Tales* and wrote it into the book. I have a couple of other comics I did around that time, a lot of them are my own version of DC's original *Who's Who* series, which I was obsessed with as a kid. If Top Shelf ever does a collected version of the *Essex County* books, maybe I can include more of Lester's work in the bonus features.

**D'Orazio:** *Tales from the Farm* seems to be a book about defining the real "heroes" in one's life. What is your definition or example of a hero?

**Lemire:** Anyone who does what they love, and does it for their own sake, and not by anyone else's agenda. Whether it be a musician, comic artist, athlete, doctor, plumber, farmer, whatever.

**D'Orazio:** Would you ever try your hand at drawing a mainstream superhero comic, given the opportunity? If so, which character would you like to draw?

**Lemire:** I would absolutely love to draw and write a mainstream comic for Marvel or DC. I would love to take a crack at Hellblazer, The Unknown Soldier, Green Lantern, Captain America. As I said, I love all the old Silver and Bronze Age DC stuff.

**D'Orazio:** How has been your experience working for Top Shelf? Do you feel they have supported your vision on this project?

**Lemire:** Chris Staros and Brett Warnok at Top Shelf have been incredible. They are the most generous guys I could ever want to work with. They create a real family-like feel at shows, and whenever we get together. I've made a lot of new friends among other Top Shelfers like Jeffrey Brown, Matt Kindt, David Yurkivich. They have been nothing but supportive of by work, and letting me do what I want.

**D'Orazio:** Your new book, out this month, is called *Ghost Stories*. It is titled as Volume 2 of the *Essex County* series, of which *Tales from the Farm* is Volume 1. Are both stories related—do the characters exist in the same general space? And can you tell us something about *Ghost Stories*?

**Lemire:** *Ghost Stories* is the second in a trilogy of books all set in Essex County, this fictionalized version of my own hometown. The characters all interconnect and the books all tie together thematically. *Ghost Stories* follows the lives of Jimmy's Grandfather and Great Uncle as they go to play hockey in Toronto in the 1950s, right up until there last days as old men on the farm.

**D'Orazio:** What's next for you after *Ghost Stories*?

*Tales from the Farm*, page 2. Credit: Jeff Lemire.

**Lemire:** I am currently working on the third volume of the trilogy, *The Country Nurse*. I should be done drawing it before Christmas, for a 2008 release. I am writing my next graphic novel as well, which I will start drawing in 2008 for an eventual release with Top Shelf. I'm also pitching another sci-fi project with Noel Tuazon (Elk's Run) around. We'll see what happens.

**D'Orazio:** Thanks for the interview, Jeff!

# A Sweet Tooth for Comics and Hockey—
# JP Interviews Writer/Artist Jeff Lemire

## JP FALLAVOLLITA / 2009

*Biff Bam Pop!*, August 19, 2009. Reprinted by permission.

Jeff Lemire has had a busy 2009. The Toronto-based comic book writer and artist, previous winner of both the Shuster and Doug Wright Awards, was nominated for an Eisner Award for his *Essex County* trilogy. The graphic novel was collected this month as both a hardcover and softcover compilation by Top Shelf Productions. Vertigo Comics, the more mature, more sophisticated imprint of DC Comics, recently published his original hardcover graphic novel, *The Nobody*, an alternate take on H. G. Wells's classic Invisible Man character. It was his first work for a major comic book publisher. In another first, this September sees the release of Lemire's ongoing monthly series, *Sweet Tooth*, also published by Vertigo.

In-between convention appearances, instore signings, and drawing sessions, I was able to catch up with one of comicdom's rising talents and ask him via email about his work, his influences, and his new series.

**JP Fallavollita:** In your work, your love for comics is evident both in the writing and in the drawing. What comics were you reading while growing up? What was it about them that captured your attention?

**Jeff Lemire:** As a kid I loved everything DC. I think this was brought on by the publication of both *Crisis on Infinite Earths* and *Who's Who*, when I was nine or ten. Those two books opened my eyes to the *massive* cast and complex multiple worlds of the DCU, and I was hooked. *Who's Who*, in particular, featured original artwork by just about every comic book artist in the industry at the time, so it was really valuable for me in terms of seeing the diverse styles of cartooning out there and learning what kind of art I did and didn't like.

George Perez was an early favorite. This led to my love affair with *The New Teen Titans*. Later I got hooked on *The Legion of Superheroes*, and fell in love with Keith Giffen's art.

**Fallavollita:** As both a writer and an artist, who are some of your main influences?

**Lemire:** To me I don't really separate writing and art because they are all a part of the same process: storytelling. I would say my main influences are David Lynch, Alan Moore, John Steinbeck, Nick Cave, H. G. Wells, Wim Wenders, Stanley Kubrick, Tom Waits, Eddie Campbell, Jack Kirby, Joe Kubert.

**Fallavollita:** Lester, the cape- and mask-wearing boy from the *Essex County* trilogy, writes and draws his own comics. In volume 1, there's a great scene where he shares his "Heroes and Villains" comic starring the characters of "Night Bird" and "Powerman" with Jimmy Lebeuf, and in volume 3, he's seen working on a "Captain Canada" comic. I imagine this is something you yourself did often as a child?

**Lemire:** Those were in fact my childhood comics reprinted as the character's. I actually have a half dozen more of those including my own *Who's Who* type encyclopedia featuring hundreds of invented superheroes.

**Fallavollita:** Hockey plays an important part in the *Essex County* stories. You've even got your bio on the back page of the book, designed as a "hockey card," which I thought was inspired. "Jeff has an outstanding shot from the point." Hockey plays an important part of your life, doesn't it?

**Lemire:** Aside from comics, my passion is hockey. Watching it, playing it, and reading about it. Ken Dryden's book *The Game* is one of my favorite books period. Making comics is a very time-intensive process, and hockey provides me with an escape. I also think it is a very big part of the Canadian identity, so I used it as a central metaphor in the book.

**Fallavollita:** *Essex County* has drawings of big, sweeping landscapes. It has been said that landscape is an important character in Canadian storytelling, and this idea seems important to you, too. What is it about landscapes?

**Lemire:** I think it is, in some ways, a romanticized view of where I grew up, and in other ways a colder, starker version as well. The way all the characters know each other, and their lives intertwine so neatly is obviously a bit idealized and manipulated to tell a "complete" story. In the real world, everyone is connected, but in much less obvious and thematic ways. Also, visually, I took the things I loved the most about the Essex County landscape (old, rusted farm equipment, tattered wooden barns, vast open fields, endless telephone lines running off into the horizon) and focused on these, almost creating an idealized, almost timeless visual shorthand for the setting. I ignored many things I didn't find particularly appealing, like the suburban sprawl and big-box retail that is slowly creeping in.

**Fallavollita:** You've got *Sweet Tooth* coming up at the end of the summer for DC's Vertigo Comics imprint which is your first monthly series. How did that project come about?

**Lemire:** As I was ending my work on *The Nobody*, I wanted to pitch a few more ideas to Vertigo. As you can tell from my previous answers, I am a bit of a fanboy, so the idea of doing my own monthly comic is a dream come true. I had a few ideas percolating that eventually merged into *Sweet Tooth*. It's my take on the well-worn genre of postapocalyptic fiction. But I really think it is an original and personal story with lots of action, adventure, horror, and human emotion.

**Fallavollita:** As *Sweet Tooth*'s release gets closer and with buzz surrounding *The Nobody*, anticipation for your first monthly series is growing and growing. You were even a panelist at this year's Comic Con in San Diego. Do you get a sense of that at all? Excited?

**Lemire:** I'm so busy working on the book and juggling being a new father that I don't have time to worry about anything else. I honestly just try to make each page and each issue better than the last, that's all I can control. The rest of it, the buzz, the press, the sales, etc. . . . I try not to think about all of that, or let it influence my work. But, yes, obviously this is a very exciting time for me.

**Fallavollita:** What themes will *Sweet Tooth* encompass?

**Lemire:** It's about fathers and sons, it's about redemption, it's about family, it's about the friendships that can form in even the darkest of places, and it's about holding onto hope in a hopeless world.

**Fallavollita:** You're about six or seven issues into the series already—you're moving at a pretty brisk pace! What's surprised you about the series so far?

**Lemire:** How unbelievably bloody it is. It's turning out to be full of brutal violence. That might be a real shock to fans of my *Essex County* work. Yet, I think it's all still very grounded in friendship and the quiet human moments that those books had. But in some ways I think that makes the violence even more shocking. Diamond actually turned down our first preview pages for PREVIEWS because it was too bloody!

**Fallavollita:** Getting away from your own creator-owned work, if there was one character you could write and draw a story around, who might it be?

**Lemire:** I love The Doom Patrol, and if all goes well you may see me draw them sooner than you think. And, I also love all of the Golden Age DC heroes. I'd *love* to do an Hourman/Dr. Midnight/Atom miniseries set in the forties.

# Jeff Lemire On DC/Vertigo's *The Nobody* & *Sweet Tooth*

## ROGER ASH / 2009

*Westfield Comics Blog*. Reprinted by permission.

Jeff Lemire is the creator of the *Essex County* trilogy. His graphic novel, *The Nobody*, was recently published by DC Comics/Vertigo and his new ongoing series, *Sweet Tooth*, is coming from Vertigo this September. Westfield's Roger Ash recently spoke with Lemire to learn more about these projects.

**Roger Ash:** What was the inspiration for *The Nobody*?

**Jeff Lemire:** I've always been a fan of H. G. Wells's books. When I was younger, *The Time Machine* and *The Invisible Man* were probably the first books I read. They left a pretty big impression on me as a reader. I've gone back to his books at different points in my life and still enjoy them. The idea of the bandaged stranger showing up in a small town, like the initial setup for *The Invisible Man* novel, is so compelling and full of possibilities. When I was finished with my *Essex County* trilogy of graphic novels, I was looking for a project that was a bit darker and more pulpy, and I thought that that would be a great setup—to take that character and spin it into my own modern smalltown story.

**Ash:** Is this an updating of the *Invisible Man* story, or did you use the novel as inspiration?

**Lemire:** It's not an adaptation of the book. Basically, it takes the idea of a stranger showing up in a small town wrapped head to toe in bandages. From there, it goes off on my own tangent. I don't really follow the plot or the characters of the novel at all. I do my own thing with it. I make a few nods to certain characters and scenes from the novel, but nothing direct. It's a public domain novel now, so I have the freedom to do that with it.

**Ash:** Who are some of the characters in the book?

**Lemire:** Besides Griffen, the bandaged stranger, the main character would be a teenaged girl named Vickie who works at the local diner that her dad owns. She's the loner in town. She longs to escape this small town she's stuck in. When the bandaged man shows up, he represents all the mystery and intrigue of the outside world. She befriends him and these two outsiders bond and form this strange friendship. In the back of her mind, she's seeing him as a way out of town. There's also her father and the other town folk who quickly become suspicious of this bandaged weirdo. Things turn bad.

**Ash:** With both *Essex County* and *The Nobody*, and it sounds like a bit with *Sweet Tooth*, you're dealing with small towns and small groups of people. What is the fascination with the small town for you?

**Lemire:** At its root, I come from a really small town. The *Essex County* books were based on the place where I grew up. Also, I find that so many novels or comics or movies today are all set in big cities or some kind of allegory for New York City. It's nice to have stories that show a different perspective. Since I'm from one of those places, I feel like I have other kinds of stories I can tell. It adds some diversity to what's coming out. I feel like there's all kinds of great stories to be told all over the world and there's no reason they all have to be set in a big city in the United States.

**Ash:** Moving on to *Sweet Tooth*, what can you tell us about the book?

**Lemire:** It's my first monthly book and my first book in color, so that's really exciting. It's ten years after some mysterious disease pretty much wiped out 90 percent of the population of the world. The world's one big ghost town. There's this little boy who's grown up in seclusion in the woods with his father and he has some animal-like features. He has antlers and deerlike features. He has never left the woods. He doesn't know anything about the world outside. In the first issue, he's forced to leave the woods for the first time and what he finds is this world that's basically been left behind and empty. The story follows him and this big, hulking, violent drifter who takes him under his wing. They have a road trip across this new American frontier.

**Ash:** I know you were probably working on the books prior to this, but when I heard about the pandemic in your story, my first thought was the swine flu (H1N1) scare.

**Lemire:** Yeah. I was already done with the sixth issue when the swine flu scare started happening. We were all glad the guy didn't have piglike features or we would have been cancelled. [*laughter*]

**Ash:** Where did the idea of the pandemic come from?

**Lemire:** I'm a fan of the great postapocalyptic science fiction stories like *Mad Max* and Tim Truman's old comic, *Scout*. I was a big fan of that book.

*The Nobody*, page 35. Credit: Jeff Lemire.

Cormac McCarthy's *The Road* novel. *Walking Dead*, too. The idea of a post-apocalyptic world is such a great setup for sci-fi stories and action-adventure stories. Somewhere inside, I always wanted to tell my own version of one of those books, but I didn't want a world that was destroyed by a nuclear war or something like that. I wanted a world that was sort of our world but left untouched and empty. I thought that was an interesting place to explore.

**Ash:** Will there be other major characters in the book?

**Lemire:** The first six-issue arc mostly follows the two main characters, the boy and the big guy. It's them making their way across the country. The big guy promises the kid that he knows of a safe place where other animal children are gathering. So, it's their quest to find this place. I can't give away too much, but at the end of the sixth issue, the story opens wide and there are all kinds of new characters and new mysteries posed.

**Ash:** The first issue of *Sweet Tooth* is also coming out at a special price. Were you involved with that decision at all?

**Lemire:** No. That was a decision made through Vertigo. *Sweet Tooth*, *The Unwritten*, and *Greek Street* are all dollar first issues. I'm really happy about it. Hopefully it'll get a lot more people to try the book than normally would have and bring a lot of attention to it.

**Ash:** Are there any other projects you're working on that you'd like to mention?

**Lemire:** The collected omnibus version of the three *Essex County* books is coming out in August from Top Shelf. It's going to be in both hardcover and softcover and it's going to have fifty-six pages of new material. I'm also in Dark Horse's *Noir* anthology, which is coming out in a month or two. And I'm working on another Top Shelf book on the side, but that one's still in the early stages so I won't be talking about it until next year.

**Ash:** Are there any closing comments you'd like to make?

**Lemire:** Buy *Sweet Tooth*! It's only a dollar!

# Multiversity Comics Presents: Jeff Lemire

## DAVID HARPER / 2010

*Multiversity Comics*, April 7, 2010. Reprinted by permission.

Today on *Multiversity Comics Presents*, we have *Sweet Tooth*'s Jeff Lemire. This writer/artist has quickly risen up the ranks in the comic world, earning accolades for releases like *Essex County* and *The Nobody*. We're proud to bring you this interview today, and if you haven't checked out his work yet I highly suggest getting on it. It's brilliant stuff.

**David Harper:** Why did you decide to pursue a career in comics?

**Jeff Lemire:** I have loved comics since I was four years old, and I've been drawing them for just as long. For me, it wasn't so much a decision to "make a career" out of comics. It was just what I wanted to do more than anything else, so I just started doing it every day. The career came later.

**Harper:** Carl Sandburg once said, "Here is the difference between Dante, Milton, and me. They wrote about hell and never saw the place. I wrote about Chicago after looking the town over for years and years." Already having written about your childhood home in Essex County, how does growing up in rural Canada continue to influence your writing?

**Lemire:** I still feel more drawn to rural settings in my books. It just seems like you can take a smalltown setting and make it into a character all of its own. New York and Chicago already have a personality that everyone knows, but you can make up a small town and imbue it with whatever traits, both physical and tonal, that you want. It's like a perfect microcosm for whatever stories you're trying to tell. And aesthetically I just like the mood and feel of sparse, wide-open spaces more than cluttered, busy city scenes.

**Harper:** What stories and creators were the most influential on your writing and artistic styles?

**Lemire:** As a storyteller, Dave McKean's *Cages* for its sparse, stripped-down yet expressive artwork. Seth's *Clyde Fans* for its wonderful sense of pacing and loneliness. All of Alan Moore's seminal works, *Watchmen*, *V for Vendetta*, *Swamp Thing*, and *From Hell*, for their incredible sense of structure and narrative depth. Eddie Campbell's Alec books for their sense of whimsy and life. The films of David Lynch for their sense of mood and atmosphere.

On a purely aesthetic or drawing level, Joe Kubert, José Muñoz, Alberto Breccia, Alex Toth, Jorge Zaffino, among many, many others.

**Harper:** Your career as a cartoonist has gotten off to a fast start, as all of your work so far has been met with high acclaim and by a passionate fan base. Have you been surprised at all by your meteoric rise?

**Lemire:** Yes, I was very surprised by how quickly things happened. All I knew was that I was creating work that I really truly cared for, and people seem to have responded to that. On the other hand, I was drawing comics every day for years before I ever showed anyone my work, so there was a lot of bad and formative work that I kept to myself until I felt I was ready to put myself out there.

**Harper:** Given that it takes place in a postapocalyptic world where human/animal hybrids exist, many of our readers wonder where this idea came from. So what are the origins of *Sweet Tooth*?

**Lemire:** It comes from a big mishmash of influences: a little bit of *Dr. Moreau*, a lot of Jack Kirby's *Kamandi* and Tim Truman's *Scout*. A bit of Cormac MacCarthy and a lot of *Essex County* in there, too. Gus and Jepperd are really just Lester and Jimmy from *Tales from the Farm*, pushed to an extreme.

**Harper:** The character of Jeppard is very intense in comparison to the more naïve and eponymous Gus. What inspired him and his twisting tale?

**Lemire:** He is Gus's opposite. Gus is the "sweet"; Jepperd is the "tooth." Putting two characters like that together creates instant tension and conflict and makes it easy to write. His brutal, visceral, and violent nature represents the shocking and dangerous nature of the world in which Gus is entering as a total innocent.

**Harper:** Gus and Jeppard have been the main members of the cast to date. Are we going to see an expansion of the supporting cast in the future?

**Lemire:** Yes, the book will become much more of an ensemble piece as we move into our third arc. Some characters we have already met will return and play bigger roles, and there will be new characters as well. But in the end this is about Gus and Jepperd.

**Harper:** We've seen Gus have premonitions in his dreams. Are we going to see more of these? How will they factor into the future of the book?

*Sweet Tooth* #3, page 1. Credit: Jeff Lemire.

**Lemire:** Yes, Gus's dreams are very important; they often predict future events either symbolically or in some cases literally. There is never anything in his dreams that is not crucial to coming events.

**Harper:** *Sweet Tooth,* on the surface at least, is much less personal than previous works, i.e., *Essex County.* How much of you would you say still shines through the characters and the events?

**Lemire:** I disagree with that. *Sweet Tooth* is just as personal to me as *Essex* was. The surface elements are slightly more artificial. I'm filtering my themes and ideas through a genre now, and using that to amplify certain things, but in the end those sci-fi and horror elements are just metaphors, just like hockey was in *Essex.*

**Harper:** Gus has run quite the gauntlet already in *Sweet Tooth,* with his dad's death, various attacks, and now his current predicament in the camp. Is it hard to be cruel to your characters?

**Lemire:** No, it's really easy to think of horrible things to do to them. But I promise, as hard as this book is, and as dark as it may yet get, there is a reason to it all. There is a purpose to it, and an end point in sight for all the characters. And, there will be lighter moments and issues coming along the way.

**Harper:** Why did you decide to story in color instead of black-and-white like previous works?

**Lemire:** Quite simply, this was a monthly Vertigo book, and they do those in color. Plus, it was great chance to try something new and work with another amazing artist and friend, José Villarrubia.

**Harper:** Do you have an idea of how many issues you want to go for *Sweet Tooth?*

**Lemire:** 1,000.

**Harper:** I read that you already have the last issue of *Sweet Tooth* written. How does having that preexisting target affect your writing style?

**Lemire:** All of my books and stories have started with the ending. That's just how I write. You have a start point and an end point for your characters, and then you just need to fill in the middle and figure out how they get from point A to B. It's all about how your characters change and grow, and the best way to show that journey.

**Harper:** You've now worked with Vertigo twice with *Sweet Tooth* and *The Nobody.* How do you feel your style and title are fitting in with that esteemed publisher?

**Lemire:** I still think that it stands alone as a really "different" book, even for Vertigo. There haven't been a lot of single writer/artist monthlies from Vertigo or DC, so just by its nature it's going to represent a singular vision more than most of their books do. That doesn't necessarily make it better or worse than their other books, but I think it does make it stand out a bit. Having said that, they have been nothing but supportive of the book. They seem to really understand what *Sweet Tooth* is and have given me the support and freedom to let it grow. And, DC proper has been really supportive, too. I've found a lot of fans among DCU writers and editorial.

**Harper:** You have another Top Shelf graphic novel in the works. Can you shed any light on it at all, and when we may expect to see it?

**Lemire:** Not yet; still in the early stages. I would say that I will probably finish it sometime in 2011.

**Harper:** On Twitter, you mentioned that you have a Marvel writing gig upcoming. Can you shed any light on what that might be?

**Lemire:** Unfortunately, I had to turn down that gig after all. I have some DCU writing gigs in the works, and with *Sweet Tooth* and my Top Shelf book, I was just too busy to take on more work. As for the DC stuff, I'm not allowed to talk about them yet, but I will get a chance to try my hand at writing a few established DC [heroes] that I love!

**Harper:** You also mentioned writing for DC proper on Twitter. While at Emerald City ComiCon, we overheard a couple prominent DC creators discussing your name alongside the words "Brightest Day" as one of them leafed through a copy of *Essex County*. Are you going to contribute to that high-profile project, or is your DC work different in nature?

**Lemire:** No comment . . . wouldn't that be interesting, though?

**Harper:** The title is called *Sweet Tooth* and Gus loves chocolate. What do you have a sweet tooth for?

**Lemire:** I actually don't have any sweet tooth! I never eat sweets of any kind, and have no interest in sweets at all. I have a salty meat tooth! I guess I'm more Jepperd than Gus.

**Harper:** You're not just a comic writer/artist, but also a big fan of comics in general. Is there anything in particular out there that you think comic fans are missing out on?

**Lemire:** Emi Lenox! Check out her online comic *emitown*. Also Matt Kindt is the best writer/artist working in comics and his last book from Dark Horse, *3 Story*, was a masterpiece. As for monthly stuff, I really dug the first issue of David Lapham's *Sparta USA*, and *Scalped* is the best comic ever.

# Superboy: An Interview with Writer Jeff Lemire

**ED GROSS / 2011**

*Voices from Krypton*, February 20, 2011. ComicBookMovie.com. Reprinted by permission.

In its biographical sketch of Lemire, Wikipedia offers, "Lemire was born and raised in a small farming town in Essex County, Ontario, near Lake St. Clair. Lemire attended film school, but decided to pursue comics when he realized that filmmaking did not suit his solitary personality. After self-publishing the Xeric Award-winning comic book *Lost Dogs* in 2005 via his Ashtray Press imprint, Lemire found a home at Top Shelf Productions. He produced the Eisner and Harvey Award-nominated *Essex County* trilogy for Top Shelf in 2008–2009. Lemire serializes a science fiction strip called *Fortress* in the quarterly UR Magazine.

"In 2009, the DC Comics Vertigo published Lemire's *The Nobody*, a two-color tale of identity, fear and paranoia in a small community. Lemire is currently writing and drawing the new monthly full-color Vertigo series *Sweet Tooth*. He then moved over to the DC Universe to write the one-shot *Brightest Day: Atom*, with Turkish artist Mahmud Asrar, designed to act as a springboard for an Atom story to co-feature in *Adventure Comics*. He also relaunched the *Superboy* series featuring the character Conner Kent."

In the following exclusive interview conducted by *Voices from Krypton*'s editor, Ed Gross, Lemire shares his feelings about the cloned Boy of Steel.

**Ed Gross:** Where does the whole Superman mythos stand with you?

**Jeff Lemire:** I grew up reading DC comics, so growing up I was always drawn to DC characters more than the Marvel stuff, and Superman is always at the center of that. His mythos and the different creators who've taken him on over the years have all influenced me. It's really fun to be working with some of these characters, but at the same time, I'm glad this version of

Superboy is kind of his own, separate corner of that mythos. I have a little bit more freedom to kind of do things with the character, because the original Superboy was obviously Superman as a kid and you know right away how that story is going to end up. Anything you do with the Superboy character, you kind of know down the road that it's not going to matter—you know where the future is going to end. But with this Superboy, the future is unwritten, so I can do things to change the character that will last, and I like that aspect of it.

**Gross:** How would you say the character has evolved from the point he was introduced to where he is now?

**Lemire:** Well, everyone is going to have different versions of the character that is their favorite—but for me, the original version of him, I actually found really annoying for some reason. He's like this whiny, hotshot kid, and I guess I can see the appeal of that back in the '90s, to make him stand out from the other ones, but that doesn't really appeal to me that much now. In the ten years that he's been around, the character has obviously matured as a person, and when Geoff Johns was writing the *Teen Titans* and put him in that, he really took a step forward in that respect. Then they added the component of Lex Luthor being one of his fathers to the mythos, which is a really cool twist. That's where I kind of picked it up and I'm slowly trying to build the next stage for this character as he grows towards manhood and decides what kind of Superman he wants to be when he gets to that stage.

**Gross:** What was the genesis of this take?

**Lemire:** For me, I obviously wanted to have an original take on it, because you can go back and read the old comics if you want, but I wanted to introduce something new. The way I approached that was to make Smallville itself a really big character in the book—because for me, this book is about Superboy's relationship with Smallville and how that reflects the choices he has to make for his life. I thought an interesting way to do that was to make Smallville this really quirky place that was, on the surface, a typical small town, sort of like *Twin Peaks* or something like that, but underneath it's bubbling with secrets and mysteries, and that provides great fodder for storylines. And even though each storyline is one or two issues long, it's allowing me to be this bigger mystery that's going to go on throughout the entire run, which ties to a secret history of Smallville and some of those quirky, creepy things we're talking about. I'm a big fan of shows like *The X-Files*, *Lost*, and *Twin Peaks*, and I thought it would be an interesting take on a teen superhero to put him in one of those worlds.

**Gross:** So there is a growing mythology?

**Lemire:** Yes, there is. It's touched on in most of the issues—there are one or two issues where it takes a back seat, but it's something that's slowly building and it'll come to a head in the issues coming out over the next year.

**Gross:** So your interest lies in the weirder areas rather than the typical, "Superboy takes on Brainiac"-type story.

**Lemire:** There's a lot of that out there right now, and I just feel like I want to offer something new, otherwise why do it at all when you can just go out and read those other books? I try to find an interesting take on it. And to be blunt, the part of the superhero comic I find the least interesting is sort of the fights between the superhero and the supervillain—it can get pretty tedious and pat, so I want to add something else so that when you do have those fight scenes or those action sequences, they're kind of tied to something unique and they reflect the character. This was my way of doing that.

**Gross:** When you went to DC and said, "This is my take," did anyone bat an eye?

**Lemire:** Not really, to be honest. I think they had read my work, which was not superhero work at all—it was all darker, quirkier stuff—and the fact is that they approached me to do this book; they had an idea of what they were looking for, so I don't think it's a surprise that my take was more from my field.

**Gross:** How do you view Conner Kent?

**Lemire:** Well, at the start of the series he's kind of in this nebulous spot where he's the metaphorical son of both Superman and Lex Luthor, so that's pulled him back and forth over the last year. Now he's come to this point, where my series begins, where he's put that behind him and he's his own person now, and not letting them dictate who he's going to be. That's sort of where my series starts, having him go back to Smallville, and trying to bring some normalcy to himself, trying to be a normal kid to figure himself out. Of course, being a superhero keeps getting in the way of that. I don't want to give things away, but his character is on a little bit of a journey, where he's trying to figure out who and where he's meant to be. That's totally going to reveal itself over the next year.

**Gross:** Do you see the scope being limited to Smallville?

**Lemire:** It's going to be limited to Smallville for the first year of stories, and then that story is going to naturally dovetail into a bigger story that will take him out of Smallville. I don't want to say too much more than that at this point.

**Gross:** And then when that big story happens, you'll want to get back to Smallville again?

**Lemire:** I don't want to say. I don't have the idea that I'm going to be writing this book forever—I kind of have an ending in mind where I want to leave things, and whether he stays in Smallville is kind of the ongoing question of the book. I don't want to reveal that answer yet.

**Gross:** For people who don't know this version of Superboy, how would you introduce this character to them?

**Lemire:** He's a young character who has the legacy of Superman to live up to, but he also has the legacy of Lex Luthor tainting that, so we have this superhero who's torn between being the greatest hero in the world or the greatest villain in the world, and we get to watch to see which one he leans towards as he grows into manhood. I think that's kind of fun.

**Gross:** Is that conflict something you're going to play with?

**Lemire:** I want to leave it alone at the beginning of the book, because there were some stories that had been done touching on that right before I started, so I thought I'd give it a breather. But that's the thing that's at the core of his character, so at some point that's going to come back and it's going to play a part in everything else that he's doing.

# Jeff Lemire

NOEL MURRAY / 2011

*The A. V. Club*, July 21, 2011. Reprinted by permission.

Cartoonist Jeff Lemire had some published work under his belt before Top Shelf published the 2008 graphic novel *Tales from the Farm*, but that book—the first part of Lemire's *Essex County* trilogy, about various wounded people in a rural Canadian community—was so moving and beautifully drawn that it signaled the arrival of a new, formidable talent. Since completing the *Essex County* books, Lemire has begun working regularly for DC Comics' alt imprint Vertigo, first with the graphic novel *The Nobody* (a retelling of *The Invisible Man* with an *Essex*-y twist) and then with the ongoing series *Sweet Tooth*. The latter is, on the surface, a sci-fi/horror adventure about a plague-ridden future being quickly overrun by new human-animal hybrids. But it's really the story of one of those hybrids—an antler-headed kid named Gus—and his connection to a gruff, emotionally scarred tough guy named Tommy Jepperd, who, like Gus, is struggling to get along in a terrifying new world. Lemire spoke with *The A. V. Club* about how *Sweet Tooth* is like his earlier work, and about his upcoming projects for DC and Top Shelf.

**Noel Murray:** Did the image of a kid with the antlers come before the story, or did the story suggest the image?

**Jeff Lemire:** In the case of *Sweet Tooth* and in the case of a lot of stuff I do, it all starts with the image. It may be something I sketch in my sketchbooks—something that reoccurs in the sketchbooks. Eventually a character or storyline starts to grow out of that. So that character . . . I don't know. I can't remember the genesis. Why I was drawing a boy with antlers. But he kept popping up in a sketchbook one summer, for whatever reason. You just start building a character and a pretty vague story around that. I do this all the time, and some of these things I explore further until they turn into something bigger, like *Sweet Tooth*. And some other things I just forget about. This one stuck.

Plus, I'd always wanted to do something postapocalyptic, and a longform genre piece. My indie work is mostly reality-based, focused on real life and characters. I thought it would be fun to try something really different and try to do a monthly action-adventure story that was treated sort of the same way I treated my indie work: quiet and slow-paced and focusing more on the smaller character moments than big plot moments. So I started with Gus, and the main idea just sort of popped up. It seemed like a really good starting point.

**Murray:** Was it a developed idea that you shopped around, or did Vertigo ask you for pitches?

**Lemire:** It happened really fast. I was doing a graphic novel for Vertigo called *The Nobody* and I was closing in on finishing that up. I think I was three-fourths of the way through it. I really liked working with them and they seemed to really like working with me. It was just a matter of timing. Bob Schreck, my editor on *The Nobody*, mentioned to me that they had some monthly slots to fill coming up and said that if I had any ideas for monthly stuff, I should pitch them. I kinda had this loose idea for the *Sweet Tooth* thing, which at that time I'd been planning on doing as three graphic novels, probably for Top Shelf or something. I didn't expect to do much more work for DC. But when Bob offered the chance to take on a monthly, I quickly adapted the idea. At that point, it really wasn't fully formed; it was just a bunch of vague thoughts that needed to be put together. Over the course of a weekend, I put it all into a pitch, and sent it on a Monday. I think within a week they greenlit it. That never really happens. Nothing happens that fast. It was just really lucky timing.

**Murray:** Have you found it difficult to maintain the monthly pace?

**Lemire:** No, it's not a big deal for me. The monthly schedule can be pretty grueling, but I'm lucky in that my artwork is so expressive and loose that it lends itself to being done pretty quickly. I haven't been late yet. And I can also work on other projects on the side, which is important to me. So the deadline aspect hasn't been a problem.

The one thing that does get kind of stressful once in a while is telling a story that's so long, you need a break from it. You wish you could move on to some new ideas or new characters. But I still have two or three years left with these people. Some months, that can be a burden. Usually something happens and I get a new idea or a new take on something, and that reinvigorates me. It's like a marathon. I know it's going to be worth it in the end because I know where it's all going and I know this is a story that's still really important to me. So you just sort of stick it out those tough days.

The good thing about a monthly book, too, is that when you do a graphic novel, you work on it for a couple years or a year or whatever, and then you put it out and you get feedback when it comes out and that's great, but with the monthly comic I get tons of feedback from fans and that also helps to keep you motivated.

**Murray:** So *Sweet Tooth* has a definite endpoint?

**Lemire:** It definitely has an endpoint. I've known the ending of the story right from the beginning. I can't really write anything without knowing the ending. I don't know how people do that. Even with my superhero stuff, I have to know at least where I want to take the characters and what the ending of my story with them will be. I just can't structure stories or character arcs and stuff without knowing the endpoint. In *Sweet Tooth*'s case, I've definitely always known the ending. The beginning and the ending are locked. It's just the middle part that you leave yourself room to introduce new elements and characters. At one point, the story was going to be twenty-four or twenty-six issues, and then it was going to be thirty-six, and now it's more headed toward about fifty.

**Murray:** Sometimes with longform genre pieces, like *Lost* or *Battlestar Galactica*, there are concerns that the more you fill in the middle, the further you get away from where you started and then the harder it gets to bring it back.

**Lemire:** Yeah, that's exactly my biggest . . . I'm very conscious of that. It would be pretty easy to pad the middle sections and stretch this out to seventy-five issues or something. But the more you do that, the further you get from that core idea you started with and that you want to end with. In the case of *Sweet Tooth*, that's the relationship between the character of Gus and Jepperd, and seeing them grow together. The more I throw in, the harder it is to focus on that. So I have to be very conscious that anything I do add—any characters or storylines—are all working toward that end goal, and either reflecting or bringing out that core concept. Otherwise, they're just not worth doing. I guess, technically, I could probably make the book a lot longer if I wanted to. But it just wouldn't ring true at some point. It's a delicate balance between fleshing out ideas and making the world bigger and richer, and going too far.

**Murray:** You mentioned wanting to do something set in a postapocalyptic world. Were you concerned much that those kinds of stories have been done a lot?

**Lemire:** No, I kind of like that. [*laughs*] Most genre stuff, in one form or another, has been done. That's the interesting challenge: trying to find a way of doing it in a way that makes people see it differently. I wanted to take something that's been done as much as this, and instead of treating it in the way that most people treat it, as a big plot-driven thing, instead just focus in on one or two people in that world and find the quiet moments of their life. All the big genre elements are going on around them and in the background, but that's never really what the story's about. It's all in the execution, right? Two or three people can do the exact same idea, but if you keep it really personal, something new comes out of it. My stuff tends to be pretty emotionally based, you know? I feel like this postapocalyptic setting heightens everything and makes it all more immediate and desperate. The stakes are so high for every character that it really brings out heightened emotions that I thought would be really interesting to play with. It's fertile ground for conflict and for creating really interesting characters.

**Murray:** After the *Essex County* trilogy, some were a little surprised that you would take on something like *Sweet Tooth*. But elements like the backstory of Jepperd are similar to *Essex County* in terms of the tone and even the details of his life as an ex-hockey player.

**Lemire:** That's just naturally the way I tell stories. And I think that's what my Vertigo editors wanted, that kind of quieter storytelling combined with these big action elements. That's why they approved the book.

**Murray:** And though you mentioned being able to draw quickly, *Sweet Tooth* certainly doesn't look oversimplified. There's one page, for example, in the second trade paperback where Jepperd describes how he's starting to lose the memory of his late wife's face. And there are two panels of her placed over a big drawing of Jepperd's face, such that the wrinkles in Jepperd's forehead look like antlers jutting out of his wife's head.

**Lemire:** I never noticed that. [*laughs*] That might have been a happy accident. But yeah, when I say that, that it doesn't take me that long to do, that doesn't mean I don't care about it or that I'm just flopping it out. It's just naturally an expressive style, so it just doesn't take as long for me as for those people who try to make something photorealistic. I care deeply about the book and I put a lot of myself into it every month. Those three weeks or whatever of the month that I'm drawing the book are very focused.

**Murray:** Pivoting off of *Sweet Tooth*, you've started working with DC proper on some superhero titles. Was that a career goal for you when you started drawing comics?

**Lemire:** No. No, not at all. I was, and will be, perfectly happy drawing my own stuff whenever the DC work dries up. But that's the good thing about being quick, that I have time to work on other things. And so as long as I can still do *Sweet Tooth* and still create my own work that I'm writing and drawing myself, I figured I might as well take a shot at some of this other stuff, too. The opportunity was there. And it can be pretty fun to write superheroes. The first year or so writing *Superboy* and *Atom* and everything was in a lot of ways really challenging, because I had never written for another artist, and I had never really worked within that kind of editorial system where there are so many different people involved in the creative process. It took me a while to get my feet, I think, as a writer. But with these two new books I'm doing for DC for the new line—*Frankenstein* and *Animal Man*—I feel like I'm finally coming into my own, as a writer as opposed to just a cartoonist. I'm really excited for people to read these, because it'll be the best work I've done for DC yet.

**Murray:** Did you read superhero comics a lot when you were growing up?

**Lemire:** Oh, yeah, I grew up reading that stuff. I loved it. I read it well into my teenage years. Then, in the '90s, it got to the point where superhero comics were really, really bad. [*laughs*] All flash and no substance. Then Vertigo popped up. And I was reading *Animal Man* and all that back then, so it's really cool to be working on that character now. Then as I got a bit older, I started discovering alternative and underground cartoonists and European cartoonists, so there was always something to keep me interested in comics. But yeah, superheroes were a big part of why I started reading in the first place.

**Murray:** In one of the *Sweet Tooth* issues, you wrote a little note for Marv Wolfman and George Perez.

**Lemire:** Yeah, because I ripped them right off. [*laughing*] I stole the format for the issue from a comic they did in the '80s. It's cool that you can do one of these indie-looking comics for Vertigo, but it's actually a superhero comic that influenced it. It's fun to mix all your influences into something. The cool thing about *Sweet Tooth* is that you can bring influences from the underground and alternative people that I read and also bring in some genre influences, too, from movies and comics. And kind of mash it all up. It's a fun project.

**Murray:** What do you have in the works on the non-DC/Vertigo side?

**Lemire:** I'm doing a big graphic novel for Top Shelf that'll be, in a lot of ways, the true follow-up to *Essex County*. Something with that kind of scope and style. It's called *The Underwater Welder*, and it follows this guy who works on an oil rig in a small Canadian town. He's expecting his first child, and the pressures of his job and the pressures of his impending fatherhood are building and building. Then he has a sort of weird, mind-bending encounter one day when he's diving below the sea and when he surfaces, the world he knew is gone and pretty different. It's a story about him mining his past and figuring out how to get back to his wife and his unborn son. Anyway, that's the book I'm working on actively. It's due to come out next summer.

# Jeff Lemire: The Beauty of Collaboration

**KYLE LEMMON / 2012**

*Under the Radar*, January 20, 2012. Reprinted by permission.

Two of the surprise hits of DC New 52 initiative were Jeff Lemire's trippy hor-ror series *Animal Man* and his action-packed *Frankenstein: Agent of S.H.A.D.E.* Both made a big splash for the *Sweet Tooth* scribe. Here we talk for a spell with the inspiring young writer. He dishes back his thoughts on the collaborative environment of DC Comics, reluctant heroes, ceding control to artists, and remaining silent about the Mysterious Red-Hooded Woman. Also, see our discussion with his partner in crime, Scott Snyder (*Batman, Swamp Thing*).

**Kyle Lemmon:** I was looking at the initial sales numbers for *Animal Man*, and they're quite impressive for a superhero that's not as well-known as Bat-man or Superman. Are you pretty happy with the fan reactions thus far?

**Jeff Lemire:** Oh, yeah! If this book had launched outside of the whole New 52 thing, I think we would have been lucky to even continue publishing. I couldn't imagine these sales numbers. Even in Vertigo's heyday, when they were selling 80,000 copies of *Sandman*, *Animal Man* wasn't getting even close to these numbers. It's overwhelming and really gratifying. People are really responding on a critical level and the sales numbers seem to be reflecting that.

**Lemmon:** I was just reading through a joint interview you did with Scott Snyder this morning and started thinking about the similarities between your two worlds. Both *Animal Man*'s Buddy Baker and *Swamp Thing*'s Alec Holland are somewhat reluctant heroes that are pulled into otherworldly en-vironments. Do you see any parallels between your books and Snyder's?

**Lemire:** *Swamp Thing* and *Animal Man* are definitely horror books. They're not just run-of-the-mill superhero comics. The nature of a horror story is that his antagonists reflect his greatest fears back at him. I think that's why you're getting that sense that these two guys are getting caught up in something out of control, as opposed to a traditional superhero comic where the hero is more proactive about fighting crime. Holland's and Baker's lives are being interrupted by this strange threat. They are reeling and reacting. I can see that parallel.

**Lemmon:** You mentioned in another interview that you weren't completely happy with how *The Atom* and *Superboy* books turned out. Was that just because you were getting used to writing for a larger company like DC and ceding control to other artistic entities?

**Lemire:** Yes, it was an adjustment for all of *The Atom*, and the first half of the *Superboy* run. That was the first time I was writing for another artist. Up until that point, I'd been doing comics for quite a while, but had always drawn my own stuff. It was a very different experience for me. It was also the first time working with characters that I didn't completely know or control. There were a lot of factors during that first year. I was sort of learning as I went along. There were certain aspects of both books that I really enjoyed and I thought turned out really well. There are things now that I would do differently or better. That's just how it goes in life. You get better as you get older. It was a different way of working and those books were my warmup for the New 52. I got my mistakes out of the way and I feel much more confident in myself as a writer. I think it shows. [*Animal Man* and *Frankenstein: Agent of S.H.A.D.E.*] are a step up in quality for me.

**Lemmon:** Like many DC fans, I was excited to find the hooded woman in each issue of the New 52. Do you know if there will be anymore Easter egg items like that in future issues?

**Lemire:** I think at this point the writers are past their first story arc [sixth issues] and I think what's happening is that we're naturally finding how the new world is fitting together. The more we read other people's books or cultivate the worlds in our own books, we are getting a better picture of how the wider universe will connect. I'm starting to really connect with the other things that are happening in the *Justice League Dark* line, specifically with *Swamp Thing*. Scott Snyder and I are planning a really big storyline for *Swamp Thing* and *Animal Man*. Those books will crossover in an event called "Dead World." We've been dropping little Easter eggs for that right from the beginning. We'll also be including other DC characters in our stories. Little details will come back in big ways. I can only speak to my book at this point. I don't know of any DC-wide Easter eggs that we're all supposed to incorporate into our individual runs.

**Lemmon:** I can see what you mean based on the character dialogue in the first few issues. There are mentions of the Green and the Red and the Rot was mentioned in both books.

**Lemire:** It's slowly forming. As you get into issues five, six, and seven more revelations start stacking up. The books are obviously headed in a similar direction.

**Lemmon:** I really enjoyed your *Essex County* trilogy, and both it and *Animal Man* deal with family issues on some scale. I was curious about your own family and whether any of your personal life has leaked into your stories?

**Lemire:** Obviously, as a writer you're always drawing from your personal experiences. That's just natural. I don't want to talk specifically about my family because it's kind of personal, but in terms of *Animal Man*, I had my first kid a few years ago, and Animal Man is a father in the book. I'm drawing a lot of emotions and experiences from my life and putting them into the book. I'm channeling a lot of stuff there. I can relate to him the most out of all the DC characters. His life resembles my own quite a bit.

**Lemmon:** I like the idea that Buddy's daughter is leading him into this strange world and he's the one that's kind of pulling back. He's the hero of the book, but he's afraid of being Animal Man.

**Lemire:** Any time you have a family like that in a book you can really play with the dynamics. The wife character is really starting to develop into an interesting character. Buddy's son also has a cool take since he's jealous of his sister getting all of his father's attention. He's feeling left out. It's really fun to try and make the whole family the stars of the book and not just Animal Man.

**Lemmon:** *Frankenstein: Agent of S.H.A.D.E.* is almost the complete opposite of *Animal Man*. It has more broad strokes and action scenes. How do you balance out the over-the-top action and more nuanced character development of this covert team?

**Lemire:** During the first few issues I wanted to have the action be all-out and very fun. Now I am trying to peel back the characters a bit and start to develop the history of Frankenstein as a hero. I want to show why this monster is trying to protect humanity and show the secret history of him throughout the twentieth century. I want to evolve the character beyond a two-dimensional action hero as well. His awareness and consciousness expand as he experiences humanity throughout the eras of human history. I think there's a lot of interesting potential there.

**Lemmon:** Some of the other DC New 52 writers are focusing on easy-to-digest story arcs with less of a focus on massive series and megaevents.

It's certainly easier for new comic book fans to latch onto these characters. What's your stance on that plan for your books?

**Lemire:** It's kind of specific to each book. Some characters lend themselves to longer and more involved story arcs whereas others are more suited towards shorter and more palatable arcs. *Animal Man* will be one huge story that will run for as long as my run on the book will be. *Frankenstein* will be very different. That series will have two- or three-issue storylines. They all add up to one big jigsaw puzzle. It's specific to each character and the tone of each book. I like the license that DC has given each writer. We all have the freedom to decide how we approach our titles.

**Lemmon:** Do you work from home?

**Lemire:** I have a studio about twenty minutes from my house. I bike to work every morning. I used to work at home. Like I said, I just had a kid, and it's getting harder and harder to not just spend all my time with him. I had to create a separation there.

**Lemmon:** What are some of the disadvantages and advantages of creator-owned projects, which you've done in the past, and your current work on big DC titles?

**Lemire:** There are definitely disadvantages and advantages to both. It's great to have total control for the creator-owned projects. You don't have to answer to anyone. That's thrilling and freeing. At the same time, when you're working for DC you get a collaborative energy that I don't get when I'm working alone. It's nice to be able to do both at the same time. I just want to be able to do my own thing. I can work on *Sweet Tooth* or enter into the superhero world when I call up Scott Snyder to chat about our characters.

# Jeff Lemire Brings Unique Voice to *Underwater Welder*

**VANETA ROGERS / 2012**

*Newsarama*, April 11, 2012. Reprinted by permission.

Thanks to the unexpected success of the New 52 title *Animal Man*, readers are discovering the unique voice of the comic's writer, Jeff Lemire.

Incorporating his frequent theme of families and small towns confronted by the supernatural, the writer/artist's work first won critical acclaim with his quirky smalltown series, *Essex County*.

But this year, high-profile projects like *Animal Man*, *Frankenstein: Agent of S.H.A.D.E.* and *Sweet Tooth* helped land him a 2012 Eisner nomination as Best Writer. Lemire will also be writing the first issue of DC's new *National Comics* title in July and is starting on *Justice League Dark* in May.

But readers who want to check out other work featuring both writing and art by Jeff Lemire are going to get more than one opportunity over the next few months, thanks to the upcoming release of two graphic novels showcasing his work.

In August, Lemire's new 250-page graphic novel, *The Underwater Welder*, will debut after more than four years of work by the creator, focusing on the pressure of being a new dad—and a mysterious sci-fi twist that tears the main character away from his wife. And in May, Top Shelf will rerelease Lemire's first graphic novel, *Lost Dogs*. Although it's been available as a digital comic since November, the May release is the first time that readers have had the chance to get the printed graphic novel in years.

*Newsarama* talked with Lemire to find out more about the themes behind the two new graphic novels and how important his creator-owned projects are to him.

*The Underwater Welder*, page 118. Credit: Jeff Lemire.

**Vaneta Rogers:** Wow, Jeff, this new graphic novel has been in the works for a long time. How many years have you been working on *The Underwater Welder*?

**Jeff Lemire:** Like four and half years, I think.

**Rogers:** People who know your work will see some familiar themes. But this has a pretty cool sci-fi element involved, doesn't it?

**Lemire:** Yeah, I describe it as a really emotional *Twilight Zone* episode. It's about this guy who works off a deep-sea rig off the coast of a small coastal town. So he spends a lot of his time diving underwater and working on an oil pipeline.

And then one day, when he goes down and comes back up, the world is a completely different place. It's completely changed. Something changed while he was down there.

It's about him trying to find his way back home to his wife before his baby is born.

It's kind of creepy and moody and weird. It's like a lot of my stories in that it's based on a smalltown environment, and it has a central relationship as the core, with the relationship between him and his wife and his son. But it's got a sci-fi twist and a time travel element to it.

**Rogers:** Between *Animal Man* and now *The Underwater Welder*, it's obvious you are exploring what it means to be a dad.

**Lemire:** Yeah, I'm very subtle, aren't I? No kidding.

**Rogers:** But with *The Underwater Welder*, it's obviously focused on the pressure of being a *new* dad. Was that because you came up with this concept before you were a dad?

**Lemire:** Yeah, and it's been such a long time coming that I can look back on it now and see a part of my life represented there in the book, really. When I first started working on it and came up with the original idea, I hadn't started working for DC or Vertigo yet. And I didn't have a kid yet. That wasn't even on the radar for my wife and me. We hadn't even talked about it. So I was in a completely different place personally and professionally than I was when I finished the book.

And I think, as a result, I saw the book change from its original intent and my original story grew and morphed into something completely different by the end of it. So on the page, you're going to see that, as the character goes through things, exactly what I was going through. And feelings about parenthood.

It starts off with the pressure of impending parenthood, but by the end, it becomes a celebration of accepting parenthood. It obviously all came right from my life.

I think it's something kind of special as a result. Hopefully, the realism of those emotions and that experience will come across on the page.

**Rogers:** And we'll also see a new release from you in May, when your graphic novel, *Lost Dogs*, gets a new printing. Was that your first graphic novel?

**Lemire:** It was. I did it a while before *Essex County*. It's been out of print for quite a while. I only printed 500 or 600 copies originally. But Top Shelf is releasing it.

**Rogers:** Do you think your style has evolved since you first drew it?

**Lemire:** Somewhat. It was my first book that I did, so the art style is pretty raw compared to what I do now, but I think the story really holds up.

It's about this big hulking farmer character that gets separated from his family one day. And it's about him being involved in an underground boxing ring in Victorian England and fighting his way back to his family.

There are a lot of similarities thematically in *Lost Dogs* to what I'm doing with *Animal Man*. I can really see a direct line there.

**Rogers:** As one of the rare creators who finds a way to balance the creator-owned stuff with superhero stuff, do you feel that it's important to work in both worlds?

**Lemire:** If I had to choose, at the end of the day, if I wasn't as fast as I am at drawing and couldn't handle all these projects, to me, the things like *Sweet Tooth* and these graphic novels would always be what I choose first. It comes from a different place, you know? Obviously, my own stories and my own creations are going to be more important to me than a DC character is, but that's not to say I don't love doing the DC stuff. I definitely do, and I try to put as much of myself into *Animal Man* as I do in *Sweet Tooth*. It's just that there's a different part of yourself that you put toward something you create from scratch. And of course, for me, there's the added joy I get from being able to draw my own stories. Not that I don't enjoy working with another artist. It's just that drawing is something I wouldn't want to give up.

I guess I'm lucky that I can balance everything. But I think just doing one or just doing the other wouldn't be all that satisfying to me. I love that I can do both.

# There's Nothing Else Jeff Lemire Would Rather Do

**JASON SACKS / 2012**

*Comics Bulletin*, May 15, 2012. Reprinted by permission.

Jeff Lemire has been one of the breakout stars of the DC New 52. His work on *Animal Man* and *Frankenstein* has been among the most popular and critically acclaimed work of that line. I didn't know what to expect when I talked to him at Portland's Stumptown Comics Fest in April, but it shouldn't surprise any reader of his series that Jeff was as nice, interesting, and down-to-earth as any person I've had the chance to talk to.

**Jason Sacks:** You've walked the line between the indie and commercial worlds. Do you have a preference? Do you enjoy having a foot in both worlds?

**Jeff Lemire:** Yeah, I do. I grew up reading *Spirit* comics and stuff. I have a huge affection for that stuff and specifically the DC Universe. That's something I've always loved. So it's really fun to be able to work in that world and still keep doing my indie work for Top Shelf and Vertigo. I'm just lucky that I'm fast enough that I'm able to do so many projects at once. As long as I can do both, I'm happy.

**Sacks:** You're writing three series a month, as well as writing and drawing *Sweet Tooth*?

**Lemire:** Yeah, two and a half or three, depending on what month. I am writing quite a few books, and my nine-to-five, Monday to Friday is mostly still drawing *Sweet Tooth*. That takes the most time. Scripts for the other stuff just get done when they get done—on weekends, at nights, whenever you find some time.

**Sacks:** You're living for comics. Do you love doing it?

**Lemire:** There's nothing else I've ever wanted to do or [would] rather be doing, so when you love doing it that much, it's not hard to do it all the time.

**Sacks:** You grew up in a small town in Canada. Is that why so much of *Essex County* seems to ring true?

**Lemire:** Yeah.

**Sacks:** What was it like creating comics in a community like that? It must have been hard to find kinship.

**Lemire:** Obviously my childhood was pretty isolated. I didn't know anyone else who was really reading comics at the time. I think I just escaped into comics, because there wasn't really a lot going on around that I was interested in otherwise. So I just escaped into drawing and reading comics, and that was sort of my refuge. When I got older and moved to a bigger city, I started to meet more and more people like me. It was great to be part of a community that was reading comics.

**Sacks:** Do you think your approach is different from some people's because you didn't have as many peers who were into comics when you were younger?

**Lemire:** Yeah, probably. I'm self-taught, whereas if I'd grown up around other people who were doing it, I would probably have learned certain things in life faster and not have to do so much trial and error on my own. As a result, I think I really developed a unique style because I did do so much experimenting. I didn't always know the right way to do something, so I just figured it out on my own, and I think that's where a unique voice came in.

**Sacks:** That's one of the things I like about *Essex County*, especially the earlier chapters. There was a feeling that you were just doing what came from your heart without necessarily having the filters that some professionals have. But by the end, it felt liked you had worked out some of the themes. There are some wonderful scenes that are very moving because they're personally yours.

**Lemire:** When I started *Essex County*—the first volume—I didn't know it was gonna be a trilogy or any more than just that one story. As I expanded it, I started to apply logic and figure out how it could tie together, so I think that's why you got that feeling.

**Sacks:** I keep coming back to the hockey scene, where the players are tapping the hockey sticks on the ice. It obviously comes from the smalltown Canadian experience. I think only someone who has lived in a small town in Canada can appreciate how important hockey really is.

**Lemire:** That is true. It really is a part of the community. The book itself is about family and families, and I just used the hockey team as a metaphor for another kind of family. But growing up in Canada—it's a cliché but it's a cliché because it's true—hockey's a huge part of small communities. It really brings people together. Church and hockey are the two things.

**Sacks:** *The Nobody* was an interesting book because the central story line was very superheroic but the way it was executed was very much not. It's about the loneliness of having the powers.

**Lemire:** That was a big leap: me trying to do an action-adventure/science fiction comic but still treating it in that quiet, personal sort of way. You take these big genre elements or themes and then execute them like it's an art movie or a small, quiet indie comic again, and you get an interesting tension there.

**Sacks:** They say a lot of creators keep coming back to the things that they care about the most in their life. I guess *Essex County*, *The Nobody*, and *Sweet Tooth* are a bit about being alone a lot.

**Lemire:** Yeah, isolation has been throughout all my work, I guess.

**Sacks:** I guess that comes from your childhood?

**Lemire:** Yeah, growing up on a farm like that, you can feel isolated, [but] you try not to analyze too much where the things come from. You let the work be the therapy. You don't want to overthink it and then ruin whatever's working. I think just being a cartoonist in general sort of appeals to people who enjoy being alone, because it is so time-intensive and most of the time it's just you alone at a desk. You have to be very comfortable with being isolated. I prefer being alone at times.

**Sacks:** So how did *Sweet Tooth* come about? It was a whole different level of series from *The Nobody*.

**Lemire:** It all happened really quickly. I'd done *The Nobody* at Vertigo, and they were interested in working with me on some other stuff, so they asked me to pitch a monthly book. I just—literally over the course of one weekend—sat down and took a whole bunch of different things that had been popping up in my sketchbooks and tried to meld them into some kind of a story or pitch, and that's what came out.

**Sacks:** Interesting. This isn't something you'd been working on a long time? It's a bunch of different ideas thrown together?

**Lemire:** No, it happened really quickly. Just a bunch of little different ideas forced together. The character himself was this character I'd been drawing in my sketchbooks for some reason for some months, and it really was about taking that and trying to build a story around it.

**Sacks:** There are some scenes in the series that are haunting, in the same way that the scenes in *Essex County* are haunting—slow and quietly building. It's got a different pace than a lot of the books I think of from Vertigo. Is that intentional?

**Lemire:** It's just my style, I guess. [It's] my storytelling voice, so you just try not to change it. Just try to stay true to it no matter what you're doing.

*Ghost Stories*, page 79. Credit: Jeff Lemire.

I think it did stand out and was unique compared to a lot of Vertigo stuff, so that's maybe that's why I succeeded. It didn't just fall through the cracks, and people really noticed it as something different.

**Sacks:** Can you give any hints at all of what we might expect to come up over the next few months?

**Lemire:** It's all kind of building towards the big climax in Alaska, where Sweet Tooth and all the rest of the cast of characters are heading, trying to discover his origin and [that] of the plague and the children. As that happens, we see all the different storylines that I've been playing with for the previous three years coming together into one big finale. That's definitely coming up quickly.

**Sacks:** So everything will be coming together. We are going to get an answer to what caused the plague?

**Lemire:** The big reveal at the end isn't the answer. That happens quite early. Issue 35, which is only a couple of months away, has the full answer. There's still a good chunk of story after that. It was never a book that was about the mystery. It was more about the characters. I wanted to get that out of the way and then move on for the characters to reach their natural conclusions.

**Sacks:** I like how Jeppard really changes throughout the series.

**Lemire:** He starts out as sort of a stereotypical, two-dimensional action hero cliché and then slowly becomes something much more. He becomes more and more like Sweet Tooth, really, and he softens a lot. It will be really interesting to see how that all plays out.

**Sacks:** At the same time you're doing *Sweet Tooth*, you're also doing the DC work, which is personal in a different way, I assume. First you did *Superboy*, which I really enjoyed. That's a great exploration of smalltown life, too.

**Lemire:** That's not a character I was always in love with or anything. I wasn't always dreaming of writing him. But it was an opportunity for me to get into that world and learn how to write for other artists in the shared DC Universe. I think I learned a lot on that project that I brought to *Animal Man* and *Frankenstein* last year. It was great to take another step as a writer. I was really happy with how those books turned out.

**Sacks:** What were some of the specific things you learned when working on *Superboy*?

**Lemire:** I'm so used to working on my own stuff that when I started writing *Superboy*, I was a little too specific in my art direction. I kept wanting to maintain too much control over the artists. As a result, it came out a bit stiffer than if I'd let the artists breathe and do their own thing. So when I went on to *Animal Man* and *Frankenstein*, I really kept myself away from the visual aspect of it. I just focused on character and plot and let them completely control the visual side. I think the results were a lot stronger.

**Sacks:** The art, especially on *Frankenstein*, gives the book a completely different, wild and totally over-the-top emotional energy to it. Those books are very different.

**Lemire:** They are, yes. Doing the same type of work all the time would get very boring. It's good to have something like *Sweet Tooth* and *Animal Man* that are very dark serious books, and then *Frankenstein*, which is a big, fun action comic where I can cut loose and exercise a different part of my brain.

**Sacks:** Do you generally plot ahead or let yourself really get loose?

**Lemire:** I always like to have a good solid framework to know where I'm going. Within that, you leave yourself room for new ideas as you're writing.

**Sacks:** That's especially true in *Animal Man*, where it's all coming together with the big crossover with *Swamp Thing*.

**Lemire:** That's been plotted out pretty tightly for a while, now.

**Sacks:** Have you known since you started on the book that it would lead in that direction?

**Lemire:** Not specifically what it would be, but we [Scott Snyder and I] knew we would do something together eventually. We just started planting seeds, and then as it got closer, we just figured out the specifics.

**Sacks:** Are you a fan of the work that Snyder is doing on *Swamp Thing*?

**Lemire:** Scott Snyder was a good friend of mine even before all this. Just through talking and hanging out and running ideas for each of our books off of each other, the crossover just happened. Why don't we both do this and build it together?

**Sacks:** You're also taking over *Justice League Dark*.

**Lemire:** May is my first issue, and I'm really excited about it. I'm having a blast on it. It's got all my favorite characters. Constantine is probably my favorite fictional character, so I was super-excited to get my hands on him. Surprisingly, the most fun I've had has been with Deadman, actually. He's a character I liked, but he wasn't really a favorite of mine. I really enjoy writing him.

**Sacks:** What is it about him?

**Lemire:** His working-class attitude. It's really fun to have him and Constantine bickering and playing off each other.

**Sacks:** That's a whole different side of your muscles, too.

**Lemire:** It is, yeah. It's somewhere halfway between *Animal Man* and *Frankenstein*. It has the big adventure, team book feel that *Frankenstein* has, but it's rooted more in the supernatural. More serious character studies and things like that.

**Sacks:** Were you concerned about following Milligan on the book?

**Lemire:** It's just like with *Animal Man*, since Morrison was there before me. You think too much about that, you get intimidated. So the best thing to do is just to go in there and be yourself and be confident in what you do. And be respectful of what people have done before you [while] at the same time trying to do your own thing.

**Sacks:** Has it been fun to be part of the DC New 52? That's definitely different from the work you've done for Top Shelf.

**Lemire:** It's been a whole different thing. They put so much publicity and stuff behind it. It was obviously exciting to be part of it. And then to have my books succeed was also really very gratifying.

**Sacks:** You have a book upcoming, *Underwater Welder*.

**Lemire:** *Underwater Welder* is my next big graphic novel. It comes out in August from Top Shelf. In a lot of ways, it's probably the closest thing to *Essex County* that I've done since. I'm really excited about that book, and *Justice League Dark* obviously. I just drew a Batman story with Damon Lindelof, the creator of *Lost*, [who] wrote the script. I think that will be coming out over the summer as well. It's a short story that will be exclusively available digitally, so it's pretty much new, exclusive digital material.

**Sacks:** What do you think about the way that the industry is moving into digital?

**Lemire:** Personally, I don't read digital comics. I prefer paper and like the physical book. But anything that will get more people reading comics is good with me. If digital comics make it more accessible for people who wouldn't normally make it into a comics shop to find and read my work, then I'm all for it. Anything that can help the industry grow in new directions and bring in a broader audience, I'm all for it.

# Getting to the Bottom of Top Shelf's *Underwater Welder*: An Interview with Jeff Lemire

DIAMOND STAFF / 2012

*Diamond Previews World*, July 20, 2012. Reprinted by permission.

Jeff Lemire continues to make a name for himself in the comics world. His graphic novel *Essex County* was named one of Canada's Top Five novels for 2011 in a CBC poll, and his work on DC Comics' *Animal Man* and Vertigo's soon-to-be-ending *Sweet Tooth* have garnered a wide range of critical praise.

Lemire's latest graphic novel is *The Underwater Welder* from Top Shelf Productions. The novel focuses on Jack Joseph, an underwater welder working off the coast of Nova Scotia, and soon-to-be father. As the due date moves closer, Jack finds himself under increasing pressure—not just from his impending fatherhood—but the legacy of his own father, a welder himself who disappeared when Jack was young. After a mysterious encounter under water, Jack finds himself coming to terms with his roles as both father and son.

**Diamond:** Fatherhood is at the core of *Underwater Welder*, and it's also an important thread in *Animal Man* and *Sweet Tooth*. Do you think writing about these characters and relationships has made you experience fatherhood differently?

**Jeff Lemire:** I don't think writing and creating comics has changed how I experience fatherhood. I think experiencing fatherhood has changed how I make comics. When I started out on *The Underwater Welder* four years ago, I was still not a dad myself. I think the book was really about the stress and fears of impending fatherhood that I was feeling at the time. Then, over the course of creating the book, I had my first child, a boy, and my perspective changed so dramatically that the book itself turned into something else as well. As I worked on it, it became much less about fear and pressure and much more about a celebration of fatherhood in a strange way . . . an acceptance of it. And, the same goes for *Sweet Tooth* and *Animal Man*. I don't think I could have written and drawn those books the way I have if I weren't a father myself when I started them.

**Diamond:** *Underwater Welder* seems to deal not only with the tension of the main character's impending fatherhood, but his having to explore the events that occurred with his own father as well. Was that reflective of your experience as a parent-to-be, or did that develop as part of the narrative (or possibly both)?

**Lemire:** Really, that is fictional. While I was experiencing certain stress and fear over becoming a father, I exaggerated it here and used the character and his situation as a metaphor. It's an exaggerated, fictionalized version of what I was feeling. I also wanted to get back to experimenting with weaving a narrative between past and present the way I did in *Essex County*. So all of that went into the narrative structure of *The Welder*.

**Diamond:** While there's a strong science fiction element to this book, the character interaction and emotional aspects is clearly the core of the story. Do you ever find it difficult (with this or your previous works) to balance those aspects?

**Lemire:** No, I love taking genre elements or tropes and then representing them in a new and interesting way, but putting the focus not on the big plot moments but rather the quiet character moments. It's not dissimilar to what I did in *Sweet Tooth* with the postapocalyptic/adventure genre or *Essex County* by using a sports story. To me juxtaposing that kind of genre elements whether they are sci-fi, horror, or whatever with quiet character studies creates a really interesting tension and helps present both aspects in a fresh way.

**Diamond:** You've said that this book was harder for you to finish because it was outside the regular schedule of the monthly books. Is there crossover between the pressure of bringing a child into the world and your own struggle with pressure to deliver the book?

**Lemire:** I'd like to think any work pressures I had or have are very different from my personal life, but the fact is that my work bleeds into all aspects of my life and vice versa. So I'm sure the stress and pressure I felt trying to complete *The Underwater Welder* found its way into the comic in some way.

**Diamond:** Did you know early on that this book would be about a welder, specifically? Was it a profession you had to research?

**Lemire:** I'll be totally honest . . . I did very little research into underwater diving and welding itself. I was just enamored with the visual aspects of it and use it more as a fantasy-like metaphor than a gritty, realistic study of the profession itself. In other words, I was more interested in the atmospherics of it than the details.

Though having said that I do have a bit of experience welding myself (the dry kind). When I was a teenager, I worked in a tool and die factory with my dad for six or seven years and did a lot of welding there.

**Diamond:** The town in *Underwater Welder*, Tigg's Bay, is fictional, but how different is it from an actual town in the area?

**Lemire:** It's totally fictional and unrealistic. I wanted it to feel like a true ghost town, a final outpost detached from the rest of the world. I wanted the town itself to be very much like an imaginary place between places where Jack and Susie felt totally alone.

**Diamond:** Along with your graphic novels published by Top Shelf, you also write a number of titles for DC Comics. How different are your experiences writing your own characters versus established ones? Do you find yourself having to "shift gears" creatively?

**Lemire:** I enjoy balancing the two worlds. It helps to keep my work for both mainstream comics and indie comics fresh when I can jump back and forth between them. I also like seeing aspects of both worlds start to bleed into each other.

For instance, I think the pacing of my personal work has improved. I've become more economic with space at times so that when I want certain scenes to feel "slow" or long, there is a better contrast there. That comes from having to fit stories into twenty pages each month with DC. And I always try to bring as much of my personal aesthetic and voice to my DC work as I can.

In the end I love being able to play in both worlds.

**Diamond:** Does working on these books take away from your desire to work on original ideas, or does it give you more drive to do something completely your own?

**Lemire:** Not at all. They feed each other. Doing DC stuff always gives me a lot of new ideas that I can bring into my personal work and vice versa. Like I said, I've come to thrive off of balancing work in both worlds. My personal work will always come first, though. Luckily I'm able to juggle a lot of work, but if I had to slow down and choose, it would always come back to projects like *The Underwater Welder*. Worlds that I create for myself, by myself. As fun and exciting as the DC stuff can be, there is no comparison with the creative freedom I experience while working on these types of books.

# Lemire Paints a Bittersweet Romance with *Trillium*

**JOSIE CAMPBELL / 2013**

*CBR*, June 11, 2013. Reprinted by permission.

This summer is shaping up to be a busy one for writer and artist Jeff Lemire. Beyond cowriting *Trinity War*, DC Comics' first major event since the advent of the New 52, with superstar Geoff Johns, Vertigo Comics is also releasing the Canadian writer/artist's newest creator-owned miniseries, the sci-fi romance *Trillium*.

Announced along with Scott Snyder's creator-owned miniseries *The Wake* at last year's NYCC, *Trillium* tells the story of a woman from the year 3797 and a man from 1921 who end up falling in love, a simple action that will destroy the universe. Written and drawn by Lemire, the ten-issue miniseries begins in August.

Taking a break from his convention travel, deadlines, and recently announced DC Villains Month title, Lemire took the time to speak with *Comic Book Resources* about his upcoming creator-owned miniseries, his evolving art style, and his future at Vertigo.

**Josie Campbell:** The first issue of *Trillium* is out in August and marks your return to Vertigo following the conclusion of *Sweet Tooth*. What was the inspiration for the story, and why did you specifically want it to be a sci-fi romance?

**Jeff Lemire:** It came from a couple of places; as a kid I really loved sci-fi, and I read a lot of classic sci-fi like Isaac Asimov and Arthur C. Clarke and things like that—Stanley Kubrick's *2001* was probably my favorite movie when I was younger. I saw that for the first time, and it had a pretty profound influence on me artistically. So sci-fi is something I always wanted to tackle. *Sweet Tooth* was a multiyear project, and I was talking to Mark [Doyle],

*Trillium* promo poster. Credit: Jeff Lemire.

my editor at Vertigo, about what I might want to do next. It was a couple of [ideas] that he kind of called me on as similar to things I had done in the past, and maybe it would be a good idea to do something totally different. Doing sci-fi and it being a romance would just be completely different from *Sweet Tooth* or *Essex County* or my other creator-owned stuff. I really wanted it to be super-fresh and to write something I hadn't done before. On top of that I had these unconnected ideas about a story about an explorer from the '20s who had been in the first World War and somehow those two things got mashed together into this story.

**Campbell:** Obviously, the year 3797 you're fabricating whole cloth, but what interested you about the 1920s?

**Lemire:** That time period for some reason has always held my interest, especially World War I. This is kind of a sidetrack, but a couple of weeks ago at a convention I met George Pratt, the painter and artist, and he and I were talking about that because he had done a graphic novel years ago set in World War I. We were talking about how there's just something so visceral about that time period visually that we both connect to. Particularly from a visual standpoint it's such a rich thing to draw, trench warfare. But, also, I've always been interested in that early age of exploration, of people exploring the Amazon or the Arctic. I saw that I could parallel that first great era of exploration with this sort of futurist incarnation of where they're exploring worlds. It really was me just combining the things I like! [*laughs*] I came up with a story that somehow fits it all together.

**Campbell:** Since we're talking about the visual, looking at your work, the word "bleak" always comes to my mind—there's just something very spartan and truthful about the way you draw landscapes and people. What were you trying to do with *Trillium* artistically? Will it look similar to *Sweet Tooth* or any of your previous projects?

**Lemire:** No, I think it is a lot different and I can already tell that my art's changing just on this project from what I've done. There are a couple of things that are different; first off, building the world of the future is something I've never done. Even though *Sweet Tooth* was set in the near future, it really was still our world. There wasn't this visual worldbuilding I'm doing with *Trillium* where literally I'm designing a whole planet and space stations and space suits and imagining futuristic technology, things like that. All of my stuff, really, has been set in the present. The 1920s stuff is new, too—for the first time I had to do a lot of research on costumes and architecture and things from the '20s. Both of those things have pushed me in new directions.

Also I'll be painting a lot of the book myself. José Villarrubia, who's colored my work on *Sweet Tooth*, is involved. We're doing two different styles, visually. The stuff set in the future will be watercolor painted by me; it kind of gives it a much more organic look. The stuff in the '20s [José will] be coloring, and then the two will weave together later on. So again, this is a lot of me trying to push myself visually. In each issue, I'm also trying different things with storytelling that I don't want to spoil yet, but, for instance, the first issue is kind of a flipbook, even though there are these two stories they parallel one another. So there's a lot of stuff going on visually, trying to expand myself.

**Campbell:** You're talking about doing watercolors—how do you normally work? Do you hand paint everything?

**Lemire:** Yeah! I don't do any digital work at all; I really enjoy the tactile nature of drawing and getting my hands dirty. Especially since this style is so expressive and organic anyway, I think it lends itself much more to that than digital work. I'm penciling and inking traditionally and watercoloring over that. I was actually pretty intimidated to do this because I haven't done a lot of painting and coloring of my own work, but you just have to do it to push yourself to get better at it! Luckily I have some pretty talented friends, like Matt Kindt who does *Mind MGMT* and watercolors that book. He gave me a few pointers before I got started. I'm really enjoying it; again, this is something I haven't done before, so it's all fresh for me.

**Campbell:** We know from the last time *CBR* spoke with you that a Trillium is a flower and is also the symbol for Ontario. How is it related? Why did you want to name the sci-fi romance miniseries after the flower of Ontario?

**Lemire:** I didn't! [*laughs*] It's a long story, I swear to God I spent more time trying to figure out the title for this book than I did writing it. It took us *months*; we had a number of titles that for legal reasons couldn't get cleared, all sorts of things. Eventually we narrowed it to this one element of the story, which is this flower that mysteriously appears in both the past and the present. The word "trillium" also sounded sci-fi and so it just stuck. The fact that it was Ontario's flower and everything was just a nice double meaning for me living here. Now that word has almost become part of the story itself in a weird way, so it all worked out.

**Campbell:** You're heavily entrenched in DC in the superhero world right now with *Trinity War*. What do you see as your role over at Vertigo now? Do you want to do more miniseries going forward rather than ongoing series?

**Lemire:** Honestly, I'm not sure yet. This book will take me to the end of the year in terms of finishing it. I have a couple ideas for projects I might do after, some graphic novels, some miniseries. We just kind of have to wait and see when I'm a little closer which one really starts to take hold and then I'll figure it out at that point. Right now I'm just focused on this.

**Campbell:** To expand on this question, in general do you want to keep working on superheroes or go back to creator-owned work at some point, or possibly even revisit any of your old stories?

**Lemire:** I don't think I'd ever go back to any of my old stuff; you're told to never say never, but I don't have any plans to go back to the worlds of *Sweet Tooth* or *Essex County* or anything like that. I really enjoy doing the DC stuff. I don't know if I can continue to do the amount of DC work I have been doing the last couple of years; the monthly schedule and all that stuff is pretty grueling. I think at some point in the future, I will scale back and try to focus more on creator-owned stuff, but like I said, the next year of my schedule is all I've got planned out at the moment. Ideally the goal would to get to a place to just do creator-owned work and support myself on that at some point.

**Campbell:** While we're talking Vertigo, you're also contributing to the *American Vampire* anthology. Are you writing and drawing your story?

**Lemire:** I wrote it, and my *Justice League Dark* cowriter, Ray Fawkes, drew it. Ray's also a cartoonist, and I think a lot of the DC fans don't realize he does his own graphic novels as well. It's a chance for him to showcase his art, and we had a lot of fun. We did a short story and we painted the whole thing, so it looks really cool.

**Campbell:** To end, I remember reading about the first sci-fi project you tried to write a long time ago called *Soft Malleable Underbelly*. Did writing *Trillium* bring that project up again in your mind?

**Lemire:** [*laughs*] Ah no, that one died a long time ago! Some ideas are better left in the ground, you know? That was a formative work that should remain unpublished and unexplored forever! [*laughs*]

# My Interview with Jeff Lemire

ØYVIND HOLEN / 2013

Øyvind Holen blog, June 14, 2013. Reprinted by permission.

**Øyvind Holen:** What would you say is your most important theme as a writer: wilderness, fatherhood, or ice hockey?

**Jeff Lemire:** All of them. I think it's all a product of where I grew up, in rural Canada, where it's really sparse. I've lived in Toronto for fifteen years, but I'm still more informed by things that happened early in our life. I grew up in a very isolated area in Essex County, and there wasn't a lot of other kids around. No one shared my interests, and I felt very isolated as a kid. Obviously, hockey is a big thing for the Canadian identity, and it felt like it united everyone, even the kids in the comics.

**Holen:** In your work there really is no separation between the underground and the mainstream, whereas for the older generation something like Joe Matt coloring *Batman* was made into a big sellout?

**Lemire:** I think that's typical for my generation, meaning the cartoonists who emerged in the last five or ten years. Back in the late '80s and early '90s, there was a big split between mainstream comics and the more personal, autobiographical alternative comics. I identified myself with cartoonists like Joe Matt and Seth, and they had to separate themselves from the mainstream to create an identity for themselves.

But I feel that my generation grew up reading both superhero stuff *and* independent comics, and as we developed and emerged as creators the boundaries between genre work and more personal comics went away. I don't know why, but today you see that there is just as much genre stuff in indie comics, being treated in an interesting way as slice-of-life stories and personal stories. At the same time, I feel like more and more independent writers and artists are also doing superhero stuff; everything seems to be blending together, and the walls are falling down.

**Holen:** But has it become easier today to make comics without doing any mainstream work?

**Lemire:** When I started doing comics, before *Essex County* and *Lost Dogs*, I never aspired to do superhero comics at all. I couldn't care less. The stuff I wanted to do and the stuff I was doing was so far away from superhero comics that I never anticipated getting the opportunity. As far as I was concerned, I was getting a day job and would be working on my comics in my spare time. Ironically, doing those personal books ended up opening doors for me at DC Comics. So when I was handed the opportunity, it was too fun to not be giving it my best shot, and I really enjoyed doing it, so I kept on.

**Holen:** How important was working for Vertigo on your journey from indie comics to superheroes? Vertigo is sort of a middle ground, with lots of opportunities to write personal stuff within genre as science fiction, horror, and fantasy. Was it an important bridge?

**Lemire:** I had one major benefit working at Vertigo: I was one of the artists who got the chance to both write and draw an ongoing series, along with David Lapham's *Young Liars* and Paul Pope's stuff, and that allowed me to be even more personal.

**Holen:** I guess you, as well as me, grew up on the DC superheroes who became the foundation of Vertigo?

**Lemire:** I grew up reading Alan Moore's *Swamp Thing*, *Hellblazer*, Grant Morrison's *Doom Patrol*, and *Animal Man*, which all became Vertigo books and got me into independent stuff as I grew out of the superhero stuff. And today I am writing both *Constantine* and *Animal Man*. Obviously it started with Alan Moore, and continued with Grant Morrison and Neil Gaiman, who blew things wide open. What they were doing back in the '90s is what the mainstream is like today. Obviously it was way ahead of its time.

**Holen:** How do you get assigned to superhero comics?

**Lemire:** I was writing and drawing *Sweet Tooth*, and some of the DC editors liked it, so I got the chance to do a story with The Atom. I really enjoyed that, and they kept offering me more, since I was both reliable and competent. As long as I still can do my independent stuff, superheroes are fun to do. If I had to make a choice I would obviously choose the independent comics, but as long as I am able to juggle it I'm all good.

**Holen:** What are you juggling now?

**Lemire:** I'm writing *Justice League Dark*, *Animal Man*, *Green Arrow*, and a new Vertigo book, *Trillium*, which is a science fiction series. I've plotted the first three issues of *Constantine*, and there's another DC book to be announced, but I have to cut down on the DC writing soon, because I've reached a peak. I've also written my next graphic novel, which I will start drawing as soon as I finish drawing *Trillium*. I really like having lots of different projects, and when I burn out on drawing, I can go work on a script for *Green Arrow*.

**Holen:** Have you had any offers from TV and movies?

**Lemire:** Not really. I've had some conversations, but nothing serious. I am not really interested, to be honest. I am so busy with comics, and I do really prefer comics. Working with TV or movies feels like a step backwards, creatively, because I get so much more freedom in comics, I can do what I want, and I am happy doing it. I don't know why I would do movies, except for the money, of course.

**Holen:** When do you see Hollywood digging into comics for real? Not only for the characters, but for the stories as well?

**Lemire:** I guess it was the early 2000s, when they started developing Marvel and DC properties into franchises, like the X-Men and Spider-Man movies. This was when they really did start becoming more faithful to the storylines that had been built into the comics universes over forty or fifty years. And also translating it a lot more faithfully, and obviously it seems to have struck a chord, because now it has exploded, with three or four big movies every summer, which seem to be based almost directly on comics storylines from the last five or ten years.

**Holen:** Wasn't Marvel's Ultimate line important here, because they offered an updated version of the classic storylines?

**Lemire:** It's true. All the Vertigo guys went to Marvel in the early 2000s, and writers like Brian Michael Bendis, Grant Morrison, Garth Ennis, and Mark Millar were all doing stuff that was faithful to the original stories, but also updated it and made it accessible to younger readers. And Hollywood needs things to be accessible for a mainstream audience.

**Holen:** But why do you think the movies caught on so well? Even in Norway, where the comics at best have been a marginal phenomena?

**Lemire:** I am not sure why. The interesting question is why the people who enjoy these movies don't go out and buy the comics, because that doesn't seem to be happening. But it certainly has caught on, even though I feel that Hollywood has gone a bit bankrupt creatively speaking, when they use all these rich universes with characters and stories that have been laid out for them, which they can just take and steal and appropriate for themselves.

**Holen:** There can't be many comics left that haven't been optioned for a movie?

**Lemire:** I know; everything's either been optioned or is in development. *Essex County* was optioned a while ago, but it has just been lost forever, which is fine with me. But I also feel that a lot of the people making these movies are comics fans, and it's fun to see how much comic influence there is in Hollywood. At the same time the whole superhero thing took off, it was a whole string of other stuff, like *Ghost World* and *American Splendor*, and genre things like *30 Days of Night*.

**Holen:** Who've been the most important writers in this development?

**Lemire:** The Marvel stuff is really informed by Warren Ellis and Brian Michael Bendis, who has a widescreen, cinematic storytelling approach to superheroes. Look at Ellis's work with *The Authority*, that's exactly what we see on the big screen now. I feel *The Authority* was at the vanguard, then the Ultimate line followed. But Warren Ellis moved on.

**Holen:** I guess Mark Millar stepped into Ellis's spot, he has changed the way people make comics. Every miniseries from Ellis reads like a Hollywood pitch.

**Lemire:** Yeah, absolutely. It's strange when it comes back around, and dangerous when writers and artists in comics are not influenced by anything other than other comics. They just read comics. Or see movies based on comics. I guess even *Sweet Tooth* is influenced by movies and cinematic storytelling.

**Holen:** You're also working on the DC relaunch the New 52, which is quite different and more complicated than Marvel's Ultimate universe?

**Lemire:** It's sort of a mix between a relaunch and a refiguring; it's kinda all over the place. Marvel and DC are both rebooting themselves more often, and we see it the same in the movies as well, with Spider-Man and Superman.

**Holen:** It's also interesting to witness how Grant Morrison has been less successful in Hollywood than Mark Millar? Maybe Morrison's too complicated?

**Lemire:** That's a good point, his work's a lot more complicated and a lot more ambitious. Morrison plays around with the actual language of comics, which is not easily translated into movies. I am influenced by Morrison's level of ambition, and with *Animal Man*, I'm walking in his shoes. It's hard to underestimate the influence Morrison and Alan Moore have had on the mainstream, they completely reshaped what they were working on.

**Holen:** Was it daunting to write *Animal Man*?

**Lemire:** When I first started doing the superhero stuff, with The Atom and Superboy, I was still struggling with the difference from my personal stuff and writing superheroes for another artist. Those two projects were a testing ground, where I made some mistakes. Afterwards I felt more confident; I managed to let go of the visual side and let it be more up to the artist, while I focused on the character. I was looking at Grant Morrison's stuff and representing it for a new audience; at the same time, I was putting in something of my own stuff.

Now I feel that I've breached the gap between the superhero stuff and the personal stuff, which makes it a good point where I can retreat into more personal comics, while I keep some of the audience, so I can do it fulltime. Eventually I would love to do one DC book monthly, to keep my fingers in the pot and play with the universe.

**Holen:** Tell me about *Trillium*.

**Lemire:** It's eight issues, a sci-fi love story that follows two narratives: one in the far future, with a female scientist on a distant planet on the edge of colonized space. The other story is about a British explorer in the Amazon in the 1920s. These two characters will eventually meet, and the universe starts to unravel as they crisscross across time and they fall in love. I'm not able to talk about the graphic novel I'm doing for Top Shelf, but it's definitely about ice hockey, and it's very Canadian, with no fantasy or sci-fi element. This will be my first comic since *Essex County* with a more grounded approach.

**Holen:** I guess, in ten to fifteen years, Hollywood will be using the more personal genre stuff that is being made today as fuel for their movie machine?

**Lemire:** Yes, after endless recycling and rebooting of Avengers and Justice League, the only place to go would be the independent stuff, like *Saga* and *Prophet*, the Image books that are a lot like Vertigo in style. The Vertigo titles are too complicated, both with the legal stuff with Time Warner and the connections to the DC universe. Some of today's comics are natural for TV shows, just look at *The Walking Dead*. I think you'll see more things like *The Walking Dead* turned into a TV series, today television's a lot more creative than Hollywood. *Sweet Tooth* would make more sense as a TV series than a movie.

# *CR* Holiday Interview #10—Jeff Lemire

**TOM SPURGEON / 2013**

*The Comics Reporter*, December 28, 2013. Reprinted by permission.

Back when DC Comics announced its New 52 line overhaul, one of the things that was targeted as a key element for DC to have a chance to make it successful over the long-term was the development of unique writing talent maybe a step below that of the one or two superstar creators that a big publishing push was almost certainly going to yield. I think the writer and cartoonist Jeff Lemire has stepped into that role in admirable fashion.

Lemire is one of those rare beasts in all of comics: a creator that has found a voice useful in making comics in multiple expressions of the modern conception of what comic books are and who reads them. He has worked with DC superhero-line properties like Animal Man, the Grant Morrison conception of Frankenstein's monster, and the various mystical characters constituting their "Justice League Dark." He ended one popular Vertigo title *Sweet Tooth* with a fortieth issue and launched the science fiction-oriented *Trillium* with a much-lauded initial burst of issues. He is perhaps just as well-known in the wider comics community for the alt/arts work he's done, primarily the *Essex County* trilogy but also 2012's *The Underwater Welder*. In 2014, Lemire should continue his recent work with the television series influenced conception of the Green Arrow character and write the adventures of a Justice League set in his native Canada.

I'm grateful for the time Jeff Lemire spent talking to me midmonth about juggling all of these things, and to Alex Segura and Pamela Horvath at DC for putting me in touch. Lemire is a busy man.

**Tom Spurgeon:** When I mentioned I was interviewing you for the holiday series this year, Jeff, what came back to me was variations of, "Oh, that guy has really figured out how to do alt-comics work and mainstream work." I wondered if you ever conceive of how things are going in your writing career in those terms? Do you see yourself as bridging that gap or in those terms at all? Has working in multiple comics arenas been purposeful at all?

**Jeff Lemire:** I don't know if it's purposeful. I'm pretty aware that I come from independent comics. I bring that sensibility with me. I've never really lost it. I'm still working for Top Shelf, and doing my own very personal stuff. I'm also doing stuff for Vertigo that's a little more genre-based. The superhero stuff . . . I seem to have always have a foot in all of that stuff; it just sort of blends together. Certainly I love superhero comics and I grew up reading them and I have a real affection for them and those characters. But certainly I come at it trying to bring a little bit more of a personal voice to it. I guess my natural sensibilities tend to lean towards the independent and alternative stuff.

It's trying to bring that to those books, those elements of my personality.

**Spurgeon:** When you say it wasn't purposeful, do you mean that you didn't pursue it, or do you mean that it wasn't something you even wanted?

**Lemire:** [*laughs*] I really just kind of stumbled into it. I loved it growing up, but I never, ever, ever anticipated or pursued working for DC or Marvel. In 2007 and 2008, I was still working a day job and doing *Essex County*. My real goal was to just make enough money doing stuff for Top Shelf or whatever to maybe have a parttime income in comics, and then maybe only have to work a parttime day job. [*laughs*] I never anticipated being able to do comics fulltime. I was never pursuing working for DC. I never thought my stuff—well, certainly my drawing style but also my sensibility as a storyteller—I never thought it was something that fit at DC. I didn't even bother trying. I did my own thing. Ironically, by doing my own thing and developing a voice as a cartoonist and a storyteller, I think that served me in a way that I can bring something new to superhero comics, or at least that must be what people like Dan DiDio and Geoff Johns saw in me and tapped me to start writing some of that stuff. Then it all kind of happened. Once I had the opportunity I figured, why not go ahead and try it. I discovered it is fun to do both.

**Spurgeon:** You said that you read this material as a kid, or growing up. Were the comics of this type that interested you similarly idiosyncratic? Were you attracted to the offbeat approaches to doing superheroes that preceded you? What were some works that were meaningful to you in that genre?

**Lemire:** Even when I was reading that stuff I tended to seek out the comics that had a bit more edge to it. I was reading stuff by Howard Chaykin and Frank Miller—people like that—when I was too young to be reading it, like when I was eight or nine. [*laughter*] Everyone else was reading Chris Claremont's *X-Men*, and I was reading *American Flagg!* [*laughs*], so I was always a bit drawn to that—and not just in comics. Movies and everything. I went to stuff that had a unique author's voice, for sure. That's something that's always attracted me. David Lynch films. Stanley Kubrick films. Stuff like that at a young age. You could see the authorship behind them. You could hear someone's voice. That always attracted me. I was always seeking that stuff out.

I was the right age when the first wave of Vertigo hit. I was probably thirteen, fourteen when that first wave of Vertigo hit. It kept me interested in comics. In my late teens, I dropped out of comics, stopped paying attention. I was from a small town, so there weren't any comic shops. The only stuff I had access to was on the newsstand. I became disenchanted with superhero comics. Got more into movies and music. It wasn't until I moved into the city in my early '20s—places like the Beguiling were here—where I discovered all these other cartoonists, independent and alternative cartoonists. European stuff. That [*laughs*] really got me interested in the medium and drawing again.

**Spurgeon:** Were there one or two cartoonists more significant for you than others? Were there any where you had that scales-fall-from-eyes moments, or were you more generally drinking it all in?

**Lemire:** Yeah, there was. I remember distinctly I hadn't read comics in a few years. I was in film school here in Toronto. I walked into a comic store just passing by one to see what was going on. Paul Pope's *Heavy Liquid* was coming out from Vertigo. And I was like, "What is this?" That was unlike anything I had seen from Vertigo before, from DC. His drawing style is so energetic and bold that it's hard not to want to draw after looking at his stuff. I started finding all his *THB* stuff. That kinetic drawing style of his really made me want to draw, pick up a brush for the first time and draw.

Then I started to see what else was going on. Guys like Dan Clowes and Seth. Coming to Toronto there was this weird brotherhood of Canadian cartoonists that all hung around at the time. Seth, Chester Brown, and Joe Matt . . . you would see them at the Beguiling, and that was cool. I got into that stuff. I opened my eyes to all the stuff that was out there. You get into Paul Pope and you start to see all of his influences, the European stuff like Hugo Pratt—all those guys he was into.

One door opened another. I started to see how big comics was. It wasn't just stuff I'd grown up with.

**Spurgeon:** You were a Xeric winner, am I right? For *Lost Dogs*.

**Lemire:** Yeah, I was.

**Spurgeon:** You would have been one of the later ones, I'm guessing.

**Lemire:** 2005.

*Lost Dogs*, page 14. Credit: Jeff Lemire.

**Spurgeon:** What do you remember about that experience now? I'm always interested in the Xeric winners because part of the original mandate was very much about instructing you in the way the industry worked.

**Lemire:** Yeah, it really was.

**Spurgeon:** Was the Xeric helpful for you in terms of simply understanding this industry in which you wanted to find work?

**Lemire:** It was great. I had been drawing comics at that point . . . that was 2005, and I had been taking it seriously since 2001. Working every day on stuff and trying to get my stuff together. Even though there were a few guys here drawing comics I didn't really socialize with them. I was pretty much in a vacuum; I had no idea how the industry worked: just distributing your stuff in the Diamond catalog, I had no idea how that worked. No concept at that. Doing the Xeric Grant really made me research that, and figure that side of things out.

I was working as a cook then. I would draw all day and then work all night as a cook. I had no money. I could barely pay rent. *[laughs]* So the thought of having money to print a comic or distribute it was impossible unless I had some help. When I found out Canadians could apply to the Xeric, it became the thing. I applied three or four times before I actually got it. I would never have been able to afford printing or getting something together without it. That was a really huge step for me.

**Spurgeon:** So are you one of those pros that keeps track on how the industry works, does that interest you? Or are you at a stage—and this happens, too—where you've kind of removed yourself from that kind of close attention?

**Lemire:** I don't know. When I first started doing stuff for DC, I was a lot more interested than I am now in trying to keep track of sales . . . just out of curiosity and if they were going to keep giving me work. *[laughter]* Now that I feel a little more secure in my position and in what I'm doing, I don't have time. I'm kind of detached from that side of things a bit. I don't go online as much, or engage with fans, or keep track of the business side. I find it's more of a distraction than a help. It starts to influence the way you think about the jobs you take, and that's not a good thing. Those decisions should come from creative places, not from thoughts of career and business.

**Spurgeon:** I have an *Essex County* question. It was named an "Essential Canadian Read" at one point. I guess while elements of the subject matter are clearly Canadian, I wondered if you thought about in terms of it being a work in the tradition of Canadian literature more generally.

**Lemire:** It is very much in the tradition of Canadian literature, I think, people like Margaret Laurence. It's firmly set in my Canadian experience. I take a lot of pride in being Canadian and being a Canadian storyteller. I try to explore that in as much of my work as I can. Certainly the indie stuff, but even now in some of the DC books they're letting me set some of that stuff here and explore the Canadian landscape. It's very important to me.

**Spurgeon:** Your pacing is very distinctive, Jeff, particularly in the comics that you draw as well as write. So when you say the work is in this Canadian tradition, do you mean that it also encompasses a kind of formal approach in addition to the subject matter with which it engages?

**Lemire:** I don't know if my style or my formal approach to comics would be Canadian in any way. I really think that if you look at Canadian cartoonists that preceded me, there's not a strong connection there. Guys like Seth and Chester Brown . . . there's not a lot of common ground in what they do and what I do. Even if you look at contemporaries of mine like Bryan Lee O'Malley or Darwyn Cooke, I guess—he's been around a lot longer but he emerged right before me—we're very different than one another. I don't think there's a "Canadian style." [*laughter*] I think it's more in the subject matter and how the stories have a connection to the landscape—the land itself is almost a character in my work. It's more that than a formal approach.

**Spurgeon:** You mentioned you didn't really expect a progression into Vertigo work and now mainstream superhero work . . . but you also said that you're comfortable knowing you have a place. How long did it take for you to feel comfortable? Was there a point at which you remember feeling more comfortable with that kind of storytelling? How long did it take you to find your creative feet in the commercial comics you're doing?

**Lemire:** I think it took a few projects. It really hasn't been that long. It feels longer than it really has been. My first project for DC was 2010, so we're going on four years. I did *The Atom* and *Superboy*; those projects brought with them a lot of stress in terms of how much of my own style I could fit into them. Also, how I would do it, how I would work with another artist? There was a lot of learning going on there. It wasn't until the New 52 launch, when I got *Animal Man* and *Frankenstein*, that I really felt . . . I'd made a lot of mistakes on those first two projects and kind of figured it out. When I hit those two projects and started from the ground running, I felt like that's when I found my voice as a writer of mainstream stuff. I found the right balance of injecting my own personality into the comics but also working with artists and allowing them some freedom, not giving them too much direction in terms of layout and that kind of thing. Letting them be themselves. It was *Animal Man*, really, that I think I found myself as something distinct from when I write and draw my own stuff. But there was still enough in there that it felt like me.

**Spurgeon:** One thing I'm curious about in terms of your being one of the writers that launched with New 52: How much were you guys encouraged to contribute to the overall tapestry of what they were doing? How much were you encouraged to come up with bridging concepts, say, that other writers could make use of? How much were you accessing the work of your fellow launch writers to see if there was material you could use in your books?

**Lemire:** We were given quite a bit of freedom. I think part of that is they were launching so much stuff at once that they were looking to us to really take the point on our own books. For instance, Scott Snyder and I had been good friends at that point for a couple of years. He was doing *Swamp Thing*, and I was doing *Animal Man*. So, with us pitching books at the same time, there was a lot of back and forth and thus connections between the two books. We really built our own corner there. Something like *Frankenstein* wasn't even part of their plans for their relaunch, but I had a vision for that book and plans, and they liked them. So that one came more directly from me, just as a fan of what Grant Morrison had done there. I felt like there was potential to just keep adding onto that mythology. I had a lot of chances to add to the mythology. The books were both successful, so I got to keep adding onto them.

**Spurgeon:** I talked to Scott Snyder last year, and he was like this, too: that you're kind of mindful of other writers and their strengths and weaknesses and are pretty helpful and solicitous towards one another. That might be via a direct relationship but also might take place indirectly, just in terms of being aware what other folks are up to. Is that a fair assessment?

**Lemire:** Yeah, I think my circle of friends at least are all supportive of one another. A lot of my Top Shelf friends have ended up working at DC: Matt Kindt, Rob Venditti. So there's a friendship there that goes back, and we're all very supportive of one another, and bounce ideas off of one another. Share scripts. Give each other advice. It's very helpful.

One thing when you're doing your own stuff, like with my indie stuff, and I'm writing and drawing it myself—that's a very isolated activity. Which I enjoy. But it's also nice to enter this shared universe where you can call up another writer and start bouncing ideas off of them. That sort of collaboration you miss when you're doing your own stuff. It's nice.

**Spurgeon:** Do you still have a solid relationship with Top Shelf? Are you at the point where you have an opportunity to pursue whatever it is you'd like to pursue with them given the success of and the arc of your mainstream comics writing career? Or is there some dark secret . . . ?

**Lemire:** [*laughs*] There are no dark secrets with Top Shelf. No, I'm very friendly with them. I owe those guys so much. They gave me my first shot with the *Essex County* stuff. I love working with them. They feel more like a family than a publisher at this point. I'll continue to work with them for as long as I can. My next book I'm doing with Simon & Schuster, just because that opportunity was there, but those guys were cool—Chris [Staros] and Brett [Warnock] and I have this understanding that whenever I want to do something with them the door is open. It's important to me to keep that relationship that way. I'm hoping every three or four years I can do a project with them as well.

**Spurgeon:** I was looking at a bunch of your *Animal Man* comics, and the really basic thing that struck me about that character, and maybe even in the context of all of DC's characters at this point, is that he's a family man. So that would seem to me to play into some of your interests in family dynamics, and the way that conception of family plays against its day-to-day reality: the father-son issues, the responsibility of being a father. I'm guessing that was a big entry point for you and that character.

**Lemire:** Absolutely. It was the perfect character for me at the right time. There was so much inherent to that character I was already familiar with: if you take the family aspect away from that character, what is he, really? He's some guy that can run as fast as a cheetah; it's not really that interesting. [*laughs*]

**Spurgeon:** He'd be fun at parties.

**Lemire:** Yeah! But as a superhero comic, there'd be nothing to make him special or distinctive. Or really to give the book a chance to survive. The fact that he's a father and a husband makes him different, so that's something I latched onto right away. I expanded that as far as I could. It was a perfect book for me to infuse my indie-kind of themes into.

**Spurgeon:** You do a lot of work with those themes in your comics: parenting themes outright, like in *Underwater Welder*, or maybe something that could be more broadly defined as protective relationships, like in *Sweet Tooth*. What is it about that subject that keeps you coming back? Is it the richness of that topic? Is it the concern you personally have for those matters? Is this an opportunity for you to work through some of your fears?

**Lemire:** Probably, yeah. The same time I started working at DC, literally the same time I started to do *Sweet Tooth* and *Underwater Welder*, is when I became a father. It's hard for that not to become a big part of your work. My son is five now. I've been at DC for four years . . . it's a big part of my life. It's hard to take a step back and analyze where and why you explore certain things. [*laughs*] The work itself . . . I don't think too much about it outside of the work. The father/son thing is something I've always—for whatever reason—kept coming back to. [*laughs*] I'm sure it's something deep in my psyche. I don't want to get to into on the phone. [*laughter*]

**Spurgeon:** Let me make that broader, then. One thing that interests me about writers that work in mainstream comics, having done work before that in other modes of expression for comics, is how they come to use the fantasy element of comics, the metaphorical richness that you get when you suddenly have fantasy elements that you're compelled to use in many cases. I wonder how hard it is for writers to find ways to make that serve the story, to make it serve your particular interest in specific themes or narrative outcomes. Has that come naturally to you?

**Lemire:** It comes naturally to me because I've always been drawn to that stuff. Even though *Essex County* is quite grounded in a way, there are fantasy elements or at least dreamlike elements in there. There's a magical realism to it; with *Underwater Welder* as well. I've always used genre—horror, sci-fi, or superhero stuff—and it's something which I'm very comfortable with. Almost all of my work has used it in some way, even my personal stuff. It's not a struggle for me. I see the superhero elements or with *Animal Man* the horror . . . they are really just metaphors for what it is you're exploring. If you're looking at the forces that might pull a family apart, it's easy for you to create metaphors for that.

**Spurgeon:** Do you end up enjoying the operatic, larger-than-life opportunities with those genre tools, working on this grand stage in primary colors at least part of the time?

**Lemire:** Absolutely. The superhero stuff is fun when you can cut loose. The project I'm tinkering with for Simon & Schuster and which I'll start in earnest in the New Year, that is very grounded. That is probably my book without any kind of fantastic element at all. To be able to work on that intensely for two weeks and then spend a few days working a *Justice League* script, that's [*laughs*] almost a relief after working with that tight control of the indie world. I do enjoy it.

**Spurgeon:** The *Justice League Dark* material seems to me to represent the cleanest break with your ongoing sets of concerns and your basic approaches to form, Jeff. For example, it struck me that just having that many characters to deal with, the fact that you have five to seven lead characters, that would have to make it difficult for you to employ the kind of pacing you're able to use with a smaller cast. Comic books like that one are these rampaging plot-point vehicles—story point, story point, story point. Was that a struggle for you, to juggle those concerns? There's a tentative quality to that book.

**Lemire:** That one *was* tough. *Justice League Dark* was my first team book, and like you said, there are so many different things to juggle. With *Animal Man*, it's still essentially the story of this one character. There may be a family, but it's *his* family. It's much easier for me to infuse my sensibility into that. *Justice League: Dark* was a real eyeopener in how hard certain books are to write, and how difficult it is to do certain things with such a big cast of characters and so much going on. I don't know that all of *Justice League Dark* was entirely successful for my figuring that out.

I'm doing this new *Justice League* book next year, and I learned a lot from *Justice League Dark*, just as I had initially learned with *Superboy* and *The Atom* before doing *Animal Man*. So this one should be a lot more *me*, if that makes sense. At least I hope it will be.

**Spurgeon:** You spoke of that first transition partly in terms of learning to deal with your writers, giving them more leeway to be creative. Is there something similar you learned this time, with your transition between the two team books? Is there something you're glad not to experience again?

**Lemire:** I think, in *Justice League Dark*, it wasn't so much of an artist thing as a writer thing; I was worried juggling all of the different characters and giving them "screen time" that I never had the opportunity to take a step back and approach the material the way I would otherwise approach it. I've been very conscious of taking each character in the new team book—and this sounds very simple now, but when you're dealing with so many things it's hard to see the forest for the trees—and giving them a personal arc and then working it so they each have an emotional hook and a journey. It's about making sure there's an emotional and a character point of view in addition to the plot point of view—to boil it all down in a more articulate fashion.

**Spurgeon:** I think your art is interesting. I wondered if working with a variety of different artists as a writer is helpful in how you approach your own art when you get back to it? You're drawing the last *Animal Man*. Is there something you're looking forward to in terms of getting to collaborate with Jeff Lemire the artist? What do you think your strengths are?

**Lemire:** It's hard. Much more than with my writing I'm critical of my art. Nothing's ever good enough. As soon as I finish a page, I hate it immediately. [*laughter*] I'm very hard on my art, so most days I see the misses.

**Spurgeon:** What is something you latch onto in terms of wanting to see it improve, then, Jeff?

**Lemire:** I know I'm a strong storyteller. I know I can create mood and motion. It's really about trying to refine the style while keeping the looseness and the expressiveness of it. Make it tighter in terms of anatomy: technical things, pushing myself to get a bit better. Then there are days when I just have fun drawing. Those are usually the best days. [*laughter*]

**Spurgeon:** Do you draw outside of your comics work?

**Lemire:** Yeah, I force myself to sketch at least a half-hour every day before I start my other work. Otherwise I'd never do it.

**Spurgeon:** Is drawing a part of your writing process at all?

**Lemire:** Yeah, that's funny. I'm working on *Trillium* right now, so when I sketch all I'll sketch is scenes or characters from the Simon & Schuster thing, laying the groundwork. Turning over ideas, some of which will never make the final book. I come up with stuff sketching I never would have if I sat down at a keyboard. I definitely approach stories like that visually first.

**Spurgeon:** The designs in *Trillium* are very striking. Does that come mostly out of your sketchwork in organic fashion, or is that something you have to explicitly work on?

**Lemire:** I spent a lot of time working on the design for that one, especially in terms of the worldbuilding there. With *Sweet Tooth*, despite the science fiction element it was still set in our world. With *Trillium*, I design whole worlds and the look of the tech . . . with this new book now, I remember the last six months of *Sweet Tooth* my sketchbook was full of sci-fi stuff, prepping and trying things out for *Trillium*. So overall that was six to eight months of designing before I ever started to work on the comics themselves. That was a lot of fun, actually. I also got to look at a bunch of sci-fi stuff I loved as a kid that I'd forgotten about. A lot of Moebius, a lot of stuff like that.

**Spurgeon:** That's kind of the zeitgeist, that kind of science fiction.

**Lemire:** Yeah, it's weird. The last convention I did was last June . . . I think it was June, I can't remember. Oslo. I was checking out these Norwegian cartoonists, and even all of them were doing sci-fi, space stuff. [*laughs*] Or fantasy stuff. There's a real thing right now with genre stuff. I remember ten or twelve years ago all of the indie stuff was autobio, slice-of-life stuff. It's a real shift. [*laughs*] Then there seem to be more sci-fi books coming out, stuff like *Saga*; there's a real boom right now.

**Spurgeon:** Now, you're in your late thirties.

**Lemire:** Yeah.

**Spurgeon:** It seems like comics-makers in their late thirties and early forties, their orientation is towards the vocational aspects of comics changes. They just kind of want to get to it; they want to make significant progress on the work they feel they're meant to do.

**Lemire:** Right.

**Spurgeon:** You seem comfortable where you are and you're certainly prolific. Is that just reflective of a general work ethic, or have you thought in terms of starting to build a professional legacy? Is this prolific period part of a specific orientation you have to this time in your professional life, or is it just about maximizing your opportunities as they come to you?

**Lemire:** I'm definitely right there.

About three or four years [ago], everything in my personal life felt figured out. [*laughs*] I had a kid. I had a happy marriage. We had a house. All of that stuff was taken care of, [and] now it was time to get serious producing—not as *much* work as I can, but trying to get all of these stories I want to tell told while I still can. There's definitely that sense of work now. I'm approaching midlife; there's certain things I want to accomplish, certain things I want to do and I still feel like I haven't really told my best story yet. I want to keep going until I find it. Make sure I get to tell it before I get too old to hold a pencil anymore.

# An Interview with Jeff Lemire: On the Creation of Equinox, DC Comics' First Cree Superhero

## WAASEYAA'SIN CHRISTINE SY / 2014

*Maissoneuve*, May 12, 2014. Reprinted by permission.

Jeff Lemire has created a DC Comics superhero based on a young Cree female from a northern community. That northern community is also in Canada. Her civilian name is Miyahbin, but over the past few months, through online interviews and social media buzz, we've come to know her as Equinox, a member of Justice League United.

**Waaseyaa'Sin Christine Sy:** In reading online media coverage, it's obvious that there's a keen interest in the contributions Equinox's character will make in terms of representation in comic books.

**Jeff Lemire:** For me it's been an interesting experience learning more about Cree culture and First Nations culture. I think I've said this before in an interview, but for me, whatever stories I decide to tell or books I do, it's always a way to learn something, to challenge myself. I grew up in southwestern Ontario, really far southwestern Ontario, in Essex County, and there's not a large First Nations or Aboriginal community down there. Also, it wasn't something I was ever, as a kid, really exposed to. It was just another a part of the country that I didn't really know about. You read stuff in books in school or whatever but I didn't know any Aboriginal people growing up at all, so I felt like this might be a good way to create a project that was accessible to young people who are in other communities, just to start to scratch the surface of other cultures that are out there and hopefully create something that's a positive representation. I feel like the Canadian media, when we do see things about First Nations or about First Nations culture, its either hardships they faced or negative stereotypes and things like that. My experience, while limited, in Northern Ontario and Moosonee and Moose Factory, has been so positive. I met so many amazing, welcoming, funny, warm, people, and I wanted to create a character that embodied that.

**Sy:** I think your experience speaks so much to the majority of peoples' experiences in Canada in terms of being distanced from any relationships, knowledge, or awareness of Indigenous peoples here in Turtle Island, as we call it. Your method of using a comic book and your art and creativity to create an entry for other people, a younger audience, or even audiences of all ages is really brilliant and beautiful. In terms of representation, the importance of having Equinox come out into the world can't be overstated. In thinking about her aesthetic, her beautiful outfit that you've created, you've captured the spirit and beauty of the fancy shawl dancer.

**Lemire:** Yeah, exactly. Just to be clear, I'm working with another artist on the book; I'm the writer. There's an artist from the UK named Mike McKone. Poor Mike, I think he may have been to Canada once, but certainly not Northern Ontario, and he's so out of touch with what I'm trying to do and he's been such a good sport. I'm sending him tons of reference photos from my trips. I can't believe the job he did with the character and designing the costume and everything based on no firsthand knowledge. It's pretty stunning actually. He really pulled off, I think, something beautiful, and I've only heard positive responses about the costume and her look. And the photos I did send him were based on traditional dance and things like that and he took that and instead of just interpreting it straightforwardly he put a really modern, sleek, superhero spin on it in a way that still honors it, but it's cool and new and I think he couldn't do a better job. I'm glad you agree.

**Sy:** We have Equinox's demographic and her costume, I'm just wondering if the storyline reflects the realities of Indigenous peoples?

**Lemire:** I'll be perfectly honest: it's very hard for me to get too political in a superhero comic book published by an American publisher. They're interested in me telling an entertaining story, a superhero comic, so there are certain limitations, clearly, in what I can show and I didn't really get into it in depth; it was a matter of choosing my battles. So for me, the battle I knew I could win was in creating this character, and creating a character that was full of life and positive and that would be something hopefully young people would enjoy and can hopefully educate them a little bit about Cree culture. I knew if I could do that, this would be a victory. Going beyond that is a little out of the bounds on this project but it is something I am exploring in other projects currently.

**Sy:** Well, this seed is the perfect one, so let's relish this. In thinking about the relationships Equinox has with the other characters of *Justice League United*, I'd like to hear some or your thoughts about these relationships, not necessarily details but just what your sense is of them.

**Lemire:** Just putting her in this comic and making her work as a superhero as part of this DC Comics universe has been really interesting. I try to give every character on the team, whether it's Equinox or Hawkman or whoever, a different point of view and a different personality so they all bring something different to the dynamic. I tried to think beyond her Cree heritage, being Canadian, and First Nations. What else? What's her actual personality and perspective? What does she bring to the team? I thought a neat way to approach what I'm writing was to think of her from the reader's point of view, in this crazy larger-than-life world. She's someone who grew up in a small community, an isolated community, and hasn't left it. And then, to not only leave it for the first time but to experience all these crazy, cosmic superhero traditions going on around her; so she becomes, in a weird way, the most grounded and down-to-earth character, providing readers a new point of view into this crazy universe. So that's kind of how I've approached it and in a lot of ways I think that's a good way to approach it because hopefully the creation of Equinox will bring some new readers to DC Comics who probably haven't read a lot of comics before. If I can use her as an entry point as well, into that universe, I thought that would be a smart way to approach it.

**Sy:** I like that you're using the word "grounding." In some of your interviews, I've heard you talk about her powers, about her relationships with the land, and that blew me away. I thought, this is fantastic, this is what we're ready for; we need to be hearing this.

**Lemire:** Yeah, a lot of that came from spending time in the schools with the kids up in Moose Factory and just asking them, "What kind of traits do you think a hero should have if they're from the area? What kind of powers?" And over and over again they would all say she has to have the connection with the land. Over and over again . . . so when you hear it so many times there must be something there. That's really what I hooked into in trying to come up with her powers and everything else. I'm glad that you liked that.

**Sy:** Yes. It's so important in our day and age with the environment, all the work—the wellbeing of the environment. What better way to bring out that message than through a comic book?

**Lemire:** No kidding. If there were really superheroes in the world, what's one of the things they would need to work on? It's the way we're treating our planet. The other thing is First Nations culture is so far ahead of the rest of Canada in their relationship to nature, the world, and the land, and that's something pretty inspiring.

**Sy:** I spoke with my friend in Fort Albany [James Bay area], and told her I was having this conversation with you. It was important for me to hear her thoughts because I'm not Mushkego Cree, I'm not in the James Bay area, and I'm distanced from many of the realities that motivated Shannen Koostachin, the young Cree education activist who died in a car accident in 2010 and is said to have inspired this character. I asked what she thought about this project with Equinox, and the first thing she wanted to know was what Koostachin's family thinks about it. She also shared her hope that Koostachin's memory and her work in education, work that's connected to her family, peers, and community, would not be exploited. So, in thinking about these things, exploitation and appropriation, I'm not sure if people have asked such questions of you in these areas?

**Lemire:** I actually want to clarify that. When I did the first interview for this project months ago, they asked me about Shannen Koostachin and if she was an inspiration and I said, "Oh yeah, that's a very inspiring story," and from that it sort of turned into, as the story was represented online, as though the character was inspired by Shannen. But she actually isn't, for all the reasons you just said. I would never presume to appropriate a story that is so real and then turn it into a cartoon, especially without her parents,' her family's awareness or approval. That's something I would never do. So when I said she was an inspiration for me in creating a teenage character, definitely, but it's no way based on her or drawn from her story, much for that reason. As much as I take pride in my work I would never belittle or exploit a story just to tell people some pop culture or popcorn story. Her story is much more important than that so I'm glad you brought it up.

**Sy:** I hadn't read that angle of it anywhere, so it's good that it'll be in this interview.

**Lemire:** Yeah, it's great. I'm just clarifying because as soon as I said that she was inspiring it turned into this character being based on her and I cringed thinking, "Oh, I hope her family doesn't think I'm exploiting her," because that wasn't the case at all.

**Sy:** I know you've spent a lot of time in Moose Factory and Moosonee and when we go to these new places and have cross-cultural experiences, they can often be provocative. Can you share a fun or funny story about your experience there?

**Lemire:** Oh, God, well, I don't know if this is what you're looking for, but this is the first thing that comes to mind. I knew it would be cold, but I think I was not prepared for how cold it would be. So in Toronto, I'm a big city boy, I went and got all my quote unquote "warm, super-warm clothes," and then I got there and we had to snowmobile. We had to snowmobile for, I don't know, it was a couple hours each way on this ice highway and we were with high school kids who had clearly been on snow machines their whole lives and were much more comfortable. I was so cold! I've never been that cold in my life; I thought I was going to die. And these kids are just zipping around just like it's any other day. You're like, okay, yeah . . . it was so cool to be out there with the kids. And we checked the trap lines with the kids at this camp. The kids were so into it.

**Sy:** What a fantastic experience. Will comics be sent to them or the communities?

**Lemire:** Yes, we're sending a bunch of copies and I'm donating, buying these graphic novel collections for each of the schools along the whole coast. We're just in the process of trying to make the contacts to send them up. So definitely, that's the other thing too: obviously I'm not Aboriginal or from the area, and as good as my intentions are, I can never create an authentic story. My hope, my real hope, is that maybe one of these kids I talk to or give copies to or talk about comics with, in ten or fifteen years from now, will end up making their own comics and telling their own stories. That will be the real victory of the project.

**Sy:** The story of you coming from southwestern Ontario and being really distanced from any of this, to now, is a story, too. It's a story of how it [making connections and understanding] can be done.

**Lemire:** Yeah, it's about opening a dialogue between white Canada and First Nations and trying to open those lines of communications. Using story and art as a good way to do that.

**Sy:** So how has this project changed you?

**Lemire:** When you're in the middle of something it's hard to see how you are being changed by it. I feel like this is something that I'll look back at a year or two from now and see how my life has changed in a huge way. Just in a practical way, I've made a bunch of really great friends up there and I feel like I'll be visiting every year. I already have my next trip planned to the area. And just meeting new people and sharing new experiences and stories changes us all in ways we can't fully understand when you're still in the middle of it, when you're still in the middle of the project. But it's certainly opened my eyes. Like I've said, I've never really spent any time in any Aboriginal community and being there firsthand, getting a sense of what's really going on and what the people are really like, putting a human face to all the things you see on the news and everything just changed me. It widened my perspective in a lot of ways.

**Sy:** Well, Toronto is an Aboriginal community, too.

**Lemire:** Yes, yes it is. Every community there and everything gets lost in the jumble.

**Sy:** Yes. The whole world is in Toronto, but there is a fascinating history there, too. So one more question: how do you hope this project will change us?

**Lemire:** Well, I hope it opens a dialogue with people who normally wouldn't [access it]. I guess a lot of people who read the comics are from the States and maybe they have no concept of what any of our First Nations issues are; I just don't think they have any awareness of what's going on in Northern Ontario and this is a great entry point into North America that they probably have no awareness of. Hopefully, it's a great way for kids in our country, whether they're Aboriginal or not, to just start thinking about First Nations culture and communities, and other parts of the country that they don't know about. Hopefully it will provide a positive point of view or role model into that for them.

# Using Robots as a Metaphor: An Interview with Jeff Lemire and Dustin Nguyen

KARIN L. KROSS / 2015

*Tor.com*, July 17, 2015. Reprinted by permission.

Combining elements of space opera and the Pinocchio-like adventures of an innocent robot boy, Jeff Lemire and Dustin Nguyen's *Descender* has been one of the big hits of the year in comics; before the first issue was released, Sony announced that it had secured the rights to develop a *Descender* film. Amidst the bustle of the convention floor at SDCC, I sat down with writer Jeff Lemire and artist Dustin Nguyen to talk about the place of artificial intelligence stories in the current zeitgeist, their collaborative process, and where Tim-21, his faithful robot dog, and homicidal friend and protector Driller would be going next.

**Karin L. Kross:** I feel like artificial intelligence is having a moment right now in pop culture; you mentioned *Ex Machina* in the Descender letter column recently, and even *Age of Ultron* fits to a certain extent.

**Jeff Lemire:** When I conceived Descender, I wasn't really aware of these other things coming at the same time. And it's not like you're consciously trying to be part of any kind of movement or trend, but clearly you're right, there does seem to have a little bit of a spike in pop culture, for sure. I think it's just a reflection of the time we live in. You know, you're recording this on your phone right now and it's just—technology is leaping ahead and ahead so fast now. I started in comics in 2005, ten years ago, and at that time I didn't have a cell phone. I don't even think I had a computer myself, you know. And just in those ten years, how much technology has changed. We certainly are on the cusp of some sort of—I don't know, they call it the Singularity, or whatever, but I think we're staring it down now, and I think that's why it's so present in pop culture, because it's so imminent.

**Kross:** It's kind of like this reaction to pervasiveness of stuff like a smartphone.

**Lemire:** I think so, yeah. I don't know if that's why—I just want to tell a cool sci-fi story about a robot, so I certainly didn't think of it as a reflection of anything that's going on. But I think that's why we're seeing it, sure. I mean, technology becomes a bigger part of all of our lives every day and it's just exponential, so it's not hard to see that technology eventually becoming somehow equal to us or almost a sentient thing itself.

**Kross:** Of course, with *Descender*—the tech is one thing, but it is a very human story, ultimately. What are some of the influences and ideas that you had going into it?

**Lemire:** Tim-21, the main character, is probably the most human character in the book, and I'm not so much interested in telling stories about machines as people. So in this case it's what those machines tell us about ourselves and the people around them—using robots, AI, as a metaphor for the Other, the outsider, whatever that means, whether it's racially, sexually, whatever. I think it's still a very powerful metaphor to use. I think I was just trying to use robotkind and machine-kind as this way of exploring racial relations and things like that. But on a bigger level I just wanted to tell a really great space opera, sci-fi story. Certainly Stanley Kubrick is probably the biggest influence on the book: *2001* and *A. I.* And also some manga, Urasawa's *Pluto*—stuff like that if you're looking for direct influences.

**Kross:** I was wondering, Dustin, if you could talk a little bit about some of the challenges and rewards you find in using watercolor.

**Dustin Nguyen:** I've always liked painting watercolor, and Jeff's always had this really—I use the word "handmade" feel to all his work, and I thought it was perfect to use that with him. If it were any other writer I worked with, I probably just would have gone digital, which makes it move a lot faster. It's a challenge, but it's also a good way to limit myself from overloading myself on work, because [with] watercolor, you can only work it so much before you kill it, you overdo it. So it limits me to what I can do, but at the same time, it forces me to do just the important things. And instead of going for really heavy-on design, I go for atmosphere. And I think it works really well with Jeff's work. His work is always very atmospheric, like when he worked on *Sweet Tooth*— just wandering down a barren abandoned road, it felt like you were actually there, and I think I wanted to find some of that as well with this story.

**Lemire:** I really think the watercolor decision is probably what's made the book successful because at the end of the day, there's just so many comics out

*Descender* #3, page 1. Credit: Dustin Nguyen and Jeff Lemire.

there, so many sci-fi comics. I think the watercolor look has really helped it stand out and find an audience and separate it from the pack. And it's kind of cool; it's a book about machines and is such an organic medium. So that's kind of the whole theme of the book, human and machines intermingling, represented in the drawing style—where he's drawing these very technical robots and things, but executing in this organic way.

**Nguyen:** And I have to point out—I hate to always say, "Oh, because it's painted it's a special book"; I feel bad because there's guys out there doing amazing watercolors, so I don't want to make it like that's our hook. I do enjoy a lot of the books out there, and a lot of people do it, but like Jeff said—it almost fights each other and balances each other out, with the amount of tech and doing something really organic. And a lot of the illustration, it reminds me of when you read the old manga, they would only do three or four pages in color, and the rest was in black-and-white. And I loved looking at the covers. There are mistakes, there are flaws in there, but it's all part of being the imperfect look of it that makes it fun.

**Kross:** What's a typical day, week, unit of collaborative time?

**Nguyen:** As little as possible. We don't like each other much. [*laughter*]

**Lemire:** You know, it's probably the easiest collaboration I've ever had. We talk so little. And not because we don't like each other but because we don't need to.

**Nguyen:** Yeah, we don't need to.

**Lemire:** I write the scripts and he just draws them; we don't even communicate or anything. I just trust him completely.

**Nguyen:** And he's like, "Oh, you can change anything you want," and I'm like, "Dude, the script is perfect!" It's how I feel like a lot of books need to be done: just two people.

**Lemire:** We don't get in each other's way at all; we have complete trust. I think we both have a huge amount of respect for one another in what we do and we just want each other to do that, and it just comes together perfectly.

**Nguyen:** I think if you find someone, and they're really good at what they do and you really like what they do, you should really just trust them. And the scripts come in and they're exactly what I would want to work on. There's nothing on there that I can say, "Oh, this needs a little"—no, there's nothing there, it's really exciting. I read his scripts—Kindle has this program where you can send yourself emails to the Kindle, and it transfers it to an e-format book. So I format it to look like a book and I read it like a novel. I have all his scripts in there.

**Kross:** So with the visual designs of the book, is that something that comes out the script?

**Lemire:** I give pretty vague descriptions and he just goes nuts.

**Nguyen:** I think—we talk about a lot, we talk about what we want to feel from looking at it, and that kind of thing.

**Lemire:** Yeah, I think we probably talk a lot less than other people, I mean—I want the book to look like a Dustin book so I let him design the stuff, and he's so much better at it.

**Nguyen:** And I want it to read like a Jeff book.

**Lemire:** We have a lot of common influences too, so that helps. It gives you a shorthand where you don't have to try to explain what I want. I know a lot of Jack Kirby stuff from the seventies was really influential on me in this book, like the *Eternals*, and stuff like that, those giant Celestials and things, so I'm like, "Make a Celestial, a big guy like that!"

**Nguyen:** It's easy. I think we're in a good time right now where you can talk about anything in pop culture and people will get it. We're like the same age too, which helps a lot. We weren't into the same things but we saw the same things at least.

**Kross:** Image seems to be really friendly to SF and SF storytelling; I was wondering if you had any thoughts on that.

**Lemire:** I think they've had a certain amount of success at it with *Saga* and now *Descender*, so it opens the door for other people to come and try stuff. I feel like SF comics have had a huge boom since *Saga*, because it was such a big hit. I think we're probably near the end of that wave. Something else is going to hit now. But the good stuff rises to the top. I think Image is so good at all the genre stuff because they're so hands-off. You work for the bigger companies doing general work and there's so many cooks in the kitchen. You can still do those big bombastic stories here, but it's just me and Dustin's vision, with no one interfering.

**Nguyen:** And I think content is always key. I think instead of trying to make a SF book, we wanted to make a good book that we both enjoyed.

**Lemire:** It wasn't about SF; it was about Tim and his character where he goes, and the SF stuff are the trappings around it.

**Kross:** Before the first issue even hit the stand, there was the movie happening. How did that come about?

**Lemire:** We announced the book here last year, at this show, in San Diego, and just had that promo image that's hanging up there and a brief description. And we immediately had interest from Hollywood. And that image is very evocative that Dustin did; that's really the reason why we had so much interest.

**Nguyen:** We had the first issue kind of roughed out, didn't we?

**Lemire:** Yeah.

**Nguyen:** We just had a plot.

**Lemire:** I think the reason things happened like that is that I tend to work really far ahead on everything, because I'm juggling a lot of books, so in *Descender*'s case, I already had the first arc written and the whole series mapped out—a pretty detailed series bible of the whole thing before the first issue even came out. So we were able to show producers the shape of the whole thing, and that's why the deal was done early like that. But honestly, I think it just goes back to that image Dustin did, it really seemed to capture a lot of things.

**Nguyen:** Thanks, man. It's weird, because Image said, "Hey, we need a promo for a thing," like, on a Friday, [and], "We need it by Monday."

**Lemire:** So quick, yeah.

**Nguyen:** Quick turnaround, yeah. But it was really the story; when we talked about it, we knew what we wanted to do and it was really fun.

**Lemire:** Yeah, I think it's because we had the whole thing figured out before we started, we were able to have really good conversations with those producers, and they got a real sense of what it was they were going to be buying.

**Kross:** So you said you had the whole thing planned out; I'm not going to ask the "what's going to happen next," but what are some of the general ideas and places, literal or figurative, that you're looking at going?

**Lemire:** It's always a tough one because you don't want to spoil things, but in the first issue, at the back we had the atlas of the different planets in the solar system that we're working in. There's nine different planets, and I think we want to spend a lot of time on each of them . . . we worked really hard to give each planet its own identity, its own look, its own purpose within the story, so you'll see a lot of planet-hopping and we'll see this expansive universe through the eyes of this boy. Certainly the mystery of the Harvesters is going to be ongoing, the thing that propels the narrative, but the trick with all of it is, you want to go bigger and bigger and show more and more, but you don't want to lose what it's really about, the quiet little moments between Driller and Tim, so really it's just keeping the focus on the characters despite the expanding canvas.

**Kross:** Anything you're particularly looking forward to working on?

**Nguyen:** Killing everyone, turning them into robots? [*laughter*] If I said it, it would spoil a lot.

**Lemire:** There's a desert planet in issue 6.

**Nguyen:** The gas planet would be my favorite, and it's not because I don't want to draw backgrounds; it is just the idea of a planet entirely made of gas. I've always been fascinated by planets like Uranus and I think parts of Venus. When I was little, I wanted to be an astronaut—to see different environments, and just to imagine yourself being on a planet with only gas, and gravity so low that you actually wouldn't be able to move around without floating. That stuff's fascinating to me.

**Lemire:** Yeah, it also has sentient gas creatures living on it, which is fun.

**Nguyen:** I just always laugh when I hear the words "gas creatures."

**Lemire:** Exactly.

**Nguyen:** Childish, childish.

**Kross:** Dustin, before you got here, I was asking Jeff about this moment of stories of robots and AI and was wondering about your thoughts as well.

**Nguyen:** I think it's not so much a trend, but it's just basic human fascination with something that's not about us. We think we're the only smart things in the world and everything is like, an animal, but when you have something like AI it's almost like it's part of us, because we created it but—I think it's just common human fascination with that.

# An Interview with Jeff Lemire

MICKAËL GÉREAUME / 2016

*Planet BD*, February 17, 2016. Reprinted by permission.

**Mickaël Géreaume:** Could you please introduce yourself and tell us how you began working in the comics industry?

**Jeff Lemire**: My name's Jeff Lemire and I'm a Canadian cartoonist. I started working in comics sixteen years ago, around 1999–2000. I'd gone to film school in Toronto, but, as I studied the film medium industry, I became less interested in it and more in comics, again. I grew up loving comics and drawing all the time, but there wasn't really a clear path to making a career doing comics so I tried other things but I missed drawing so much that, when I graduated film school, the first thing I did was drawing comics again. I spent several years just developing my voice, practicing, until I did *Essex County*, a book I did in 2005, 2006. It was the first book I really felt I'd found my voice as an author. So I started to publish those with Top Shelf, a small publisher in America, and, from there, I went on to work for Vertigo, with *Sweet Tooth*. And then I started writing superhero comics as well from DC and now Marvel. Now my career is kind of split in two halves where I do mainstream superhero stuff and I still do my more personal work on the side.

**Géreaume:** What have been your influences, artistically speaking?

**Lemire:** It's always changing. At different points of my life and career I find different artists. As a child, I only had access to Marvel and DC superhero comics. That's what I grew up reading . . . and copying. But then as I got older, I started to develop my own style as I started to discover more European cartoonists who were more stylistic, more impressionistic, more expressive than the American comics. It suited me more. The big ones were probably . . . when I was really developing my style, the person I always looked at the most was probably Dave McKean, who did *Cages*. It was sort of my bible, I just love that book.

**Géreaume:** He's a genius!

**Lemire:** Yeah, he's a genius. So that's the thing I aspired to. Although I could never reach it, just the expressiveness of his linework . . .

**Géreaume:** Have you met him?

**Lemire:** I've never met him.

**Géreaume:** He's a nice guy.

**Lemire:** Yeah, I'm sure he is. Dave McKean was sort of my big touchstone. But, I mean, Paul Pope also—just the urgency of his brushwork was really inspiring when I was first starting. And I discovered a lot of European cartoonists like Hugo Pratt, José Muñoz. So many! [*laughs*] And now all the time I discover new people and new inspirations.

**Géreaume:** Meeting Dave McKean is very easy. All you have to do is to follow Neil Gaiman. They hang together half the time.

**Lemire:** [*laughs*]

**Géreaume:** From the beginning, you've been balancing between indie comics and mainstream. Do you have a specific approach to each type?

**Lemire:** Not really. I try to bring as much of myself as I can to the superhero stuff as well. It's just a different process. You're working with more people, it's more of a collaboration, so my voice is only one of several in the making of the final product, you know? So we're collaborating and my voice, my style is mixing with whoever the artist is, whereas doing my independent work is much more direct. It's my voice. Especially when I'm drawing my own stuff, it's just one person, it's a more distinct, more direct vision, I guess.

**Géreaume:** In each and every one of your comics, you try and go for new approaches to narration and visuals. For example, in *Trillium*, you roughed up some readers by forcing them to turn their book upside down to follow the two protagonists' intertwined destinies, and in *Green Arrow*, the visual edition was out of the ordinary. Is that a goal you set up for yourself, each time?

**Lemire:** Yeah, yeah. It's usually a personal challenge. Like, when you've been working in a medium for a certain amount of time, like I've been drawing comics every day for fifteen years now, you've got to find new ways to keep it fresh for yourself, each day, you know? Or else, you get bored. So you challenge yourself to try to find new ways of using the medium to communicate and challenge the readers. I feel you have a responsibility, as a cartoonist, to do everything you can to fully explore the medium, its potential. It's a language like any other and the more you use it, the more you learn different ways of using the language. It's mostly to keep me from being bored, as if I'm not bored, the reader is likely not bored either. [*laughs*]

**Géreaume:** Lately, the first books of *Sweet Tooth* and *Descender* both came out in France. Could you please present those two books to our readers?

**Lemire:** *Sweet Tooth* is, I guess, a science fiction, postapocalyptic story. It's about a group of children who are hybrids, half-animal, half-human, in the wake of a plague that's wiped out most of humanity. They may hold the secret to either curing the plague or to whatever caused the plague, so different factions of people are hunting them, and the book tells of the road trip these kids take across postapocalyptic America. And well . . . I don't know, I figure that's it. [*laughs*]

**Géreaume:** And *Descender*?

**Lemire:** *Descender* is a sci-fi, space-opera book that I'm doing with artist Dustin Nguyen, and it's a big, sprawling epic of robots on the run in space . . . it's a universe where robots have been outlawed and they're hunted down, killed, and destroyed. It follows one robot, a young boy-robot and his companions, as they're sort of trying to find their way in this universe that hunts and fears them.

**Géreaume:** *Sweet Tooth*'s first TPB was published last December, in France. There's a very dramatic scene in it where the children are in prison. It's a very dark moment, like a throwback to World War II. Do you also challenge yourself to reach at the readers' emotions, like that?

**Lemire:** To me, the stories always gravitate to ones that are emotionally charged, that I can invest in, emotionally. These are the stories I like to create as well. I want to touch the readers and affect them, emotionally, have them engage with the characters. And sometimes, that means doing very dark and terrible things to your characters, but, usually, my stories end up in an optimistic place. I may put my characters through hell, but they end up coming out in an optimistic place.

**Géreaume:** You really made an impressive entrance at Marvel Comics with *All-New Hawkeye*, *Extraordinary X-Men*, *Old Man Logan*, and *Moon Knight*. How did you get to work for Marvel and how did you manage to find yourself at the helm of all these titles?

**Lemire:** [*laughs*] Well, I'd been working at DC comics for four or five years and I think I'd built a name for myself on *Green Arrow* and *Animal Man*. Then, last year, I felt it was time for a change, for various reasons. I met Axel Alonso, the editor in chief at Marvel Comics, and we talked about different things I might have worked on. *Hawkeye* was the first thing he wanted me to do and I didn't want to do it because Matt Fraction and David Aja's run was so special. It was very daunting to try to live up to it. So I was skeptical and I hesitated to take it on but then I came up with that idea of exploring Hawkeye's childhood. It seemed like something that I like to do with a lot of my characters. So, once I had an idea that I felt strong about, I decided to do *Hawkeye* and I think they were all very happy with how it turned out. And then it was just a matter of timing when the new *X-Men* came to be. They needed a new writer for *X-Men* and I was there. [*laughs*]

**Géreaume:** You're the new Bendis.

**Lemire:** [*laughs*]

**Géreaume:** I read *All-New Hawkeye* yesterday, and I think you found a right balance between Matt's established character and a new vision. And Ramon Perez's art is very powerful.

**Lemire:** Everyone loved Matt and David's run on the series so I just didn't want to do something totally different to betray the readers. I wanted it to feel like the same characters that they'd invested in. But I didn't want to copy what they did either, I wanted it to be personal to me. So I've tried to find a balance between continuing with the kind of feeling they had going but also bring as much as possible of my own voice as well as Ramon's into it.

**Géreaume:** About *Descender*: when I read what it's about, I wondered why you picked Dustin to illustrate that. It's weird to see his style on this kind of story. Did you choose to work with him or was it a chance encounter?

**Lemire:** It's a great mix. Dustin and I had been both working at DC for a long time, but we never worked together. We always admired each other's work. So, when I left DC, he was also looking to do some creator-owned projects and it was perfect timing that we got to work together. It's such an effortless collaboration, I feel like we share brains and we hardly communicate at all! We just have the same influences, the same way of telling a story. It's a perfect mix of two creators; it almost feels like destiny that we got to work together. When I used to look at Dustin's stuff, I always loved when he did watercolor—his private work was mostly watercolor—and I knew he wanted to do a full comic in watercolor. I felt it was interesting for *Descender* because . . . I mean, it's a story about machines and technology, which is usually illustrated in a very precise, clean way, but he's doing it in a very organic way, with watercolor. In a weird way, that mix of technology with the organic watercolor medium almost perfectly symbolizes the character of Tim—a machine, yet so human—it just works very well.

**Géreaume:** I know you do the covers on *Descender* but, in general, how do you choose to illustrate a particular title?

**Lemire:** I can write a number of titles at the same time, but I can only ever draw one thing at a time because it's very time-consuming. I'm already working on a new graphic novel that will come out in May. I've been working on it for the last three years which is about when we started doing *Descender*, so I've been kind of busy. [*laughs*] But I wanted to do more creator-owned stuff. So, working with people like Dustin allows me to do more than one creator-owned project at a time. And after my graphic novel, I'll probably do a new Image book that I'll write and draw. . . . Yeah, I can only really do one book at a time, and if I'm going to invest as much time as it takes to draw something, I'd rather it be something that I own and create myself rather than a Marvel or DC property.

**Géreaume:** I don't know if this is still going on but you've been allegedly working with Scott Snyder on a new book. Could you tell us a bit about it?

**Lemire:** Yes, it's pretty exciting. I've just finished another graphic novel called *Roughneck* which will come out from Futuropolis in May and then I'm working right now drawing a book that Scott is writing which is called *A.D.: After Death*. It will be with Image Comics in the US. It's not a series; it's a graphic novel. It's sort of growing all the time and it started off at a hundred pages and it's getting bigger. It's science fiction, located in a future where death has been genetically cured and it follows that society of people who are basically immortal. One of them in particular has everything he's ever wanted, he's immortal but he's very unhappy so it kind of explores him as he tries to escape all this. It's very interesting, and we're doing it in this strange format which will be prose, like a novel this guy is writing and I'm illustrating just illustrations, not comics, and the other half will be in comics form so it's a mixture of everything Scott does and everything I do.

**Géreaume:** Do you collaborate on the writing with Scott?

**Lemire:** No, Scott does all the writing and I'm drawing.

**Géreaume:** So it's the first time you're only illustrating a book?

**Lemire:** Yeah, I've done a couple of short stories with others that I didn't write, but I've never drawn something this long that someone else wrote, so it's interesting.

**Géreaume:** Doesn't it feel weird?

**Lemire:** It's challenging in a good way because it forces me to do things that I wouldn't do if I was writing myself and it pushed me in different directions that I would never have taken on my own, visually. So it's helped me grow, I think my artwork has leaped a lot on these next two projects, from *Sweet Tooth* and things. . . . And it's kind of fun to try to interpret Scott's vision. We're really good friends, Scott and I, we've known each other for a while and we talk about so many things. I know him so well that I know his intentions and what he wants. It's very easy, like—we don't need to communicate too much; I know what he wants.

**Géreaume:** Last question regarding your work: I love *Trillium*. How do you look back on this series?

**Lemire:** I'm very proud of it. I think that, in a weird way, *Descender* would never have been had I not done *Trillium* because *Trillium* was my first incursion into hard sci-fi. I loved the worldbuilding so much, doing it, that I wanted to do more and that led to *Descender*, which is bigger in scope than *Trillium*. And I really loved the experimentation of *Trillium*, with the format. Yeah, I'm really proud of it.

**Géreaume:** Were you given the power to get inside the head of someone famous, living or deceased, in order to understand his art or his techniques or just how his or her mind works, who would you choose and why?

**Lemire:** David Lynch, the film director. Ever since I was a kid, his work has affected me more deeply than anyone else's. I almost can't explain it, it's just so powerful to me, so influential. He's my hero. But, artistically? Definitively Dave McKean. [*laughs*] Because he's so versatile, he can do so many different things and do them so well. If I could rob his talent, that would be great.

# *Outright Geekery* Interviews . . . Jeff Lemire

**SARAH ELIZABETH CAMP / 2016**

*Outright Geekery*, June 27, 2016. Reprinted by permission.

Today, *Outright Geekery* is proud to bring you a special interview with comics writer and illustrator Jeff Lemire! Lemire is known for such works as *Essex County*, *Sweet Tooth*, and *Descender* in addition to a continually growing body of work that stretches from independent titles to titles with Marvel, DC, and Image Comics. This particular interview comes in the aftermath of Lemire's newest endeavor, *Black Hammer*, a new ongoing series published through Dark Horse Comics with artist Dean Ormston, colorist Dave Stewart, and letterer Todd Klein.

**Sarah Elizabeth Camp:** As you can probably guess, a number of the contributors for *Outright Geekery* have been heavily anticipating the release of your newest title, *Black Hammer*. That being said, how does it feel to be writing a superhero narrative that is entirely new?

**Jeff Lemire:** I actually came up with *Black Hammer* back in 2007–2008 as I was finishing my *Essex County* graphic novels. At the time, I planned on doing it as my own next graphic novel that I would write and draw. Back then, I was still only doing indie comics and I never anticipated a day when I would actually be working on mainstream superhero comics like I am now. So, Black Hammer was sort of my way of expressing my love for the superhero genre, but filtering it through my own indie style.

Then, as things developed in my career, *Black Hammer* got put on the backburner so I could focus on doing *Sweet Tooth* at Vertigo. And, that also led to me writing a lot of mainstream superhero comics since then. But I never forgot *Black Hammer* and would pull it out and tinker with it once a year or so. But it became obvious that I would never have time to draw it myself, with all

*Black Hammer* #2, cover. Credit: Dean Ormston and Jeff Lemire.

the other projects I have lined up to draw now, so I started thinking of doing it with a collaborator.

Dean was one of the first artists I thought of. I've loved his work since his *Books of Magick: Life During Wartime* series at Vertigo and had the chance to meet him at a comics festival in Leeds a few years back. Luckily Dean liked the project and came on board.

So, while it still remains a love letter to the superhero genre, I'm adding my own experiences working into superhero books into the mix of that original concept now, too.

**Camp:** This may seem like a silly question, but in relation to the above question: where do you get your inspiration from? When writing a narrative dealing with superheroes, how do you keep it fresh?

**Lemire:** I get to draw from the entire history of comics and superheroes. It's hard not to be inspired by that. I get to take everything I love and then mix it together into something new. And I don't need to worry about continuity or editorial interference. I get to do whatever I want. But above all that, I really just love the characters. Forget all the superhero stuff; I just love these characters as people and love exploring them.

**Camp:** With the series being titled *Black Hammer*, and Weber's daughter being revealed as a woman of color, one could assume that this titular character—while absent—is an African American superhero. What can you tell us about him, without giving too much away of course? What/who were your inspirations for this kind of character?

**Lemire:** That's tricky because both Black Hammer and his daughter, Lucy, are *key* characters in the book and central to the mysteries of *Black Hammer*. What I can say is that, like all the characters in *BH*, Black Hammer was inspired from a very specific part of comic book history. So, he was pulled from the '70s Blaxploitation superhero archetype, like Luke Cage or Black Lightning. But, like all the other characters, he will be revealed to be something much more than that, a real, fully rounded character that transcended these genre trappings and stereotypes. And as for Lucy . . . I can't say anything else. She is very much the core character of *Black Hammer*.

**Camp:** Do you and your creative team anticipate making *Black Hammer* an ongoing series, or will it be a limited run like *Sweet Tooth*, *Trillium*, or *Plutona*?

**Lemire:** It is an ongoing series. I already have eighteen full scripts written!

**Camp:** The first issue was masterfully done, just the right amount of tease without giving too much away! What can readers expect in the future of *Black Hammer*? Specifically, I'm thinking along the lines of Madame Dragonfly, Abraham Slam, and the real zinger for me—Joe Weber's daughter?

**Lemire:** The first arc will continue to explore and reveal more about each character, while also showing key moments from their "in continuity" adventures as superheroes, which will add backstory and subtext to the present day narrative. The first arc is six issues long, and each issue will shine a light on one of the character's pasts.

**Camp:** Within the comics realm, I'm sure you're no stranger to current discussions and discourses regarding representation with a capital "R." How do you feel *Black Hammer* will fit into that discussion, if at all?

**Lemire:** I am aware of this, but I don't concern myself with it. I just want to tell the best story I can with the best characters I can. And if I do that right, this naturally lends itself to creating a diverse cast of characters that represent all the different aspects of the world around us.

**Camp:** You have such an extensive body of work that you have contributed to the comics world over the years, this may seem like an odd or misplaced question, but how do you, as the creator/writer/illustrator, view audience reception during the creative process?

**Lemire:** I don't say this to be dismissive of my readers, or of comic audiences, but the truth is I don't think about the audience all that much. I'm my own worst critic. I am trying to challenge myself with each project to grow and to be the best writer and cartoonist I can be. If you start thinking about what audiences want your natural creative compass can start to get really skewed. Comic audiences are incredibly diverse and complex. You can't please everyone. I have to be true to myself, and if I'm proud of the work I do, chances are other people will be, too.

# Jeff Lemire Follows His Secret Path

**TOM POWER / 2017**

*CBC Q*, April 20, 2017. Reprinted by permission.

**Tom Power:** Jeff, congratulations on the book.

**Jeff Lemire:** Thank you.

**Power:** I read it last night. I want to talk a little bit more about graphic novels a little bit later, but first I know you said that each book really marks the place you were in when you made it. And I know that's not geographically [*laughs*] but as a person. *Roughneck* is a book about this former NHL player. He's drinking and he's fighting and he's dealing with his family; he's in trouble with the law. I'm interested, given that you say these books reflect where you are, where were you when you wrote *Roughneck*?

**Lemire:** Yeah, it was an interesting time for me. I think I actually started *Roughneck* quite a while ago. It's been done for over a year. But there was some . . . we held onto it because *Secret Path* came out first and we didn't want to put them out at the same time. So, I think I started working on the book by like 2012, 2013. I was going through some stuff myself. I was kind of dealing with some things in my life I was trying to change, much like Derek, the character in the book. But, aside from that, there's a whole heap of fiction put on it as well. He's his own character in his own world and you kind of create metaphors for things you're dealing with.

**Power:** Yeah, exactly, but what about this particular story—why did you want to tell this particular story?

**Lemire:** I'm trying to think back. At the time I had done *Essex County*— well, now it's been about ten or twelve years since I did that book but . . .

**Power:** Wow, it doesn't seem that long ago. [*laughs*]

**Lemire:** I know, it's crazy. After that—especially when I go to the States— everyone sees it as sort of this epitome of Canadian fiction or something. And that kind of lingered, that it is Canadian fiction. I love the book, I'm very proud of *Essex County* and I wouldn't do anything differently. But now I feel like my awareness of the country of Canada and what Canada is, is so much broader than it was back then, instead of this sort of idealized world of hockey and small towns . . .

**Power:** What changed there?

**Lemire:** I think I just started opening my mind a bit more to what other cultures—First Nations and Indigenous people in Canada—were going through and how that had been something that wasn't even on my radar in the past and it sort of suddenly came on my radar. I don't know how that started, but it just became something I became very concerned with and troubled by. And you know, certainly reading different authors like Richard Wagamese and Joseph Boyden and other people sort of started me down the path of becoming more aware of what was going on in the North and in the First Nation communities. And I just felt like if I was going to do another Canadian story it would be good to not just touch on the idealized Canada but also the other parts of Canada that maybe I didn't know enough about.

**Power:** I want to talk a little bit about those influences a little bit later. But first, I was thinking while I was reading this that the other day we had Jay Baruchel into the studio. Jay was in promoting *Goon 2*, which is, of course, a very different take on the hockey goon, on the hockey enforcer. And Derek, the character in *Roughneck*, is a fighter, he's a fighter in hockey, and I know you've touched upon that kind of story in your work before. Just as an author, just as a creative person, what is it about the hockey enforcer that we find so interesting?

**Lemire:** Going back to the first question, I think one thing I kind of just forgot until you said that was that was the summer I started working on this book was the summer I think four ex-enforcers committed suicide or died that summer. It was the summer Wade Belak committed suicide and Boughner, I think, as well. Those four stories about those men really hit me, and I really started thinking about what that life of violence does to a guy. These are young men who grow up playing hockey, and they quickly find their path in the game is to be the tough guy, to fight, to do that every night and if they want to stay in the game and be vital . . . it is a life of violence. And then, when the game kind of leaves them behind, they're still left with that violence inside them but nowhere to put it. And that became a fascinating idea to me, to create a main character.

**Power:** And often they're not remembered in the same way. If you look at the non-hockey fan list of hockey players who they know—you think of Mario Lemiuex, you think of Wayne Gretzky, you think of Chris Chelios. You

*Roughneck*, page 20. Credit: Jeff Lemire.

don't hear names like Boughner, you don't hear names like Marty McSorley. You don't hear, you know it's . . .

**Lemire:** Or if you do, it's for some infamous on-ice thing like Marty McSorley that happened that isn't a great memory. There are the rare occasions, there's people like Tie Domi who kind of created a sense of celebrity around himself, who transcended being the tough guy. But for most of the part, these guys are soldiers who do what they need to do for their teammates, and then the game leaves them behind and they're forgotten.

**Power:** And damaged.

**Lemire:** And damaged physically, mentally, emotionally, and that became a fascinating and really intriguing entry point into a character study for me with Derek.

**Power:** Also, I was so curious about Derek's childhood, because I know that his childhood is a key part of the man that be becomes. I don't want to give away too much, but you see sort of the familial reasons that he was encouraged to be an enforcer, to fight rather than to skate. The theme of what happens to us as children and how it impacts us when we grow up is a huge part of *Roughneck*. I don't want to give away too much again, I'm trying not to do really spoilers here, but it's hard because some of the most impactful moments are moments where your characters are standing on the road and are looking at themselves as children. And I'm realizing that looking at children is something that is synonymous with a lot of your books, a lot of your work. Why is childhood something you want to explore?

**Lemire:** I'm not saying anything earthshattering here, but the things you experience as a kid impact you. You feel everything so much deeper as a kid. You're not jaded by the world yet. So everything, the good and the bad, is so exciting or so terrible [*laughs*], depending on what you're experiencing. And those feelings are so intense compared to what we feel as adults. I feel like things get dulled down as we get older. And I find that I love writing that from that point of view of a child who just feels everything so intensely and everything is so important to them.

**Power:** But also the loss of the innocence seems to be something that you use.

**Lemire:** Yeah, it's good and bad, right? Yeah, that's part of childhood— leaving childhood behind—and that's so heartbreaking to me. Especially as a father now myself, I have an eight-year-old son, and watching him grow and slowly go from being a baby to a toddler to now into a kid and you see him leaving parts of that behind and that can be heartbreaking. You just want him

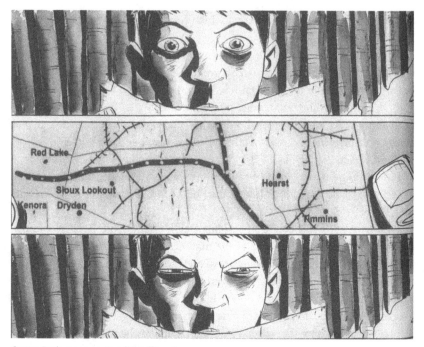

*Secret Path*, page 33. Credit: Jeff Lemire.

to stay that one age forever. You want him to be innocent, you want him to be so excited about everything and so innocent, and I find that so sad. [*laughs*]

**Power:** The world turns us into adults, whether we want it to or not. I heard a great interview with a great band called Dawes; they're a band from California, and the lead singer said he wrote this song because his little brother was six or seven years old, and this is the radio, and he said the "F" word for the first time. And he said, "Oh man, like something was left behind the first time you curse like that."

**Lemire:** Yeah, and I feel like if you look at someone like Derek and his sister in the book, they both grew up with very troubled childhoods and they both looked for a way out and unfortunately they both took avenues that weren't healthy. And now it's a time as adults where they can kind of get some perspective and hopefully sort of find some . . . a new way of living. That was the other sort of theme I was interested in.

**Power:** I want to talk a little bit about *Secret Path* and *Roughneck*. You mentioned that you were writing *Roughneck* when Gord Downie approached you to draw *Secret Path* [and] you kind of put *Roughneck* to the side and concentrated on *Secret Path*. Congratulations, by the way, on the Juno Awards for that project.

**Lemire:** Oh, thanks, I only got into comics to win music awards, so it really worked out for me.

**Power:** Well, I'm glad. [*laughs*] When you said that *Secret Path* and *Roughneck* are kind of linked, that they complement one another . . .

**Lemire:** They really are.

**Power:** What do you mean by that?

**Lemire:** Well, I mean I was creating them at the same time, so they can't help but be linked aesthetically; visually, especially they look almost the same [*laughs*]. I was about halfway, I think exactly halfway, through *Roughneck* when I met with Gord and his brother Mike for the first time at my studio and they kind of laid out their idea for doing the *Secret Path* and told me about Chanie Wenjak, and they asked what I was working on at the moment and I kind of explained about *Roughneck* and the thematic parallels and things. They both kind of smiled to themselves. Knowing I was already working on a book about the North and about First Nations and then they were presenting this *Secret Path* to me; it all seemed fated that we work on it together at that time.

**Power:** Sorry, was it hard to put it away? Was it hard to stop this project to start something else?

**Lemire:** Writing comics is pretty grueling, day in, day out, page after page; it's pretty tedious. So after a hundred and something pages of drawing it every day it was kind of nice to have an excuse to take a break. [*laughs*]

**Power:** Right, 'cause it's not like traditional writing. And I know I'm going to sound like I don't really know that much about it, but I guess when you write a traditional novel you're sitting there with a word processor in front and you're typing. This is something so different.

**Lemire:** Drawing a page of comics is a lot of hard work, and doing it every day—it's a grind. And you kind of have to keep your eye on the bigger picture and the bigger story you're telling because you can get really caught up in the details of what a particular face looks like that day and you're not drawing it properly and stuff and you can get too much tunnel vision on the details, so it's nice to step back. And I think doing *Secret Path* gave me a whole new perspective on . . .

**Power:** What do you mean?

**Lemire:** It was interesting. I've only ever written linear narrative where I write a script for myself and I'm drawing and I'm dialoguing it and following a plot. And then Gord came and all of sudden I was adapting music. And music is so . . . it's like poetry, it's completely different. It's nonlinear, it's not literal. It's so metaphorical, his lyrics and stuff. And so, suddenly a completely different way of me processing how to illustrate and how to visualize things that were less, less specific, less linear, more poetic, and it really opened up a lot of creative visual avenues for me that I then brought back into *Roughneck*, going back to it.

**Power:** Some of the more interesting things, conversations, that happened around *Secret Path*—were you and Gord talking about how in many ways this wasn't your story to tell. And you had to be very cautious in the way that you told it. *Roughneck* again deals with Indigenous issues. I should say if you're listening to this on the radio, not watching it, you're not an Indigenous person, you're a white person from Southern Ontario. What do you see as your role in speaking about Indigenous issues in your work?

**Lemire:** I don't know that I have a role. And I don't even know if we should have done the books, to be honest with you.

**Power:** Do you ever feel that way?

**Lemire:** I always feel that way, yeah. It's not my story to tell. None of these stories are.

**Power:** So what keeps you doing it?

**Lemire:** Because you get it in your head, you fall in love with the story and you just have to do it for better or for worse. It's not going to let you go, you know. This character of Derek and his sister come to life inside me, and just like Chaney, the fictional version of Chaney, did. And once they're in there you just got to get it out, so.

**Power:** What a strange feeling that must be to work so hard on something and then release it and then go, "I don't really know if I should be putting this out?"

**Lemire:** Well, yeah, it is strange. And it's something new for me because I really don't feel like these are my stories to tell. But at the same time, you look at the impact *Secret Path* has had and the fact that it's going to be in I think every school in Ontario next year and you'll have all these children learning about residential schools who had never heard of them before. Gord and I grew up not learning about them in school at all, which is why we wanted to do it in the first place. And then you look at that and I think, "Well, it was worth it, you know." Maybe it's not my story to tell but it's done some good and also the fact that Chaney's family, the Wenjak sisters, embraced us and endorsed the project and supported everything we did; it makes me feel like it's okay that we did it. You know, if his family's okay with it, then I'm okay with it.

**Power:** I could only imagine there must be so many, so many conflicts and this is such a beautiful book. I was looking in the back page of the book and I see, under the thank yous, Joseph Boyden there and you mention reading Richard Wagamese and reading Joseph Boyden as encouraging you to tell stories from the North of this country, to tell some Indigenous stories. But obviously, with the questions surrounding Joseph Boyden's heritage in the past year or so, I'm wondering if that made you change your mentality around these things?

**Lemire:** A little bit, yeah. I don't know how much you want to get into Joseph's situation . . .

**Power:** As much as you want to.

**Lemire:** [*laughs*] You know, I'll be honest: I don't know Joseph that well. I know Gord much better than I know Joseph, and I met Joseph a few times and I really liked his writing. I don't know enough about his . . . the details of his heritage.

**Power:** I'm more interested about you. Here you get this inspiration from this person . . .

**Lemire:** Well, there's a big difference between the way Gord and I presented our work and the way Joseph presents his work. Joseph presents himself as someone who's part of the community and a spokesman for the community, I think, and I don't think Gord and I have ever said that we are, you know. So there's a big difference, I think, there . . . I think that is the difference.

**Power:** But I can only imagine—I don't want to harp on it—but I can only imagine that after finding influence from someone and then seeing questions around that heritage, it must change you a little bit, or mess with you a little bit.

**Lemire:** Yeah. Yeah, I think it changed my perspective on his work for sure.

**Power:** What is it about First Nations culture, Indigenous culture and heritage that you want to bring to people's attention?

**Lemire:** Well, I think the . . . I think it's, it's something that . . . it's not something that happened in the past. This is something that's happening right now.

**Power:** As we speak.

**Lemire:** There are people suffering in our country and we're not doing anything about it. So if I can do anything through art to raise awareness to that, I think that's a good thing. I think it's that simple.

**Power:** I'll tell you this: the *Secret Path* was the first graphic novel I ever bought. I'll be honest with you: it's a really, really new genre for me.

**Lemire:** Okay.

**Power:** I apologize.

**Lemire:** [*laughs*] That's okay. I do not stand . . . I do not represent all graphic novelists. [*laughs*]

**Power:** [*laughs*] But, but as a graphic novelist and as a very acclaimed one, and as someone . . .

**Lemire:** I love hearing that; that's my favorite things to hear. My favorite thing about my career is that I don't just have fan boys reading my stuff, and God bless them 'cause they help provide my living.

**Power:** [*laughs*] They help put the gas in the car.

**Lemire:** And I love them and I'm one of them. But, I love that when I do signings at shows, I have this mixture of people reading my *X-Men* comics coming up with big stacks of that to be signed. And then people who have never, literally have never read a comic book before coming up and getting this thing signed. And I love that somehow my work has found this bridge between those two things. That's not very common.

**Power:** But to that, and I'm hoping I can ask you a really kind of basic question for someone like you, but a very new question for someone like me. And I think if you're listening to this right now you may have not read a graphic novel before *Secret Path* or maybe not all. What can graphic novels do to address very, very complex issues, like the ones you explore in both *Secret Path* and now in *Roughneck*?

**Lemire:** Well, it's a big question. The stuff I do isn't always for kids, but one thing, one real benefit of graphic novels is it's a great way to get kids reading who may not read normally. And that's certainly not the only attribute of the medium that I think we should focus on, but it is a great gateway for kids and a great way to introduce kids to difficult subjects. And then more on a creative, artistic side—the medium it to me is limitless. It combines the best aspects of literature and visual art into something completely different and new, and it's a completely different language that I think is limitless, what you can do with it. I love reading fiction, but if you look at a good graphic novel you're not just looking at words on a page, you're looking at somebody's . . . those drawings are coming right from somebody's hand. It's like seeing somebody's handwriting and somebody's fingerprint right on the page telling you that story, in a way that person can do with their particular drawing style. That was what drew me to comics so much in the first place: seeing all these different artists in different ways they draw and these personal styles. I find it so compelling and fascinating to see. It's just so visceral, and it feels more tangible than reading prose to me.

**Power:** I think that with this you have a very big publisher behind you now for this book, and I can only imagine that the pressure must be on, or there's a lot more hands in your pocket than maybe there used to be. And this could be a time where someone at your stature, and your stature is growing, could be tempted to do a story about a more American-based town but from what I can tell about you, you still want to tell Canadian stories. Why is that so important to you?

**Lemire:** Well, yeah, I think there was some disappointment on some issues in the US, when I first pitched this. I think they wanted something that wasn't so specifically Canadian. But I've got to be true to what I'm interested in at the moment.

**Power:** Why is that so interesting to you?

**Lemire:** Well, this is where I live. This is the country I live in. These are the stories I'm interested in. And you always draw from your own life in some ways. So, I love telling stories set in Canada and show different sides of the country, and I feel a little responsibility as a Canadian cartoonist to do that because there aren't a lot of us who can, who are in the position where we can tell any story we want to tell. I love Canada, good and bad, and it's constantly a source of inspiration for me.

**Power:** Well, Jeff Lemire, I've read two graphic novels and they've both been yours. So thank you.

**Lemire:** [*laughs*] Guess you should stop there. It doesn't get any better.

# Jeff Lemire

ANDREW KUNKA AND DEREK PARKER ROYAL / 2017

*Comics Alternative*, May 5, 2017. Reprinted by permission.

**Derek Parker Royal:** We're pleased to have on the *Comics Alternative* Jeff Lemire. His new book *Roughneck* has just recently come out from Simon & Schuster's Gallery 13. He also has a brand new series with Image, *Royal City*, the second issue of which has just recently come out. Jeff, welcome to the *Comics Alternative*.

**Jeff Lemire:** Thanks for having me guys; nice to be here.

**Andrew Kunka:** Yep, thanks for joining us.

**Royal:** We've talked about a lot of your work on this podcast, and it's not often that we get a creator who has not one but two new works that come out around the same time. And I want to start off with one of those, *Royal City*. I found it really interesting that in the very back of that first issue you do a kind of a two-page introduction to this new series and some thoughts that you have about it. And you say at one point something that I find is fascinating: you say that you really don't want people to call this a slice-of-life book, even though it does recall the kind of storytelling that we got earlier in your career, right, with the *Essex County* stories, that people tend to call slice-of-life. But you say that, and I'm reading you here, it says, "To me slice-of-life is code for boring to retailers and readers." So, you really made your mark early on with these more realistically based narratives, but you've done a lot of work in a variety of different genres since then. I guess a two-part question: one, how does it feel to get back to this more, if we want to call it a realistic—I will not call it a slice-of-life—mode of storytelling with both *Royal City* and *Roughneck*? And second, what is it about the slice-of-life or realism designation that kind of bores people?

**Lemire:** I'll answer the second part first. I personally have no problem with the whole slice-of-life description or comics that are not genre-based and based in reality, more humanistic grounded storytelling. At the end of the day, that's the stuff I love to do. When you're doing a standalone graphic novel, like *Roughneck* or *Essex County*, it's one thing, but when you're doing a monthly comic that comes out and it's on the stands next to countless sci-fi series, horror series, all the superhero stuff, I think to a lot of retailers and a lot of fans, not to me personally, but to a lot of those people who are the bread and butter of that monthly audience, maybe calling something "slice-of-life" seems sort of boring to them. So that was more what I was implying. But to me, as I said a minute ago, I love more grounded, realistic humanistic storytelling, and I think the best stuff I've done in genre work, whether it superhero stuff or for Marvel or DC or things like *Descender* and *Black Hammer*, tends to be very character-driven stuff anyway.

I guess getting to the first part of your question: I started off doing stuff like *Essex County*, and then a book called *The Nobody*, which were very grounded kind of books. And then, my career kind of took unexpected turns where I had all these opportunities to work for Vertigo and I did *Sweet Tooth*, and then that led to doing mainstream superhero stuff for DC and then later Marvel. So, the last ten years or so of my career, eight years since *Essex County*, I've mostly been doing genre stuff. And I love genre work, I love doing sci-fi and *Trillium* and *Descender* and all that stuff. But there was certainly over the last couple of years—I think around 2012 actually when I started *Roughneck*—I did have sort of a yearning to go back to more of the kind of storytelling I started my career with, with *Essex* and stuff. Doing all that genre stuff is fun, but I really wanted to kind of get back to more grounded, more realistic kind of storytelling. So, for me, *Roughneck* and *Royal City* kind of reflect that desire to kind of go back and have that little place outside of all the sci-fi and the superheroes and everything, which I love, but it's nice to have a place that's a little more grounded, where I can really dig in and tell more human stories.

**Kunka:** That's interesting because I was just saying—I don't want to jump ahead too far into *Royal City*—but in the second issue there's that panel at the bottom of the first page where Pat's talking to his wife and it looks like she's on another planet, and I thought, "Oh no, is this going to be like a *Trillium* crossover into *Royal City*," but, no, she's on a movie set. But it feels like having that on the page turn seems to be calling, maybe calling out to some of your regular readers who might for a moment think you're going into another genre.

**Lemire:** Yeah, I was just having some fun. And I honestly realized after the fact that I think the character in *Trillium*, not the spacewoman woman Nika but the other character, his name is Pike, and then the family in *Royal City* is the Pike family, so maybe he's their ancestor or whatever. Yeah, I was just having some fun, 'cause people always ask me if all my personal, creator-owned stuff is like in a shared universe of whatever, so I was just having a little bit of fun [laughs], throwing out a weird meta *Trillium* crossover is the Pat/Pike, the main character's wife is filming the *Trillium* movie, so it's kind of fun. I hope Vertigo doesn't see that, and then I'll probably get into legal trouble. But we'll see.

**Royal:** It's like you're interlinking your stories like you did with the *Essex County* narratives.

**Lemire:** Yeah, it's kind of playing off that. I don't think that in my mind all my stuff does connect in that way, really. I can see *Roughneck* being in the same world as *Essex County*, perhaps, but beyond that they all tend to be their own little self-contained universe.

**Royal:** Now, in that essay at the end of issue one of *Royal City* that we referenced a second ago, you mention *Roughneck* and so, which had you conceived of first: was it *Royal City* or *Roughneck*, or did these come to your head at about the same time?

**Lemire:** Yeah, it's like the timeline on that—it's a bit strange. So, actually I started working on *Roughneck* probably 2012, and I actually finished *Roughneck* quite a while ago. It was I think finished end of 2014 or early 2015. So, at least two years ago, I finished that book but due to various publishing machinations with Simon & Schuster and other things going on, they decided to hold onto *Roughneck* and not publish it until just recently, just in April. So there's a two-year gap where *Roughneck* was done but sitting on a shelf, and that's when I started working on other things. I did *A.D.* with Scott Snyder first and then *Royal City* was sort of the third consecutive project there after *Roughneck*, *A.D.*, and then *Royal City*.

**Kunka:** So how is it kind of in that realm of promoting a book that you've been done with now for two years?

**Lemire:** [laughs] Yeah, it's strange. It helps that I like the book nice enough, I'm still proud of it and sort of stand behind what I wanted to do. So, it's not hard to get back into thinking about it again. But generally, when I finish a project I move on fairly quickly into the next thing and kind of just never really look back. But yeah, it is sort of funny to all of a sudden go back and have to be talking about something creatively I was done with a couple of years ago. I think the fact that I'm doing *Royal City* now, and in a way *Roughneck* led to *Royal City* just because it was kind of a return to this sort of storytelling and getting away from genre-based stuff, so I feel like it's all sort of flowing together nicely. So, it's good timing really.

**Royal:** Yeah, because *Royal City*—I mean, the two issues that are out now—they do have very much the same kind of feel of what you have in *Roughneck*. But you also mention *A.D.: After Death* that you were doing with Scott Snyder. I guess we should get the last part of that pretty darn soon, right?

**Lemire:** Yeah, it's done, I promise. We were a little late on the third one. Scott and I are both pretty busy. We got the first two done and then the schedule kind of caught up to us. But it is done and at the printers. So I think the third volume, I think it comes out maybe in a week or two. I have them, they just sent me my comps, so I know it's coming really soon anyway.

**Royal:** To me [A.D.] is kind of an in-between story, between your genre work and the more realistically based stuff, like *Roughneck* and *Royal City*. There are parts of *A.D.* that have the same kind of feel as, again *Royal City* or *Roughneck*, but on the other hand, there's something really science fiction-y about it, that you could put in with, let's say, *Black Hammer* or *Trillium*.

**Lemire:** Yeah, I mean a lot of that comes from Scott as well, obviously. He wrote that, conceived it. And then the project really evolved a lot from when Scott first told me about the idea for *A.D.* It was a few years ago, and at that time it was a very small story, it was pretty much a straight genre story, kind of a heist, a sci-fi heist story that would be like maybe twenty or thirty pages, like a short story really. And then we started working on it, and it just sort of kept growing and growing. And then Scott really wanted to get back to doing prose work 'cause that's what he was doing before he did comics and I think he was missing writing prose a bit, and we talked about that and we kind of found a way to include that sort of storytelling in the comic. And it really evolved into what it is now, which I think you're right: it really does straddle that line between really grounded intimate storytelling and then just more kind of bombastic science fiction world that the book is set in. Just like with my career, I kind of love bouncing between both those things. I love science fiction and superheroes, but I still like grounding it. I guess the book really does reflect my career in a weird way.

**Kunka:** Do you find you have a readership that crosses over between your genre work, your science fiction work, and the stuff like *Essex County*, *Roughneck*, and *Royal City*?

**Lemire:** I think I'm really lucky that I do. I think you talk to a lot of creators who do creator-owned stuff and then do stuff for Marvel or DC, and commonly, when I talk to them anyway, it's often the complaint that the people reading the Marvel stuff, the DC stuff aren't crossing over and reading their creator-owned work. But I do find that my audience does sort of follow

me, where I'm very grateful, obviously. They've especially followed me between things like *Trillium* and *Sweet Tooth*, my creator-owned stuff, and then
things like *Essex* and *Roughneck*. Some of the Marvel stuff you get . . . there is
a large portion of the Marvel or DC fanbase who only read those characters
and aren't interested in other things. But I do find that a lot of my fans seem
to be willing to follow me wherever I go, thankfully. And that's great.

**Kunka:** That actually led me back to something that Derek was asking
about with this essay in the back of *Royal City* #1: [like] you also mention
that with *Essex County* and *Roughneck*, this book doesn't have overt genre
elements or high concept and it's not a standalone graphic novel. So, I'm wondering how you pitch something like that, and is part of your ability to do
something like *Royal City* at this stage in your career due to the fact that you
do have this loyal fanbase and readership that will follow you to a book like
*Royal City*?

**Lemire:** Yeah, I'm really lucky at this point where I don't really need to
pitch stuff to Eric [Stephenson] at Image anymore. And that's not to say he's
going to automatically greenlight anything I want to do, but I think he has a
lot of faith in me and he kind of knows that I have enough of a following that
if I do launch a book it will probably succeed [and] really sustain itself. So I
am in a really fortunate position where I can take a risk now. Having done so
much Marvel and DC stuff over the last five or six years, or however long it's
been, and then even the success of *Descender*, where those things are kind of
doing so well that even if *Royal City* crashes and burns, I'll be okay. [*laughs*] So
creatively, it opens you up where you can do whatever you want and do your
dream book like *Royal City* and hope for the best.

**Royal:** Now, you mentioned that *Roughneck* is something that you had
been sitting on for quite a while; that does feel like a story that could have
come out of *Essex County*. Were there kernels of that idea that you had considered in the early days when you were working on those *Essex County* stories?

**Lemire:** No, it really came a lot later. Like I said earlier, I had been doing so
much sci-fi stuff, and even my creator-owned stuff after *Essex* was very sci-fi-
based with *Sweet Tooth* and *Trillium*, so it was really me trying to get back to
that kind of storytelling, but none of the elements that became *Roughneck*
were really things I had conceived of earlier or were lingering. They were all
fairly new things, stuff that all percolated in my head around that summer of
2012, when I was kind of thinking of what to do next.

**Royal:** I was thinking primarily in terms of the hockey. Were you a hockey
player as a kid?

*Royal City* #4, page 2. Credit: Jeff Lemire.

**Lemire:** I was, and I still play every week pretty much. I love the game, and it's always a big part of my life. For me, hockey is kind of my one escape from comics—my whole life is comics at this point. [*laughs*] It's all I do every day and most nights. So, watching hockey or playing is sort of my one thing every week where I can just shut that comics part of my brain off and do something else for a couple of hours, so I really enjoy it. But after *Essex* I felt like I had gotten that out of my system, telling stories about hockey. But then that summer of 2012, when I was kind of looking around for the next thing that would kind of catch me, for my next graphic novel, that summer—it was either that summer or the summer before—there were four, I believe four, NHL hockey tough guys, sort of enforcers, the guys who go out and fight every night, who all died of tragic circumstances this one summer. Either from suicide or substance abuse, and it became a big story here in Canada, about how these NHL enforcers are sort of living this really violent lifestyle and then many times it leads to brain damage. And then when the game leaves them behind, when they get too old to play anymore, they're left very damaged and a lot of that violence that they kind of had an outlet for when they were playing the game, often turns inward and it can be very tragic. Anyways, that summer that story was really in the air here, and it struck me as a really fascinating and kind of tragic character study. So that was sort of the roots of what *Roughneck* stemmed from.

**Royal:** That's the dilemma that the protagonist Derek finds himself in?

**Lemire:** Yeah, exactly. I basically constructed a narrative about one of these guys, a fictional version of one of these guys. These are themes that are very close to my heart, themes of addiction and cycles of violence in families. So, it all kind of gelled together and became this story.

**Royal:** And then the addition of Derek's sister Beth, who in many ways is linked to some of the struggles that Derek is going through in terms of his past, the relationship with the father, anger and all that. But then she comes with her own baggage that is at least not immediately directly linked to her past with the family.

**Lemire:** I think in some ways it is because her father was a very violent man, abusive, and probably an alcoholic, and those tended to be the men she was attracted to growing up, which seems strange, but it's so often the case: that you find yourself stuck in these cycles of repeating it in a family. So having a female point of view in the story with his sister, I just wanted to show the way the violence can shape people in different ways. For Derek, he had an outlet with it with hockey, for a while anyway, and it became one thing for him. And for her, as a woman, it became something else. And it was just hopefully a way to show how violence can affect a family, not just one person, but men and women, and it affects everyone differently. But it all kind of stems from the same trauma, the same childhood things that they both kind of went through.

**Kunka:** I don't know how much I can share about this, but my one hockey claim to fame is that when I was in college I dated a girl—on one date—whose previous boyfriend was Tony Twist.

**Lemire:** [*laughs*]

**Kunka:** So that's got a comic overlap, too. And I went to her dorm . . .

**Lemire:** Do you know the comic overlap of that?

**Kunka:** Yeah, yeah.

**Lemire:** The Tony Twist thing, isn't that [Todd] McFarlane, right? The pseudonym or something?

**Kunka:** Yeah, yeah. I said when I went to her room and she had like a shrine to him, he was playing for Peoria at the time and it was clear that she wasn't over him, and I didn't want to mess around with that so. . . .

**Lemire:** Yeah, you don't want to mess around with Tony Twist; man, he was a tough character. [*laughs*]

**Kunka:** I bring that up every once in a while when hockey comes up. Other than playing hockey in my backyard on a creek—I grew up in North Dakota and played hockey on a creek in my backyard with my brother, and *Essex County* really hit me with a lot of that.

**Lemire:** Well, you're practically Canadian then . . .

[*laughter*]

**Kunka:** Yeah, I don't know where the accents fall on the scale.

**Lemire:** Yeah, well, I think if you've played on a creek outdoors, that's all you need to get a Canadian citizenship.

**Kunka:** Really, that would be really useful right now.

**Lemire:** [*laughs*] Yeah, it sure would.

**Kunka:** So other than the stuff being kind of in the news at the time that you were coming up with *Roughneck*, were there other things about the thug and hockey that attracted you to that character?

**Lemire:** I've always kind of liked writing those tough guy characters, those damaged tough guys. I think it goes right back to *Sweet Tooth*; the character Jeppard is pretty much that as well. And in *Essex*, the Jimmy character, if you're familiar with that book. So, I've always liked those big, kind of damaged tough guy characters. They're a lot of fun to write. I tend to enjoy the voice of those guys, writing their voice and stuff. So, it was already a natural fit for me when these stories were kind of popping. And then there's other things that kind of came into *Roughneck* as well. At the time, I was reading a lot of Indigenous Canadian writers here, novelists and really kind of educating myself a lot more about Indigenous culture in Canada and our First Nations and things that I was kind of very ignorant to. Growing up in mostly a white community in Southern Ontario here, I didn't really have a lot of exposure to Native culture. And reading these different authors that summer, I started to realize how little I knew about this huge part of our country and our history. So that was kind of part of that that went into *Roughneck* as well. And I spent some time up in the north, Northern Ontario here on a few First Nations reserves and communities, some isolated communities, doing research and kind of getting to know people in the communities at the time that I was working on the book, so that all fed back into it as well and kind of gave me a setting to go along with the character stuff I was talking about earlier.

**Kunka:** There's something really—I don't know, emotionally charged and fascinating—about the type of character that you're dealing here with Derek, who's someone who had this great success at one time and then comes back to his hometown and is still kind of revered in the town. And he's still able to, for example, kind of get away with things because of his connection to the local cop and stuff like that. But it feels like that's such an interesting character to catch them at that point in their lives, after this great success and celebrity has passed and what their life is like following up on that.

**Lemire:** Yeah, I find it really fascinating, too, to see these people who had this really exciting kind of life at one point, and were heroes to many people, and then to kind of catch them on the flipside of that when they're kind of beat down and broken. I think in a lot of ways you can even see that in other things I've done too. Like even *Black Hammer*, you have this group of superheroes. They're superheroes, there's nothing cooler than that [*laughs*], but we're catching them ten years later when they're all kind of lost and broken and that life has left them behind. I find there is something very compelling about that; I agree, yeah. I certainly enjoy writing those characters even though it's not always fun and happy; it can still be really interesting I think, from a character point of view for sure.

**Kunka:** Yeah, and then Pat Pike in *Royal City* seems to be in that area maybe? We haven't seen a lot of him yet but . . .

**Lemire:** Yeah, he certainly is fading glory, yeah, absolutely. You're right on that.

**Royal:** You mentioned earlier your reading of stories on Indigenous populations in Canada. And I know that your book that came out last year with Simon & Schuster, the one that you did with Gord Downie, *Secret Path*, definitely deals with that topic. It's also, though, in *Roughneck*, but it's maybe a little more in the background, if I guess that's accurate. Because we learn that Derek and Beth's mother was Native American, and then Al, a character who becomes quite prominent in the last half of the book especially, also has links to that community. And that becomes significant, but I don't think it's an overriding concern in *Roughneck*, or am I not seeing its importance as much as I should?

**Lemire:** No, it's there. I tried to walk a really fine line there where it is a big part of the story. Derek and Beth, the characters, they're half-Cree and that was their mother. And it's a part of their heritage, their background, that they didn't really know a lot about. You know, their mom for various reasons didn't speak a lot about it, so they were kind of just raised white. But as the story goes on it becomes more important to them. They start to connect more with their mother and that side of their background and start to see the beauty in that culture and how it can help them heal. So I think it is important. But I think the line I tried to walk as a writer, especially as a white writer writing about another culture, is it can be very easy to overdo it and to fall into cliché. So, I tried to keep it as—I don't know what the right word is, just like not overdo it, I guess, and not to turn them into these clichéd Native characters, but make them feel like well-rounded people, like it was one part of a more complicated person.

**Royal:** I want to ask you about the use of color in *Roughneck*, because the vast majority of this book is in kind of a greyish-light-blue wash, which I think adds to the tone. It's rather somber. We've been talking about Derek as kind of a down-and-out character who had once had success as a hockey player but now he's kind of coming back to his—acknowledging a past that he hasn't really lived up to. And so, I think the greyish tones really work well. Yet there are strategic moments throughout this narrative where you bring in a variety of color, and I was wondering if you could speak to your ideas about the uses of color in this story?

**Lemire:** Yeah, well, it's kind of a two-part answer. There's the creative artistic answer and then there's the practical one. I guess, at the time I had just finished *Trillium*, I believe, when I started working on *Roughneck*. And *Trillium* was the first time where I started watercoloring a little bit of my own artwork. Up until that point, my earlier stuff was black-and-white, and then when I did *Sweet Tooth*, José Villarrubia colored it for me, because I didn't really have a mind for color. But then my friend Matt Kindt started watercoloring all his own stuff. And I would be at conventions with him and watching him do it, and it looked so fun. So, when I started working at *Trillium* I really wanted to—I didn't really know a lot about painting and color, but the only way to learn is obviously to do it and make some mistakes. So, I painted half of *Trillium*, and I learned a lot on the page doing that. So I knew I wanted to continue it on my next book but I wasn't really fully ready to commit to fully painting a—whatever it is, I don't know how long *Roughneck* is now, I forget, a 260-page book or whatever it was—it just felt a bit overwhelming to me. So, from a practical point of view, it seemed like a strategic way to use color sparingly. And so that's the practical answer. The creative one: the blue tone really does help set the book where I wanted to set it. It feels very cold and isolated, and I felt like that really reflected it. And then I feel like it's kind of a reverse of what you might expect, where usually that kind of clichéd flashback thing is to always see it as black-and-white or a sepia tone, but I thought of maybe flipping that: when we do flashbacks, that's the stuff that's full color. Almost like those experiences from our past were so vibrant and were so important, and now years later the lives have been become so dulled down and damaged. Just like when you're younger you kind of feel stuff a little more intensely than you do when you're an adult. Creatively that was kind of my thinking, of kind of flipping that using color for the flashbacks for that reason.

**Royal:** And then there's the use of red for the violence.

**Lemire:** When you're doing that blue, that cold blue tone, when you throw red on that without any other color it pops obviously right off the page. And violence is such a part of comics. Like whenever you do superhero comics or anything, there's always fighting and violence and it becomes cartoony, it becomes a different kind of thing. But I wanted the violence in this book to be very visceral and ugly. And for none of it . . . whenever someone beat someone else up, or used violence in the book, I wanted it to feel like it was dangerous. And inflicting pain and ugly. So, I felt like that really harsh use of red could be a way to just really accentuate that.

**Kunka:** Yeah, and the one character in the story, which takes place in the present time as the story's unfolding, that's represented in red, or I guess any color, is Beth's boyfriend, Wade.

**Lemire:** Yeah, yeah. He's sort of this walking timebomb, right. So yeah, that felt like a way to link the violence of Derek with this other character who he clearly hates but has something in common with. Symbolically you have this dangerous kind of thing looming, and he's approaching and getting closer as the book goes on. And we've already established the red as sort of a symbolic of danger and violence and everything else.

**Kunka:** I think the use of color too, and when you were talking about how it works and flashbacks, also works in the one scene I'm thinking of where

Beth is walking down the road and she's remembering this traumatic event from her childhood that happened and it's happening with her, kind of side by side with her in these smaller panels. That's something I really like that you do and other work—I'm thinking of *Underwater Welder*, too—where you have two different time frames happening simultaneously on the page.

**Lemire:** Yeah, and that's something you can only really do in comics. Like in film or television you have to cut back and forth right, you can't—I mean, I guess you could superimpose things but it doesn't really work well on the screen generally. But in comics you can do that; that's one of the beautiful things about the language of comics that you can take advantage of, where you can, actually on the same page, in the same viewing experience, juxtapose multiple things at the same time. You can't do that in prose, with novels; you can't do it in film. So, what always excited me about making comics was doing things like that where you really have those moments where you kind of use that language of comics to do things that no other medium can do. And I love that.

**Royal:** I do want to say, though, that there was a successful use of this in film that immediately came to mind, and that is Woody Allen's *Annie Hall*, the scene where Alvy is visiting Annie's family, and then there is a flashback to Alvy's family having dinner. And so there's that split-screen and, if you recall, the two families communicate through . . .

**Lemire:** There you go. [*laughs*]

**Royal:** . . . not only between the two panels but also through time.

**Lemire:** That's cool, yeah. There you go. I guess I'm wrong. But yeah generally, generally speaking it doesn't work well on film.

[*laughter*]

**Royal:** But if you're wrong, you're wrong because of Woody Allen, and that's a good reason.

**Lemire:** There you go. Yeah, that's alright. There's always exceptions to the rule, right.

**Kunka:** It does something that comics, maybe we could say, does better than other media, which is show how traumatic memory is, like a relived experience. People who have suffered from trauma and go back into those memories are physically feeling exactly the same way that they did under the trauma, and so to be able to show that as such a vibrant and present moment there, I think really captures what that experience is like.

**Lemire:** Yeah, and I think the advantage comics has, if we're just talking about the way you can do things like that—yeah, we can do a split-screen like what Woody Allen did in the film or whatever, but the dimensions of a film screen or television screen are never going to change whereas. I mean, technically the dimensions of the pages you have in comics don't change, but you can play with the layout so much and limitlessly with different panels on a comic spread or page, in so many different ways, where you don't really have that freedom on film, even if you are juxtaposing images for the most part. So I do think there is a real strength there with comics.

**Royal:** Now, you studied film for a while early in your career, right?

**Lemire:** Yeah, I did. Comics were always kind of my first love, and I grew up drawing and making comics all the time. But I came from a really small town in Canada. Trying to make a living or a career out of comic books just didn't even seem remotely possible. There was no avenue to pursue that. But I did have some friends who had moved to Toronto, where I am now, to study film. I saw what they were doing and I love movies too, so I thought, well maybe. I'd love to tell stories. There was a really booming film industry here so, if nothing else you can find work in the industry as a technician or something and make a career out of it. And then maybe eventually find a way to tell my own stories with film or something. But in the way that when you're seventeen, you only have a vague idea of what you're doing [*laughs*], that's kind of where I went. So yeah, I ended up moving here and taking a film program in Toronto for four years. And I learned a lot about storytelling and about writing and stuff, but the more, the further along I went in the film program here, the more and more I just started falling in love with comics again, especially in the city here, I was exposed to better comic shops and started to find all kinds of comics that I hadn't read as a kid. European stuff, and underground stuff, and alternative comics. I just started to really fall in love with drawing again and with the medium and with the potential of the medium to the point where I think in my fourth year I really just kind of stopped going to all my classes and [was] just staying home and drawing comics all the time. Which, in hindsight, could have really blown up in my face. But it worked out. [*laughs*]

**Kunka:** We're kind of jumping around a little bit here, but when we were also talking about this idea of the past informing the present and things to do in comics, I was also thinking of how we're getting in *Royal City* this character Tommy, who is the brother of the Pike siblings who form the main characters in the story, and how each character sees Tommy differently.

**Lemire:** Yeah, and I think that's true when we lose somebody, a family member or someone you're close to, whoever was close to that person or whoever it is in the family that thinks back or remembers that person, they probably all think of different times, different moments, different relationships they had with that person. So, it seemed to me that if you had a family they would all kind of . . . the first thing they would think of when they thought of their lost son or sibling would probably be a different point in their family's history or their personal relationship with Tommy. So they all kind of had a different one. And then that's the way to sort of visualize it, is they all see him and interact with him as a different person, really. And I don't want to get too much more into that 'cause it really starts to expand and evolve as the series goes on and it does lead, it leads somewhere else which may be even a bit stranger than that. Yeah, and I have said in the past, it's not a genre book. It's not really a supernatural book, but there is something strange going on in the town. [*laughs*] And I do find myself being pulled more to that strangeness the further along I get in the series. So it is kind of evolving quite a bit from my original intent. In a good way, I think.

**Royal:** Well, that's one of the things I liked about that first issue is, almost from the very beginning, you get a sense that there's going to be some strangeness going on in what seems to be at least on the surface kind of a realistic narrative when Peter goes to his workshop and he's tinkering with the radios, which I'm hoping we'll learn more about all those radios. And then we hear the static and Tommy calling out to his father. Those are in the opening pages and when I first read that I thought, "Okay, this is not just a straight realistic narrative. This is going to be a weird wacky ride."

**Lemire:** I think that's part too of what I was alluding to, when that comment you brought on the opening of our interview about the slice-of-life thing, is that even *Essex County* and maybe not so much *Roughneck*, but definitely *Essex County* and for a 100 percent *Underwater Welder*, there was a real strong sense of magical realism to both those books. Even though they were grounded humanistic stories, there's a lot of magical realism in both of them. And I think *Royal City*'s the same. *Royal City* maybe is now, I don't want to spoil anything but as I'm getting into the second arc here myself working on it, some of those magical realist elements are starting to really walk the line between supernatural and magical realism. So, there is definitely something strange going on in the town. [*laughs*] And I'm kind of loving it. But yeah, I don't think it's distracting from the human stories I wanted to tell, if anything it's reflecting them and enhancing them. I just love the idea, if we have this one world where on the surface everything is a normal family and a normal place, but there seems to be another world within that world that is there, and it's interesting to explore as well.

**Kunka:** Now, with the characters in the Pike family that we see in *Royal City* so far, are they going to be the regular characters throughout this ongoing series or is *Royal City* going to kind of be this focus of the series?

**Lemire:** Yeah, my intent with the series is to kind of do something like what [Ed] Brubaker and [Sean] Phillips did with *Criminal*, where they had the *Criminal* kind of head title of *Criminal* and then each arc would be different characters, and maybe the main characters from one of their arcs would become just supporting or background characters in another arc. So, it's all taking place in the same world, but you're kind of telling different stories. And I'm not going to go quite to that extent where every arc is a different story. The Pike family, their saga, their story, I have it plotted out now to be about twenty issues. So that's going to be at least four arcs. But I do think it can be the thing where when I finish that, when I finish the Pike story, I can take a little break, do something else, and then come back and do another story, set in *Royal City* with completely different characters. Or come back to the Pike family again years later and see where they're at, let them age with me, in the way that Jaime Hernandez and Gilbert [Hernandez] do [in] *Love and Rockets*. So, for me it feels like this place now that I have where the story potential is kind of limitless and I can do different things. But, depending on whatever I really want to do and where I am at with my life, and my career, at least for these first couple years it will be the story of the Pike family. It's a pretty extensive story. And it's pretty tightly plotted at this point.

**Royal:** So you say you've mapped out the Pike family and their story may take up, let's say, the first four story arcs.

**Lemire:** Yeah, like four trades, twenty issues roughly.

**Royal:** Okay. So, do you have in your head maybe an ideal number of issues for *Royal City* that you want to eventually get to, or are things just completely open-ended?

**Lemire:** Yeah, it's open. I think I'll do these twenty issues and probably take a break and do something else and then come back to it. Like I said, hopefully it can be a thing I just come back to whenever I want. So it could be something that goes on throughout my career, or different stories set in that town. At least this initial run I'm thinking twenty issues.

**Kunka:** That's great because, you know, when you mentioned Gilbert and Jaime's stuff, and I've been teaching their stuff lately, and I always find myself, especially when talking about Jaime's stuff, to say to the students you really don't understand what it's like to have read this book for thirty years.

**Lemire:** Yeah, it's magic. [*laughs*]

**Kunka:** Yeah, I don't want to make this seem too ambitious, but to think about getting in on *Royal City* now, and then seeing where it goes over the course of years and years.

**Lemire:** Yeah, that's the idea for me, too. And it really was inspired by Jaime's work, where he has made all these other characters that you've been following for thirty years. And to read that, like you said to them, "I've been reading that for this long," like I have and you have, you're so invested in those characters. They're like so real to us and like nothing else in comics really, that there isn't anything like that. It's a magical thing, a beautiful thing, and I'm no Jaime Hernandez, but if I could have this thing where we follow this family throughout my life as a creator and I keep coming back to them, it could be really cool to see them reflecting different things I'm going through in my life at different stages. I'm forty now. The characters, the siblings are all around my age now, so twenty years from now I could tell more stories with them when they're in their sixties and they would be experiencing totally different things. And the stories would be about different things, I would think, than they are now. So it could be really fascinating.

**Royal:** One of the mistakes I try not to make with narratives like this is, let's say you have, as not the protagonist [but] a major character, someone who is a writer or a writer-figure . . . I mean, in the first issue of *Royal City* when we're introduced to Pat, it's like okay, he's the writer, I wonder if this is a stand-in for Jeff Lemire, who is the writer of *Royal City*. And then we learn that not only are things set in a town called Royal City but that Pat has even written a book called *Royal City*. And so then I started to wonder, "Okay, is this going to get all metafictionally twisty in a fun way."

**Lemire:** [*laughs*] Well, I'm having some fun 'cause my first book was *Essex County* and I grew up in Essex County, Ontario, Canada. So, Pat to me—I've never done that before where I have an actual doppelganger, like I'm actually writing myself. Some writers do it all the time, but I've never really done that. And I don't really want to. [*laughs*] But I thought it would be fun instead of having someone as a surrogate for me like Pat, to sort of imagine my career going really off the roof. Just kind of imagining me making all the worst decisions I could have made throughout my life rather than the right decisions. And then having a character that is that. So Pat is pretty much me, that we kind of started at the same spot but he—whereas I made I think good decisions personally and professionally [*laughs*]—Pat keeps making the wrong ones. And it's sort of like this guilty fun of exploring my self-destructive nature, but not having to actually do it in real life. So [*laughs*] . . .

**Royal:** No repercussions.

**Lemire:** Yeah, exactly.

**Kunka:** So, I think another aspect of *Royal City* that we're getting to is the sister in the family. Sorry, drawing a blank on names.

**Royal:** Tara.

**Lemire:** Yep, that's right Tara Pike, yeah.

**Kunka:** And the idea that *Royal City* is basically built on this manufacturing industry that's been leaving for years, which is a thing we've seen a lot of in a lot of cities. When we first see her, [she's] talking about modernizing the city a bit by introducing a golf course and a resort. So is that another concern of *Royal City*, is dealing with a city that, or community that's in transition like this?

**Lemire:** It absolutely is, yeah. I really love that as a setting 'cause, like you alluded to, that's happening all over North America right now, where you have these, not the major cities, not like Chicago, Toronto, New York, but you have these smaller cities all over, we have them here in Canada and you have them over there where they were built around industry and they were these booming midsized North American cities in the '50s, '60s, '70s. And then now, obviously, [the] economy has changed so much and everything is being outsourced and these small towns are just dying off. And the youth are all leaving for the bigger cities and the towns are kind of just rusting away and leaving these factories and industrial waste behind. And that to me was such a great setting for a comic, to see this city in transition, like you say. And we also have this family who kind of reflects it in a lot of ways, where they're kind of dying off and killing [and] destroying each others' relationships and they're a family very much in transition as well. So they kind of reflect one another. But yeah, I love that idea of a dying industrial town as my setting. I grew up in one. Near where I grew up, Windsor was right across from Detroit, so it's an auto city and it's sort of in transition like this as well. So it's something I know well and [I] worked in factories, auto factories and plants and shops all throughout high school and university, while I was going to university and stuff. So, I always wanted to do stories that were at least partially set in that kind of blue-collar factory world. Someone like Pat, who's completely escaped it like I did, now he's coming back. I think I'm rambling now. Do you remember what your original question was? [*laughs*]

**Kunka:** No, you're dealing with it. I was just thinking because I live in South Carolina now and I see all these towns that were once like kind of booming textile cities but also the way . . . I have different routes I can drive, I have about an hour commute, and sometimes I can go through these small towns that were clearly, even earlier were really booming tobacco towns, so there would be these massive tobacco, like warehouses and stuff, and beautiful old houses and beautiful old buildings that are all abandoned.

**Lemire:** Yeah, there's something amazing about that, too, visually for me to draw that stuff, like these abandoned factories and stuff; we'll see more of those as we go on. There's something kind of beautiful in that industrial decay as well, just for a purely aesthetic point of view, that I love drawing. I think your question was about Tara the sister; she's sort of the one who's still fighting for the future. She wants to bring change and she wants to modernize it, find ways to keep this town alive. But, of course, the flip side of that is kind of accepting that the past is over and the way they used to live is dying and a lot of people there can't let go of that. So she's sort of facing that conflict.

**Kunka:** And that conflict manifests itself in her home life too, that that's one of the things she'd be sacrificing is her husband's job to this modernization.

**Lemire:** Yeah, which seems terrible, but in the long run she knows they would both make money if her thing went through. But his male pride probably can't accept that. I don't want to spoil too much because the third issue, which will come out very soon, is actually pretty much completely focused on her and her husband and exactly what we're talking about so. [*laughs*]

**Kunka:** Oh, good.

**Royal:** We know what you're saying, Jeff, about the focus on the cities that had once been thriving, productive, and then over the past several decades have just lost it, lost populations, lost their youth, lost their industry. I can't help but think of what you were talking about earlier especially within the context of *Roughneck*, that characters such as Derek or, let's say, with Jimmy in *Essex County*—those figures that at one point had been if not at the top, then at least that they were on their way there. But then something happens, or a variety of things happen, and they're kind of like husks of what they had been, or what they had wanted to see themselves. That's not that different from what you were describing in terms of these cities.

**Lemire:** Yeah, I had never thought of that. But that's really true. Yeah, that's interesting. [*laughs*]

**Royal:** Another connection between *Roughneck* and *Royal City* that we haven't made yet is your protagonist in *Roughneck* is called Derek and the *Royal City* takes place in ROYAL City. So I feel personally drawn to your recent storytelling.

**Lemire:** You've cracked the code, man. I was just stalking you for years. It's all subliminal love notes to you.

[*laughter*]

**Royal:** And it couldn't have been cracked before this interview.

**Lemire:** No, this was it. It's very important. My work is done, I don't have to do issue four, we're good.

[*laughter*]

**Kunka:** And Derek, you really are a shadow of your former self anyway.

**Lemire:** I've heard you described as a rotting husk, so . . .

[*laughter*]

**Royal:** That's where I excel, as a rotting husk. Well, let's talk about another series you have going on right now. We've talked about *Royal City*, the new *Roughneck*. We've talked a little about *A.D.: After Death*. *Descender* is something that we've gone on about, what—almost two years now, right?

**Lemire:** The book's been really successful critically, and sales have been great. I think it's one of those things where Dustin's such a machine that we've been able to put that book out without being late every month. And it almost gets taken for granted a little bit with some of the newer stuff I'm doing. But it's certainly still absolutely one of my passion projects. I love the world of *Descender*, and I love working with Dustin [Nguyen] and, yeah, I love that book, I love having a big science fiction universe to play in. Having spent all this time talking about *Royal City* and *Roughneck* and everything, I do really love sci-fi as well. And having a big fun space opera like this is really a fun place to visit every month for me.

**Royal:** What's the genesis of this series?

**Lemire:** A couple of places. I had done stuff like *Sweet Tooth*, but I hadn't really done space opera, sci-fi before. I had *Sweet Tooth* finished, and I really—okay, I'll be brutally honest, this is what happened. [*laughs*] So, I actually pitched *Adam Strange* to DC, right around the time I was doing *Superboy*, I think. So this was before The New 52 out of DC. I pitched an *Adam Strange* series. And everyone really liked it, but they were doing the whole New 52 relaunch and so it just wasn't a good time to do it. So, it kind of got shelved. And my *Adam Strange* pitch actually kind of became *Trillium*. I kind of sort of morphed it and it evolved and kind of grew into something else. But the genesis of it was this *Adam Strange* thing. So, after *Sweet Tooth* I kind of twisted this *Adam Strange* pitch into *Trillium* and made it a creator-owned thing, and it really didn't resemble *Adam Strange* anymore by the time I actually got to doing it. But I kind of fell in love with the worldbuilding of that. When I was working on *Trillium*, I fell in love with doing space opera and sci-fi and kind of building this planet, and this culture around this planet. It was so much fun doing that stuff behind the scenes and I knew that I wanted to do more and I knew I wanted to do it on a bigger scale. So when I finished *Trillium*, I started making notes for a bigger sci-fi thing, which became *Descender*. Around that time, I knew Dustin from working at DC; I was doing superhero stuff and Dustin was doing a lot of *Batman* stuff, but he and I had never worked together, even though we really liked each other's work. And my exclusive contract to DC was coming up at the same time as his and we were like, "Well, we should do something creator-owned." At the time Image books were really booming with *Wicked + Divine* and *Bitch Planet* and all these books were launching and having so much success—*Saga* and everything. We thought we'd give it a shot doing an Image book, and I had all these sci-fi ideas floating around so I sat down and kind of really worked them into the story. And I'd always wanted to do something about robots. Big mythologies surrounding robots and so I guess those were all the seeds of *Descender*.

**Kunka:** And you did get to do *Adam Strange* ultimately anyway, right?

**Lemire:** Yeah, I kind of did. I didn't really get to do the version I wanted to do. [*laughs*] I do love those old DC characters, that's for sure.

**Royal:** Well, I mean, have you and Dustin talked about how long you would like to sustain *Descender*? The more we get, the more I get into it, the more I see the potential for years and years of story here. I don't know what would happen if it ended any time soon.

**Lemire:** [*laughs*] Well, it's a no. It's not ending soon. I do have the end, though, and right now what is sure, we're on—I think Dustin and I are working on issue 26, I think.

**Royal:** 21 is out.

**Lemire:** 21 is out, and we're working on 26, so we're one arc ahead on what's coming up. So we're on the next arc. And right now, I have the whole series plotted out with an ending, and it ends around issue 40. But having said that, when we started at issue 1, the same ending was plotted out and it was about twenty issues. So, it's like you say: the more I get into it, the more I start adding new characters and new side plots and it keeps growing. So, forty issues now could easily become sixty. And who knows—yeah, it does seem very expansive, the universe. Even if we end the story of Tim-21 and his whole robot mythology that we're doing, I could even see going on, going off and doing other things in the same world too because I think we both love working with each other and love the world.

**Royal:** And the key for me was, in those initial issues, you ran at the back a rough guide to the various worlds. And so I remember Andy and I reviewed that when it first came out, that first issue of *Descender*, and we commented on that and wondered if this was going to be a series that was going to be going on for the long haul.

**Lemire:** Yeah, like I said, I'd done so much worldbuilding before we started even working on the book. I gave Dustin this massive bible where it had all these different planets worked out and their cultures and their atmospheres.

[*laughs*] I had built this whole universe. So I think it certainly is a big canvas. I think we could do a lot of stuff in it. And the story will continue to grow and grow. That's the fun of space operas and sci-fi, that you're not limited to one world—you have the whole universe at your disposal and you can kind of make it up as you go. There's been a couple things in that atlas of worlds that you're talking about that was in the first issue or first couple issues, that when I actually get to those worlds, thirty issues later, whatever I wrote in issue 1 doesn't really fit anymore. So I'm going to have to retroactively change a couple of those descriptions when we do the hardcovers or something. 'Cause I've had to tweak it a little bit, but . . .

**Royal:** So there will be hardcover deluxe editions?

**Lemire:** At some point, yes. Like I can't say anymore at this moment. But, yeah, there are. We have been discussing it, absolutely. If you follow [Dustin] on Instagram or whatever, you'll see every day he posts all these incredible little sketches and stuff he does of Tim-21 and everything that aren't even part of the book, they're just stuff he's doodling on the side. He has so much of that stuff that it would be a shame not to do some kind of hardcover or where we can have all this stuff showcased in the back or something.

**Kunka:** We just had Matt Kindt on the show and . . .

**Lemire:** Oh, I'm sorry . . .

[*laughter*]

**Kunka:** We ended up talking about his Valiant work. So, I wanted to bring up *Bloodshot* because I've been really enjoying your work on *Bloodshot*. And we're heading into a new series, right, with *Bloodshot Salvation*?

**Lemire:** When Warren Simons, the editor at Valiant, and I first started talking about me working with them a couple of years ago—I can't remember when it was now, like two or three years ago now—and we talked about *Bloodshot* and I had some ideas for that. And I pitched him at the time what would have been a twenty-issue run. Which was really the *Bloodshot Reborn* story that I ended up doing. And I didn't really see any more story beyond that. I felt like when I got to the end the *Bloodshot Reborn*, *Bloodshot U.S.A.* stuff that I did last year, that was kind of the end of my run and my story, the character. I finished that stuff, and I kind of was away from it for a few months and Warren and I would talk about other things I might want to do, and a few things came up but then I just kept going back to those characters and started getting new ideas [*laughs*] and I kind of missed them. When you invest twenty issues into something and especially with *Bloodshot*, I felt like it was a real blank canvas when I got it and I really tried to expand the mythology and build his world as much as I could. I had laid all this great framework down and it felt like a shame not to keep going with some of that stuff. So, we talked more and then the end result is this new series *Bloodshot Salvation*, which really picks up where the last series left off but it takes things in [another direction]. We don't want to just do the same story over and over. So, I think it really does break new ground as the next chapter in the story of *Bloodshot* and the supporting cast that I introduced.

**Kunka:** Now, when you mention as supporting cast, is that going to include the character find of 2015, Blood Squirt? [*laughs*]

**Lemire:** Ah, Blood Squirt. The origins of Blood Squirt are when Warren, Matt Kindt, and I—this is Seattle Emerald City Comic Con three or four years ago, whenever we were going to do *The Valiant*, Matt and I, and I was going to do *Bloodshot* afterwards. And I kept joking around about this stupid Blood Squirt character over dinner. And they were laughing and laughing, I don't even know. There were far filthier *Bloodshot* jokes or Blood Squirt jokes that didn't make it into the comic.

[*laughter*]

**Lemire:** And then I was writing the pitch for the actual series, and then I just got this crazy idea to actually put this ridiculous Blood Squirt character into the story. And I put it in the pitch, and I think Warren thought I was kidding when he read the pitch. And I'm like, "I'm not kidding, I really want to put it in." [*laughs*] That's how he made it in. But I'm kind of glad. I don't know if Squirt's going to be in. He hasn't found his way into my plans yet, but that doesn't mean he won't. There's always a spot for him [*laughs*].

**Kunka:** Did you draw that character in those pages?

**Lemire:** Yes, I did. In the original, the first four issues I did. And then after that I got too busy and whomever the artists were on those issues I had to kind of look at what I'd done and sort of ape all of it. But yeah, originally I did draw it.

**Kunka:** Now, you recently talked about *Bloodshot Salvation* where you were pretty honest about the fact that you had a certain direction that you were going to go with it and then you changed that direction?

**Lemire:** I did, yeah—I mean, there's no reason not to be honest about it. It's all process. None of this stuff kind of comes from nowhere. It all comes from working on stuff over time. I don't want to get too political on the podcast or anything, but when certain elections happened and . . .

[*laughter*]

**Royal:** That's okay, we get political.

**Lemire:** We know when Trump won, I was really, like many people, kind of shaken, shooken, or whatever the word is. Still am a little bit by it. And at the time I got really angry and I was working on *Salvation*, and I kind of worked this stuff into the initial *Bloodshot Salvation*; that's where it would have been *Bloodshot* vs. the alt-right and white supremacists and things like that. And we kind of started working on it, and it didn't really feel right. I think it was just me kind of shoehorning something in that didn't really fit what I really wanted to do. And then a couple of months passed and I wrote the first couple scripts in that direction, and then I looked back on them and they just felt like such a heavy-handed sort of—it just didn't feel subtle or intelligent. It just felt like really obvious. Luckily, I work really far ahead. I've already written almost ten issues of *Salvation* at this point. The joy of working that far ahead was none of the artists had started drawing and Warren had a lot of time, and I just said, "You know, Warren, we announced the book and yet we kind of announced the alt-right stuff, and it was just not sitting well with me that weekend we were at Con." I was with Warren, and I just said, "It just feels lazy, it just feels really heavy-handed and just sort of lazy, and it doesn't really feel right." And so I went back and I just kind of started pulling all of that stuff out of the story. It's kind of like a sculpture: you keep trimming stuff away and you start to see what the real shape is underneath it. And I kind of found what the real story was that I really was initially excited about. And it wasn't that stuff. So I kind of went back and got rid of a lot of stuff and reshaped the series and now I love it. I'm really proud of it. Happy with it and excited about it. But yeah, I think there's definitely a place for political allegory and using superheroes and comics to do that, but in this particular instance it just wasn't feeling smart or good. So, it didn't—it's not going to go that way.

**Royal:** Yeah, something else Donald Trump almost screwed up.

**Kunka:** He almost screwed up *Bloodshot*.

[*laughter*]

**Lemire:** He almost ruined *Bloodshot*.

[*laughter*]

**Royal:** See, we're saying this now, but two weeks from now, when we're at war with North Korea and having the world destroyed, you know it'll sound rather callous.

**Lemire:** [*laughs*] That's right, we'll all be dead and won't know the difference.

[*laughter*]

**Kunka:** Yeah, I'm sure we've said things in the podcast in October 2016 that look callous now.

[*laughter*]

**Royal:** You were talking about working with superheroes, and I mean—we can talk about what you've done with DC, what you've done with Marvel,

[but] I'm much more interested in what you do with the superhero genre of your own, your creator-owned stuff. And I found it interesting that, at least from the outside, it seems that *Black Hammer* and *Plutona* were forming at around the same time. Is that true?

**Lemire:** No, actually, that's not true at all. Both of those have a very different origin. I think they came out at the same—the idea sort of became concrete at the same time, when I was finishing up my first contract with DC and kind of just starting on Marvel. So, I had this little limbo period. There were a couple months where I wasn't doing a lot of DC or Marvel stuff, and I almost had a backlash in a way to some of that stuff and I think that's why I wanted to do my own superhero stuff. But we were talking way back in this interview about how you had asked me if *Roughneck* and some of those ideas were around when I was doing *Essex County*. And I said no, but actually *Black Hammer* was. *Black Hammer* was the next thing I came up with after *Essex County*, back in 2007, 2008.

**Royal:** Really?

**Lemire:** Yeah, and that was going to be the next thing I did. I was going to draw it myself, it was going to be a graphic novel. Because at that time, *Essex County* was—it was Top Shelf who published it and it was an indie book and I love superhero comics, I have always loved DC comics, especially the whole mythology, and I grew up reading that stuff and that's what made me fall in love with comics in the first place. But I never thought back then, in 2007, that I would actually get a chance to write quote-unquote "real superhero comics." I never thought I'd work for DC and Marvel; I was just this indie cartoonist. But I wanted to do something with superheroes so I came up with this idea, basically superheroes meets *Essex County*, my love letter to all the superheroes that I loved growing up, but kind of placing them in that kind of more grounded, quiet farming community in Essex County and doing this sort of spin on it. And I had drawn all these characters and the whole pitch and everything in 2008, and I pitched it to Dark Horse. Diana Schutz was working at Dark Horse at the time, and she really loved *Essex County*, so she had asked me to pitch some stuff. And I pitched her *Black Hammer* and she greenlit it, and then, at the same time, Bob Schreck greenlit *Sweet Tooth*, which I'd also pitched at Vertigo and I kind of had to make a choice and I ended up doing *Sweet Tooth*. And *Black Hammer* just kind of got shelved.

But I always loved that idea, and I started to really love the characters that I had come up with, and every couple years I'd kind of pull out that sketch book and dust it off and add some stuff to it, or look at them. And then in 2013 or '14, I just realized that with *Sweet Tooth* and then *Roughneck* and all the other stuff I was doing, I would never get a chance to draw *Black Hammer*. But I still really wanted to do it. And so I decided to try to find another artist to work with me and just write it. And I had talked to Dean Ormston a few times at conventions, and we really hit it off. And I've always been [a] huge fan of his stuff he had done at Vertigo, and it felt like he was super-underrated. One day, I just kind of out of the blue got excited about *Black Hammer* again and sent him my old stuff and said, "Would you want to do this?" So, that was sort of the origins of *Black Hammer*.

And then *Plutona* was a completely separate thing. Actually that was Emi—the artist Emi Lenox—[who had] that idea of those kids finding a dead superhero in the woods. We were hanging out at San Diego Comic Con three years ago or something and having coffee and she said that she had this idea and she told me about it and I loved it. Just that day over coffee we kind of started like just jamming on the story of *Plutona* and we kind of plotted the whole thing just for fun over coffee. And then we thought, "Oh, we should do this." So yeah, so those two books, even though they came out at the same time, and they're both sort of creator-owner, alternative takes on superhero stuff, they kind of had very different origins.

**Royal:** Well, did you and Emi plan from the very beginning for *Plutona* to be a kind of a miniseries limited to five issues?

**Lemire:** Yeah, it was always a really short thing. It was always just this one small sort of like a little indie movie—never meant to be a bigger ongoing thing. That was it. And since we finished the book we've had a couple of conversations. We're like, "Well, we could do a sequel," and we kind of threw some ideas out but none of it felt right. And so I think we're just going to let it sit and just let it be what it is. Having said that, I am currently writing the screenplay for *Plutona* as an option. I haven't left the world yet anyway. I get to kind of go back and sort of reinterpret it now, and just trying to stay really true to the comic, but as it is, the comic itself wouldn't fill a two-hour film, so I've had to expand a few little things here and there, and kind of turn it into a bit more of a quest. Instead of them automatically finding the body in Act One, it's more of a quest to look for the body. That opens up a lot of stuff for me. But yeah, I've been having a lot of fun still living in that world anyway.

**Royal:** A superhero *Stand by Me*.

**Lemire:** That's it, man. It was pretty much that simple when Emi pitched it. I don't know if you guys know the film *Mean Creek*, but she loves that movie *Mean Creek*, and I love *Stand by Me*, and then we just started riffing on it, so yeah, it's a lot of fun.

**Royal:** I was asking about your original idea to have this as a limited series because, I remember when *Plutona* was first listed in *PREVIEWS* and Andy and I were discussing this. I think we got the impression this was going to be an ongoing series and then a couple of months later when they did announce that there was going to be an end point, that there was just going to be five issues, I had wondered was this a change in plans; is it not selling that well? Sometimes publishers will not let you know that something is a miniseries or a limited series for, I guess, a variety of different reasons.

**Lemire:** I figured it was just a miscommunication. Honestly, I'd already written the whole five-issue thing with the ending before we even solicited it. So, it was never, ever meant to be anything else. It may have just been sort of a poor communication on the solicitation stuff that made it feel ongoing. But yeah, no there was no change of course.

**Royal:** As if you have time to work on other things, but is there something that you're starting to formulate now that we may see in the not too distant future that you can actually share with us?

**Lemire:** Yeah, well, there is one. I mean, well, there's a number of things. I'm always developing ideas and sometimes I take a couple of years to get ready. So there's a couple of things you know, but the one that's closest is probably this book *Family Tree* that I'm writing and Phil Hester is going to draw for Image. It's going to come out in the fall. And I've written the first four scripts, and I think Phil will start drawing soon. I hadn't really done a real horror book yet and I really wanted to do something that was kind of horror, or a weird horror story. And I had really loved doing *Animal Man* at DC; of all the superhero stuff I've done, that was one of my favorites. And one thing I loved about that book was that it was a superhero book but . . . I really just kind of wrote it as a horror comic. [*laughs*] And I loved doing that book, and I wanted to get back to doing something that had a similar vibe to my *Animal Man* stuff but that would be my own. It's the story of this little girl who literally starts to transform into a tree one day. And her brother and her mom and her perhaps crazy grandfather take her and they go on this insane road trip trying to figure out what the hell's happening to her and why. And they're being chased by these cultists who want to kill her or do something else with her. It turns into this whole kind of vast horror mythology that I've kind of been working on. So that book's going to be really fun and a different flavor for me as well.

**Royal:** And so in addition to looking forward to that, we have other issues of *Royal City*, the final installment in *A.D.: After Death*, your Marvel, and especially your Valiant work.

**Lemire:** My Marvel stuff's winding down. I'm done with Marvel for the foreseeable future. So, *Old Man Logan*, the last couple of issues are coming now and we've made the last issue [which] comes out this month. I wrote a twelve-issue run on *Thanos*, which is about halfway done now. So yeah, that stuff's winding down. And then kind of focusing over on all the creator-owned stuff for a little while.

**Kunka:** Well, Jeff, we want to thank you for coming on the *Comics Alternative*. We had a great time talking with you. And we haven't mentioned it yet, but you were a part of this podcast almost from the very beginning. We started out in 2012 with an idea that every now and again we would do what we would call an artist spotlight, or a creator spotlight, where we would use an episode to focus on just one creator, an artist or an artist illustrator and look at their body of work. And the very first one we did was on you. It was back in August of 2012; it was our sixth episode, and at the time, we thought that we had almost too much to discuss because we were really into *Sweet Tooth* by that point, there was *Essex County*, *Nobody*, *Lost Dogs* had just come out again from Top Shelf, *Underwater Welder* had just come out, and so we thought, "Oh my God, there's too much to discuss here." We didn't do many creator spotlights after that. But can you imagine if we wanted to do something like that today with everything you've done, it would have been impossible.

**Lemire:** Yeah, I know. I'm busy [*laughs*] doing a lot of stuff. But when you love what you do, it's hard to say no. I keep getting all these great opportunities to work with great artists like Dean and Dustin and Phil, and in addition to doing my own stuff that I draw myself. So, it's hard to say no to the chance to work with such talented people. And to make comics—that's what I love more than anything in the world, is making comics. I guess the end result is this kind of massive body of work I'm putting together which is really nice, so . . .

**Royal:** Well, thanks for sharing all that with us.

**Kunka:** Yeah, thanks. I really enjoyed talking to you and talking about your new work because I love *Roughneck*, and *Royal City* is really shaping up to be one of my favorite books right now.

**Lemire:** Yeah, thanks. *Royal City*, a little spoiler or not a spoiler but just a teaser: the first arc is five issues, and then issue 6, the series takes a major, major jump, and I'll just leave it at that. But it's almost a different series for a couple of issues and it's been really fun to do.

# Jeff Lemire: I Am Thinking of Nothing More Than Comics

**ANDREA FIAMMA / 2017**

*Fumettologica*, November 16, 2017. © Andrea Fiamma and Fumettologica.

Polite, softspoken, and very tall. These are the first three things that you notice when you talk to Jeff Lemire. The author of *Essex County, Roughneck, Descender, Black Hammer, Sweet Tooth*, and all the other superhero comics (he worked for DC, Marvel, Valiant, Dark Horse, Top Shelf, and Image) was at the last edition of Lucca Comics & Games, brought by one of his Italian publishers, Bao Publishing.

We sat down with him to talk about the craft of his work, his creative process, and how he hated working on the *X-Men*.

**Andrea Fiamma:** So, how's your normal day of work?

**Jeff Lemire:** My Monday to Friday in my studio is mostly spent drawing, because I'm also drawing a book every month and drawing takes much longer than writing, so my daytime is mostly spent drawing and then at night I try to write one script a week. A couple of hours each night I'll just work on a script, and in that way, I'm able to do five books a month plus whatever I'm drawing.

**Fiamma:** That's a lot work.

**Lemire:** It is, but I love what I do; it's my passion. It's all I want to do; even in my free time, I love to do it. And I find having different projects and different genres allows me to stay fresh; instead, if I just did one thing I would get bored. Being able to do *Descender* and then superheroes and then other things allows me to never really burn out on anything, 'cause I'm doing so much different stuff.

**Fiamma:** *X-Men* has to come out, though. Do you find difficulties writing on command?

**Lemire:** For example, I spend one month where I work just on the *X-Men* and nothing else, and I might write three or four issues of the *X-Men* and then I get to put it away for a couple of months until I get inspired again. In that way, I have never written on command like you said, or force myself to be inspired. If I get far enough ahead I can just go to something when I actually feel like working on it or I'm excited about it, or I get a new idea.

Staying far ahead allows me the luxury of only working on something when I'm excited about it. Mostly. Once in a while you might get a deadline where you have to write, but I usually manage to stay far ahead so I can pick and choose and really only work when I feel like.

**Fiamma:** And what is it like when you actually have to write something because of the deadline?

**Lemire:** It's miserable. I don't ever get in that situation. I'm really good with time management, so I honestly can't think about the last time I was on a deadline where I had to write something. I'm usually three or four months ahead of where I need to be, because I hate that feeling. I never let myself get there.

I tend to do projects that are very different from one another; I try not to work on anything that's too similar. If I'm working on *Descendent* or *Royal City*, it's just a matter of getting my head in that world again and the world sort of tells me what the story is. I never have to force it.

**Fiamma:** Is it stressing different muscles writing personal works vs. work-for-hire?

**Lemire:** I guess so. I try to approach it the same way; what makes the Marvel stuff successful for me is that I try to bring the same amount of myself to it that I bring to my creator-owned works. I hate to separate them, because you start creating work that feels artificial or forced. But, I mean, by the nature they tend to be a little different, a little more freedom on your work, take the story wherever you want, don't have to get approval every time. I think that freedom gives you a bit of confidence that helps you.

**Fiamma:** Doing superhero stuff gives you the same pleasure?

**Lemire:** To be honest, I grew up reading superhero comics and I love them. I was really excited to write stuff for Marvel and DC for the first few years that I did it, but lately I'm feeling burnout on it, so I think I'm gonna move away from that stuff and just do creator-owned.

And then all the superhero stories that I wanna do, I can kinda do them in *Black Hammer* now, which is my own superhero universe. I'm in a really good spot where I can finally take a break from that stuff. It was fun for a few years, but now it's starting to feel like work and I don't like that.

**Fiamma:** Was it a rush decision or something that was slowly building in your head?

**Lemire:** You never do anything on a rush, it was something that built up over a year or so where I just felt it wasn't the place for me anymore. I felt that I've done the stuff I wanted to do and I wanted to move on. I'm doing a couple of smaller projects for DC right now, but even those are sort of eccentric weird side projects. I don't know if I really wanna do any big books like *Batman* or *Superman*. I don't feel passionate about it anymore. Ideally, a year from now, I'll just be doing my own stuff.

**Fiamma:** For a while?

**Lemire:** Probably. Maybe I just need a break, to be honest, 'cause I've done so much. I started writing superhero comics for DC in 2010, so for the last seven years I've written a lot of comics for Marvel or DC, and I feel burnout on it. I'll take just a couple of years to do my own work and I'll see how I'll feel—you never know. Maybe I'll love doing that and I'll never go back, but I do love those characters, so probably I just need a couple of years to rest.

**Fiamma:** Where do guys like Bendis take the energy to them for so many years?

**Lemire:** I don't know. If I had to just do Marvel or DC work, I probably would quit; I wouldn't do comics anymore, just because it's too similar—I just don't have enough freedom to do the kind of stories I want to do or the kind of stories I wanted to do when I first started making comics. I want to get back to do just that stuff.

**Fiamma:** Did you find constraints in that? Or at some point you were censoring yourself because you knew that they would not accept that idea?

**Lemire:** Little bit of both. It depends on the projects. Certain books like *Moon Knight*—total freedom. They never gave me any notes and you can kinda see it in the work. It's the best thing I did.

**Fiamma:** Do you feel that was your best work, for Marvel?

**Lemire:** Yeah, for sure. And then the *X-Men* stuff was kind of a nightmare, to the honest. Really difficult, I came in, and they already had storylines in place I had to use that I probably wouldn't came up with myself, and I felt editorial was very restricting in what they wanted. And too many notes. And then you start second-guessing yourself. It's just not a good situation. That wasn't a great experience, but on the flipside, doing *Moon Knight* was really fun.

So it just depends on the editor and on the project and the property, but sometimes it can get a bit restricting and then, like you said, if you're working with these kind of editors and stuff you're not writing from a place of confidence. Will they like this, or this? You never have that feeling when you're working on your creator-owned works.

**Fiamma:** How do you see yourself in the comic book industry?

**Lemire:** I don't think too much about that stuff. I'm so worried of what my next project is and doing something good. I just worry about the book that I'm working on that day. I mean, I know my books sell well enough that I can keep doing what I want to do and that's really the most important part. I recognize that certain things that I've done stood the test of time. *Essex County* is still very vital today, so I can see that and it's flattering and gratifying. I do see that I have a strong readership.

I'm lucky enough that I can do something like *Descender*, which is sci-fi, or *Royal City*, which is very emotional, and my readership seems to follow me from one thing to another. So, that's very fortunate for me. But in terms of the bigger context, I don't think too much of that.

**Fiamma:** Your style is very peculiar, sketchy, and immediate on the page. How did you find it? Do you think about the line or is it immediate to do?

**Lemire:** It's funny because my artwork does look very spontaneous, but I actually spend a lot more time laboring over my artwork and thinking about my artwork than I do with my writing.

My writing is very spontaneous. [*laughs*] I write a script in a few hours, just like a stream of consciousness, whereas the art is very labored and I have to work really hard at it.

And it just came from the fact that five years before I ever published anything where I was drawing comics every day, really bad comics, and going in different directions that weren't me and that's the only way to find what is you: going the wrong way and going back and be a really good self-critic and recognize when you're doing something that isn't honest. Over those years, I gradually developed a style that felt natural to me and the artists I always admired were really expressive and you could really see their personality in the artwork.

I don't have that photorealistic sensibility, I don't have that ability, so it's just from recognizing what you do well, which is for me, create mood and emotion, and going in that direction. Also, I didn't know anyone from the comic book scene in Toronto, I was in a vacuum and maybe that's where my style came from too, which was that I was self-taught and not influenced by anyone else. All of that probably helped to make whatever style I have.

**Fiamma:** In those early books what kind of styles were you aiming at?

**Lemire:** At that time, I didn't know anybody else who made comics, so I was on my own. I didn't go to art school, so I was just teaching myself, trying to figure out what kind of tools to use, even that alone changes how you draw. It took me a while to figure out cartoonists use brushes, which pens they use or don't. So even changing tools, my style would change dramatically and my early stuff was very unprofessional. I didn't use brushes, I didn't know how to spot black, so things were very different. And then you also fall in love with different artists when you're younger and you try to draw like someone else sometimes, so you go a couple months copying someone else's style.

**Fiamma:** Who did you copy?

**Lemire:** The guy I was obsessed with in that period, the early 2000s, was Dave McKean, especially *Cages*. I got inspired a lot by his expressiveness and spontaneity of his line work, but I also spent too much time trying too much to be like him and he's a much better draftsman than I'll ever be. So there was some bad works there.

**Fiamma:** Now, do you feel you've reached a point where your style is cemented?

**Lemire:** I have my style now; you draw the way you draw. But there are always refinements, playing with different media. I just started in the last two years watercoloring my artworks. You find new ways to do things, but still maintain what's working.

**Fiamma:** How are you doing with that technique?

**Lemire:** I love it. I don't think I'll ever go back to not doing them. It adds an all new layer to the work that wasn't there before. That's been really fun in the last three years experimenting with that. I'm still learning and adding and just . . .

**Fiamma:** Go with flow!

**Lemire:** Yeah, go with flow. Trial and error; I'm trying things that work for me and my style.

**Fiamma:** And in the writing? Did you just learn by doing it?

**Lemire:** I just started writing things that I could draw. I just did that and then, it wasn't until 2010 that I got hired to write something for another artist for the first time and that took me a couple of years to figure out what stories I wanted to tell with another artist.

And then I did *Animal Man* and that was the time where I figured out how to put the pieces together, but I don't overthink the writing at all. I spend a lot of time plotting and working on the plot and then when I actually write the script I try to keep it very emotional and spontaneous.

**Fiamma:** Like your drawing.

**Lemire:** Yes, there's the common element. I think that immediacy [is] a good thing. Especially with writing, the risk is to overthink everything. You can spend weeks overthinking a scene and a dialogue and then you look back at the first draft and it's just as good as the last. I don't know, I just get it out there.

**Fiamma:** You managed to do an astonishing amount of work in the last seven years.

**Lemire:** I've been exclusive at DC for five years, and my contract ended and I decided that I wanted to try other things and work with other people. I approached different publishers, and all of sudden I was doing one book for Dark Horse, one for Valiant, one for Image, one for Marvel. Now I narrow down to just a couple and I'm not really doing any work-for-hire stuff.

And every company has good thing and bad things. Valiant was wonderful, Image is just you on your own. Dark Horse was super-supportive; I have a great editor there.

**Fiamma:** On top of that, you even did some animation work with the adaptation of *Secret Path*, the comic book based on the concept album by Gord Downie.

**Lemire:** It was an incredible project doing that comic book. Gord gave me all the songs and let me do my thing. Then he would come every couple of weeks and if something wasn't feeling right for what he had in mind he would tell me, but for the most part trusted me. We work closely on it; emotionally we got very close. Gord passed away two or three weeks ago so it's been really hard. But concerning the animation special, I've no interest in animation.

**Fiamma:** You wouldn't like to try directing?

**Lemire:** Not really. I've done a little screenwriting just for fun, I wrote the screenplay for the feature adaption of *Plutona*. That was fun, because it was my story. It's for the same guys that are working on *The Underwater Welder* with Ryan Gosling. Seven of my books are in different stages of development. *Descender* seems to be moving. There's a screenplay, there's now a director attached, an Italian director actually.

**Fiamma:** Who?

**Lemire:** I can't say. But yeah, *Essex County* seems very close to put into production on television, but then again there's no official word, so who knows. And the others are all in different stages, early ones. I'm not too involved with them. I don't really care if they'll happen.

But I don't aspire to do that, but it was fun to try. Comics give me so much freedom that I don't really have interest in other things. The only reason I would do it would be for money and that's not a good reason for doing anything.

**Fiamma:** You don't seem very eager to see your comic books on the big screen.

**Lemire:** Let's be honest: how many movies are made every year and how many of them are actually good? Not many, right? First of all, the chances of getting made are very small and then the chances that it gets made and it's actually good . . . it's almost impossible.

It's heartbreaking to be too invested. For me, it would be too hard. And if something happens and it's good, that's amazing. It's not a priority. My priority is comics. It's everything I want to do.

# An Interview with Our Best Writer of 2017, Jeff Lemire

## BRIAN SALVATORE / 2018

*Multiversity Comics*, January 4, 2018. Reprinted by permission.

As revealed at the end of last year, the *Multiversity* staff voted Jeff Lemire as the best writer of 2017. Not only that, but his *Black Hammer* garnered the number one ongoing series spot from both the staff and readers, and *Royal City* was one of our best new series as well. Clearly, we feel that Jeff was doing some great work this year.

I reached out to Jeff after the staff voting for "Best Writer" was done, and hoped that he would be up for an interview. Thankfully, he was. We spent the better part of an hour on the phone, talking about his 2017, and what we could look forward to in 2018.

**Brian Salvatore:** I was doing just some tallying this morning and it's insane how many books you worked on in 2017. You had three creator-owned ongoings, *Black Hammer*, *Descender*, and *Royal City*. You had an OGN in *Roughneck*. You did the *Bloodshot* stuff at Valiant and you did, I believe, six different Marvel books: *Death of X*, *Extraordinary X-Men*, *Moon Knight*, *Old Man Logan*, *Thanos*, and *IvX*. Just from a time-management standpoint, how many hours a day are you writing comics?

**Jeff Lemire:** This is the most common question I get because my output is so crazy. I actually work very sane, very regular hours. I'm just super-organized. Generally—and I know this interview's supposed to be about by writing—but just as a way of answering the question fully, my Monday to Friday is spent at my studio or I'm drawing most of the day so it'll be, I usually get to my studio around 8 a.m. and I draw all day. I do an eight-hour day, 8 till 4. Then my writing, I generally—honestly, I do it on a weekend or an hour or two here or there at night during the week after my son goes to bed. It's really not that crazy and even on the weekend, I don't really work fulltime or anything. It'll just be a couple hours here and there if my family's busy doing other things or whatever. It's not super-crazy.

Drawing takes the bulk of my time, so that's my Monday to Friday and then I try to write one script a week. Doing it that way, you can write four books a month and then draw one. That's the method. In terms of sometimes it seems like there are more than four books a month coming out, I realize that but I stagger them. For instance, I might write a whole arc of *Desecender* in one month or something. I might just get really into the world of *Descender* and write five or six issues and then I'll put *Descender* away for three, four, five months until I get really excited about it again. It allows you to stagger projects. While there may be six or seven books coming out every month, I'm not actually writing six or seven books every [month], I'm only writing usually three or four.

Getting ahead like that allows me never to have to worry about deadlines. If I'm not really feeling something, if I'm not really super-excited about *Thanos* or *Descender* that month, I don't have to force myself to work on it and just to work on it just to get a script done. I can wait until I get new ideas and get really excited and that keeps me fresh, too, 'cause then I'm never working just to work. I'm working 'cause I'm really into something. That shows always in the work.

**Salvatore:** Absolutely. I wonder if because you are an artist as well as a writer, do you think that your scripts leave more room for artists to do their thing? And because of that, do you think that you can churn out scripts in a faster way than if somebody's meticulously plotting out every panel?

**Lemire:** Yes. Yeah, there's a lot of truth to that. I've spoken to Matt Kindt about this 'cause Matt is also a cartoonist and he and I are both superfast and prolific. We often when we're alone we often say, "I don't understand how some writers can only do one or two books a month and seem to barely get those done." Because it doesn't take that long. We talked about it, and it is—there's something to what you said where because we draw, we're used to breaking a story down in our heads visually in a way, it's become so inherent to us that we don't have to—there might be some shortcuts to the thought process that we automatically take without thinking about it now. Other writers who don't draw have to spend more time on that. I don't know, I'm talking out of my ass here. There might be something to what you said. You probably said it in a more articulate way than me but . . .

**Salvatore:** I can't imagine that would be the case.

**Lemire:** I do think that me and Matt, since we draw our own stuff, we're already fulfilling that side of our creative side so I don't feel the need to visually control all the books I'm writing. I just try to work with artists who I love and let them be themselves and do what they do. My art direction tends to be very sparse because I know having drawn scripts that other people have written, the more freedom I have, the more of myself I can bring and the better the work is. I learned that a long time ago. It's all about working with people you trust. I tend to work with the same artists a lot, who I know we have chemistry and my scripts can be really sparse in terms of art direction and giving direction on layout, things like that. I don't really do a lot of that. It's more focusing on character and pacing and things, plot.

**Salvatore:** That's really interesting. You talk about working with people you trust and I definitely see that. You do have a number of collaborators who now have been working with you for a long time. You see really great fruitful things come out of that. *Descender* this year really took a step forward. I loved that book beforehand but it seems like there's this unspoken telepathy right now that's happening in the creation of that book where every issue just seems to be a little bit deeper and a little bit more comfortable than the issue before and that obviously can only happen over a period of time. It was really great to see that, and it's great that you're letting these artists do their own thing because it does show in the work. Or at least I think it shows in the work.

**Lemire:** The big secret to being a good comic book writer is just having a good artist. Comics are a visual medium first, and I'm not saying being a writer isn't important, but a really great comic book script drawn poorly is not going to be a very good comic book. But a really mediocre comic book script drawn greatly is still going to be a pretty good comic. It really comes down to the artist you're working with and how your storytelling styles tend to come together. When I work with Dustin [Nguyen] or [Andrea] Sorrentino or Dean Ormston on *Black Hammer*, I found collaborators there that we together create a third creator who's better than either of us are alone. We don't have to talk that much, we just trust each other and we each give each other what we need and we don't overdo it and the work it just seems to come really naturally.

**Salvatore:** You mentioned *Black Hammer*, and that's where I want to take the conversation right now. What's so cool about *Black Hammer* from a reader's perspective is that you've created these worlds, whether in your graphic novels or in your creator-owned series, that feel incredibly lived in. I loved reading those books and wondering about what's happening on the periphery. But with *Black Hammer,* it's the first that I feel like we're not just getting a look at a story, we're getting a look at an entire world. As a writer, how do you approach building not just the story involving five or ten or fifteen different characters but building up this entire world? Is that a different challenge for you? Is that fun? Is that terrifying? What happens with that?

**Lemire:** Yeah, it's not terrifying, it's super-fun. That's the joy of writing— worldbuilding and doing this stuff. *Black Hammer* is a very specific project and because I have the advantage of seventy years of superhero comic book history to draw from. It's not like I'm building something in a vacuum. I have thousands upon thousands of amazing comic books out there that I've loved reading and grew up with as this basis to draw ideas from and that makes it really easy and really fun. You can pick and choose things from various eras of comic book history or various artists, writers that you love and ingest them and then do your own spin on them or combine different things into a new character. Honestly, it's just like a kid in a playground. I'm just having fun with it. That makes me want to build the whole world.

You start with the core cast who are stuck on the farm or whatever—those five superheroes—and then the more you see of their backstories, the more the world just slowly gets built up and up to a point where now we're doing spinoff miniseries because there's just, I'm getting more ideas for characters who are on the periphery of the main story who have their own story that carry their own little miniseries or whatever. We're going to do a whole bunch of different satellite books around the main series just to build the world more. That doesn't come from me wanting to cash in or wanting to—I certainly don't need more work. It comes from just honestly having all these other stories I can't wait to tell and all these great artists I get to work with. It's just so fun, that book. It's probably the most effortless and just the most, in some ways the most rewarding project I've ever done.

**Salvatore:** Wow.

**Lemire:** There's something about that world of *Black Hammer* that it just feels like it's more than anything than I've ever done. It captures everything I love about comics. It has everything I love about superhero comics in it. But it's also done in a way that really reflects indie comics and alternative comics and the stuff I grew up creating myself. It combines both aesthetics into something unique. I love the world so much. Those characters are so real to me now.

**Salvatore:** This may not seem like the most natural comparison and it's perhaps colored by the fact that they're both Dark Horse properties: this reminds me of the start of the Mignolaverse. Mike Mignola when he created

Hellboy, talked about putting all of his favorite things about comics in one book. It started off as this one thing and it just grew and grew and grew and now there are all of these satellite miniseries and worlds and all that. This feels like the start of something like that for you. Can you see this being something you're still playing with ten or twenty years down the road?

**Lemire:** Yeah, I really think that being at Dark Horse didn't hurt either 'cause you're in the neighborhood of Mike Mignola so you see that it's definitely an inspiration. Talking to the editors there and stuff, you're like, you realize we can do what he did. It's very inspiring what he did 'cause like him, he had been doing a lot stuff at Marvel and DC when he first started his career and probably wasn't completely satisfied creatively. And then to, when he did *Hellboy*, he got to cut loose and he had no more restrictions and he could just put everything he loved into this thing. You can see it. That's what happened with *Black Hammer*. I'd been doing a lot of superhero comics over the last five or six years at DC and Marvel and some of those experiences were awesome and some were a little more up and down. As it's going to be when you do a lot of stuff.

But then I could finally do a superhero comic that was just all my own and I could just literally take everything I loved and not have to worry about anyone else's books. I could just make my own little world and pour everything into it. I can definitely see the *Black Hammer* universe going on for quite a while. I know that the main story, the story *Black Hammer* proper that I'm doing with Dean has a definite ending. I've already written it actually so I know it. It's not coming any time too soon, but I know what it is. The surrounding universe and these other characters, I could see telling stories in that for a decade from now still happily being coming up with new stuff to do in that world.

**Salvatore:** That's super-exciting to hear as a fan of that book. It's incredibly exciting to hear that there's that much fertile ground there to be planted in.

**Lemire:** Just to tease and stuff. We haven't; we've only announced the Sherlock Frankenstein spinoff so far which just started coming out. There's actually, at this point, four or five other *Black Hammer* miniseries being drawn and already written.

**Salvatore:** Wow.

**Lemire:** It's all coming.

**Salvatore:** That's exciting stuff. That's really cool. Let's shift away for a minute from the creator-owned stuff. Let's talk about Valiant, because you've been one of the cornerstone creators of Valiant for the last few years and you've specifically carved out this really interesting role with Bloodshot. I have been a fan of your work before you went to *Bloodshot*, and I had read

*Bloodshot* as a kid in the '90s. I couldn't think of a creator that I felt less would have fit with *Bloodshot* than you. I've been so wrong, and I'm so happy how wrong I was about that. It's not the most natural fit for you. You and I talked at New York Comic Con a number of years ago right when you were starting with *Bloodshot*. We got into the things that appealed to you about the character. I'm interested now, three or four years later with the body of *Bloodshot* work under your belt now, what's it about that character that keeps being rewarding for you and what can folks look forward to in the next few months of *Bloodshot*?

**Lemire:** Bloodshot was interesting because I'm with you: it's a character that has zero appeal to me. I'll be honest with you. I just couldn't care less about that character when I was offered it. I never really read the old '90s Valiant stuff and the character of Bloodshot himself was everything I didn't like about superhero comics. He was this ultraviolent action hero. It was two-dimensional, I thought. It just didn't appeal to me at all. But then I started thinking, it's almost like a challenge when someone offers you one of these characters. You're like, well, how can I take this thing and make it something that does appeal to me? As soon as you start thinking that way, that's when you suddenly start building stories. Once the stories start coming if you fall in love with them it's almost like you have to do them. *Bloodshot* was like that.

Bloodshot was so cold and so violent and inhuman. It just did not appeal to me. My challenge was well how do I take this thing that is cold and inhuman and make it relatable and make me care about it and the reader care about him as a person, and the story just grew from there. I planned on doing twelve issues or something back when I got it, but now I've done, when I'm done with what I'm doing now, it'll be closer to forty or something issues we've done. Fifty or something and he just became this—I'm getting off track, but he just became this character who I could explore [in] any genre with, which became really exciting—where one arc could be like an almost like a supernatural detective story, and then the next arc it could be like an '80s action movie like Predator and then the next arc it could be a horror story.

He could always be at the center of this and through these different genres I could explore different sides of his personality and that's what I'm continuing to do with the new series *Bloodshot Salvation*. The first arc is this really intense emotional revenge story; that's the one's that coming out right now. The next arc shifts and becomes a real supernatural horror story where we get into the dead side and then the third arc will be a crazy, I shouldn't say too much but it will involve a lot of science fiction elements, we'll say that. It's just this thing where Valiant gave me so much freedom to make that character my own that any idea I came up with they seemed to support. Then that makes you, that keeps you excited. When you have no restraints on what you can do it just keeps you charged up. Well, now I can do this. Let me try this. It just kept going and the character became really alive to me. I really built out a supporting cast in his mythology and I felt very invested in what I had built so you want to keep building.

**Salvatore:** I find it so fascinating that you and Kindt have found such a home there because again, I'm thirty-five, when I was ten or twelve or whatever, I was reading Valiant comics as a shitty kid who liked violence and didn't go for some of the more nuanced things. You guys are such different creators for that but I love how you've been able to bring your sensibilities into these books. I read a ton of comics in my role at Multiversity, and there's something about the Valiant books that just feel so well considered. Nothing seems to happen that isn't really well considered.

**Lemire:** I'll tell you that the reason for that is twofold. The first reason is that it's still a very small universe. They've been very smart about limiting the amount of product they put out even though they could try to flood it with more. They keep their output each month to around seven titles or something. As a result, the universe stays small enough that it's very controllable. That's not the right word. It's like what you said: everything that happens really matters. Everything is very considered, and it's easy to coordinate with the other books in the line without having them restrict you. We can build together rather than having fifty titles where you're stepping on each other's toes just because there's so much stuff going on. That's why it feels so cohesive.

But then the second reason, the most important reason is that Warren Simons is the editor-in-chief and as much as the creator's visions it's Warren's vision as well. He's been so good about who he's cast as the creative teams on those books. He gives us so much freedom and he encourages us to be ourselves and to bring the best of what we do to the work. You almost feel like you're doing a creator-owned book really with these characters. You can see that with what Matt's doing on *XO Manowar* and with what I've done on *Bloodshot*.

**Salvatore:** Absolutely.

**Lemire:** Anyways, Warren's definitely one of the best editors I've ever worked with in comics, and it shows in the books.

**Salvatore:** That actually pivots nicely to something I want to talk with you about. Because you've done work for so many different publishers and because you're keeping so many different things going at once, what is your relationship like with your editors? Do you want an editor who's checking in with you? Do you want to be left alone?

**Lemire:** It varies from project to project. In general, I'm a very organized and self-motivated person—I always have been—so I don't need someone checking up on me all the time. I get the work done on time. I've never been late. In that aspect I don't need someone breathing down my neck. I do find, because I came to comics in a spot where I was already writing and drawing my own graphic novels originally, I have my own voice at this point. I do better with less in terms of an editor. I don't need to get on the phone and hash out the story with someone all the time. I do better when I'm left to my own devices. For the most part the editors that I work best with are people like Warren or when I was doing stuff with Vertigo with Will Dennis and Mark Doyle and those guys where I had a vision for the book and they trust it and they let me do my thing. When I run into a roadblock then I can call them but they don't force their vision on the book.

The worst experiences I've had are things where you get an editor who, and I'm not going to say which books these were, who they are—you sometimes you get editors who wish they were writers and they want to put their fingers in every decision and cowrite and question every plot point. At that point, it's like they're just—then you start second-guessing yourself, you're just not writing from a good spot anymore. You're not writing with confidence and you're not allowed to do what you do well. I tend to do better with less. That's why I like creator-owned books. I really don't have an editor; I just handle it myself. I actually am going to bring Will Dennis into some of my Image stuff just because now I'm doing so much stuff it's getting hard to keep track of deadlines and artists.

Again, I guess the short answer is I do my best work with less editorial input. Just having someone there to support my vision and when I do need help I reach out to them. Someone who's not trying to impose their vision on what I do.

**Salvatore:** You were doing so much at Marvel this past year, whether it some of the Inhumans or *X-Men* stuff or it was finishing up your *Moon Knight* run or *Old Man Logan* with Andrea Sorrentino. Just talking about Marvel work in general, you've worked for both Marvel and DC, what's one of the differences in working with Marvel versus working with the Distinguished Competition? Not good or bad, what's different about working for those two places?

**Lemire:** I don't know. That's a really good question to answer 'cause as far as the work itself, it's not that much different. It just—you're working on a different universe. I'm naturally much more comfortable in the DC universe just 'cause those are the books I read growing up so I know the history, and I have that sentimental attachment to the DC stuff that I don't necessarily have to the Marvel stuff. Creatively it's not different; it all just depends, there's different personalities, different editors at both companies and that can influence things. Work-for-hire stuff for the big two is, it can be great and it can be sometimes frustrating. It just depends what editors you get, what character you're on, what artist you get paired with. My Marvel stuff on a whole was pretty positive. *Moon Knight* and *Old Man Logan* and *Thanos* were all great.

The *X-Men* stuff was a bit more challenging just because it's such a big machine, and there's so many people involved. That can get a bit, that can just be more challenging in some ways. I don't know if that answered your question. There's not a huge difference between the two. Like I said, there's different personalities at each company and that affects things both good and bad.

**Salvatore:** I'm interested—you're going to understand the spirit in which I'm asking this question, or somebody who's had so much success with creator-owned stuff, with graphic novels, what's the appeal of still doing work-for-hire at this point in your career?

**Lemire:** It's a great question. I ask myself that a lot sometimes. I'm at a really great spot in my career right now where, maybe four or five years ago, I was still establishing myself with mainstream comic book readers because I had done a lot of indie stuff and had success there, but in the more mainstream crowd, if you want to call it that, I was still establishing myself. I did stuff at DC with *Green Arrow* and *Animal Man* and then stuff at Marvel, where I established a name there as well. In terms of broadening my readership that was really valuable. It helped bring more readers to my independent work and it helped me launch a bunch of Image books that have now been successful. Now I'm at a really good spot where, to be completely honest with you, if I didn't want to do anything for Marvel or DC right now; financially I don't need to. I'm making a really good living off all my creator-owned stuff and that's what I always dreamed of.

I guess the only reason I continue to do it is 'cause I just love doing it. I really do love getting my hands on one of these characters, whether it be Moon Knight or Green Arrow or whatever and trying to bring my vision to it and do something interesting with it. I find it challenging and rewarding when it works. It's just a lot of fun to work. I guess maybe the key thing is when you're doing creator-owned stuff as fulfilling as it is, it's also all you. Whereas you go to the Marvel or DC universe and you get to collaborate on a different level that you don't get in your creator-owned stuff. I get to be part of a shared universe and get to work with different artists and writers and editors and stuff. It's a little more collaborative and a little more of a community feel that you don't always get.

**Salvatore:** It's more like being in a band than being a solo artist.

**Lemire:** Yeah, I don't know. As long as I continue to enjoy it I'll do it. I still have a lot of fun doing it.

**Salvatore:** Let's go over to Image for just a couple minutes here. *Descender* started before this year obviously, but you launched *Royal City* this year. I was talking to a friend of mine about the book and he said that it just to him it feels like the evolution of your creator-owned stories have led you to *Royal City*. He said it just feels like a culmination. I thought that was a great way to put it. It feels like the next evolution of your creator-owned stories. Talk about that book and what working on that book is doing for you creatively right now.

**Lemire:** I started off, when I started making comics fifteen, twenty years ago, I don't know how long it's been now, but I was just by myself. I was writing and drawing my own material. I didn't know anybody in comics. I didn't really have any hope of ever being published and I didn't care; I just wanted to do what I wanted to do. I started doing stuff in—I did stuff like *Essex County*, and all my early work that was just my own little universe and my own place where I could go.

As much as since then I've loved everything I've done, and even things like *Sweet Tooth* and *Trillium*, which were very much the same thing, it was me writing and drawing in my own little world. In the last five, six years, I've done so much genre work, whether it be superheroes or science fiction, that I really was starting to feel like I needed to ground myself again and get back at least with one project, get back to the kind of stories I was telling early on. Like *Essex County*, where it wasn't so genre- or high-concept-based, but it was more grounded in the real world. Real people, real problems, real life.

*Royal City* came from me trying to in some ways go back to those roots. But like you said, *Essex County* was a book I did ten, twelve years ago that was really about my childhood and where I grew up. *Royal City* is now me approaching the same sort of storytelling but instead of telling a story about my past, it's telling more of a story about where I am now in my life as a forty-year-old man with a child and married. I have different concerns and different ideas than I did when I was twenty-seven and writing *Essex County*. I can see it being the evolution of, in way. I get that 'cause it is like *Essex County* but *Essex County* ten years later, with ten years more life experience under me and different perspectives.

When I go into that world of *Royal City*, it's really my escape from everything. It's my own little place and it's I don't have to worry about anything. I tell these stories of these people and live in this world. I just love it.

**Salvatore:** I can sense when reading it how much the book means to you. That's a similar vibe that I got from *Roughneck*. It's obviously different in a way, but it felt very personal and it felt like there was a story there that you wanted to tell and it wasn't necessarily, like you said, a genre story or high-concept story; it was just more of a slice-of-life little story. How do you approach crafting a graphic novel versus crafting an ongoing series? Is it just that one of them is open-ended and one of is more finite or is there something else to it?

**Lemire:** There's a few things that go into those decisions. I started off doing graphic novels, like *Essex* and then *Underwater Welder*, and I hadn't done one in a while. I had done *Sweet Tooth* and *Trillium*, but those were both monthly comics and I was starting to feel like I need—I just want to get back to getting back to doing a book where it's a self-contained thing. It's not open-ended. It's a complete story. I hadn't done that in a while so I just had the craving to do it again with *Roughneck*. And then I did *Roughneck* and I got it out of my system and I missed—I realized, "Well, the monthly comic thing has so many rewards." As opposed to a graphic novel, where you work for two or three years on this thing every day and then it comes out and it gets a little press for a couple weeks when it comes out and then it just goes. People find it or they don't.

It sits on a shelf and that's cool, but the monthly comic . . . every single month, you get that comic coming out. And then you get this constant feedback every time a new issue comes out, and you get feedback, it reenergizes you and keeps you going and so instead of something that coming and going it's more . . . it has a presence that continues for a longer period of time, and it feels like a bigger thing. And then yeah, it does allow you to be more open-ended and go in different place, whereas once you get on the tracks with a graphic novel, you know where you're going and you have to go there. Sure, you can discover new things along the way but not to the extent you can with a monthly book where you can really explore different things and really take the story in different directions.

A lot of that came too from the last half-decade, decade or so—television has really become a much more viable storytelling medium than film in a lot of ways because film now becomes all about these big franchises, popcorn movies. Whereas if you want real intelligent challenging storytelling it tends to be with television now. That's the stuff I'm watching and getting inspired by, so instead of doing a graphic novel, I started to think, "Well, what if there was a monthly comic that's more like some of these dramas I was watching on television like *Transparent* or *Six Feet Under*, things that I love where I could get deeper into these characters?" Instead of having two hours to get into a character, suddenly you have multiple seasons, fifteen hours each, to explore characters.

It just seems so much more, seems to have so much more potential for me in terms of exploring these characters and stuff to try that as a comic. Because monthly comics tend to be very high-concept, very genre-driven, I love the challenge of doing one that wasn't to see if it could survive out there. And Eric Stephenson [of Image Comics] really was excited about that too, because there isn't a lot of that out there. It felt like something different and challenging in a lot of ways.

**Salvatore:** You mentioned *Six Feet Under*, which is my favorite show of all time. I actually think that that's a great touchstone for *Royal City*. I haven't thought of that yet. Now I'm going to have to convert my *Six Feet Under*–loving friends. That's really cool.

**Lemire:** It's a huge influence on the book and on me. It's one of my all-time favorite pieces of art as well. I love that show and I watch it fairly regularly. I'll rewatch it. It was a really big influence on *Royal City*.

**Salvatore:** Two last things before I let you go. The first thing is, I want you to talk about some of your favorite comics of 2017 or creators that came on your radar. What is one of the things that you've enjoyed reading this past year?

**Lemire:** There's been a couple really cool discoveries for me of new cartoonists that I've really enjoyed. To be completely honest, I don't read a ton of monthly comics right now. I tend to wait; things I really like, I'll just wait and read the trades because I don't have as much time to read comics as I used to. The monthly stuff, the stuff I follow, I tend to follow certain creators. I'll read Jason Aaron's stuff 'cause I have of tons of respect for him as a storyteller. I love his stuff. I love *Southern Bastards* and *The God Damned*, and *The Mighty Thor* is a great superhero comic.

I really like *Paper Girls* a lot. I got into that this year. I follow Matt Kindt's stuff, too. *Dept H* and his Valiant stuff I really enjoy. His *Divinity* stuff at Valiant was great. That's stuff definitely comes to mind, monthly stuff. The stuff that hits me a bit more this year were a few graphic novels generally like myself. Tillie Walden is a creator who has limitless potential and talent and she released that book *Spinning* this year.

**Salvatore:** So great, so great.

**Lemire:** Everyone should be reading her stuff. She's fantastic. I was just in Italy for the Lucca Fest, and I was sitting next to this cartoonist who was doing sketches and I was watching her draw and her stuff was amazing and I got to know her. Her name is Flavia Biondi, I hope I'm saying that right. I don't know what her books are called 'cause they're just in Italian in the moment. Lion Forge is going to be publishing them in English soon. If you can remember that name, you should keep an eye for her; her stuff's really good. I also read a Nick Cave biography, graphic novel by Richard Kleist. I really enjoyed that as well. There's been some cool stuff that I have read this year. Comics-wise.

**Salvatore:** And then lastly, in 2018 you've come back to DC with *The Terrifics* and *Inferior Five*. Give us a little hint of what your 2018's going to look like and maybe if there's anything about those stories that you think might be enticing to our readers, lay it out there.

**Lemire:** I'll talk about those two books and then there was one more I wanted to talk about actually. *The Terrifics*, really it's obvious what we're doing there. We're trying to take everything we loved about the *Fantastic Four* and capture that spirit. I love *Fantastic Four*, I love the family feel of *Fantastic Four*, and I love those early Jack Kirby, Stan Lee comics—they're the template for what all superhero came from. They're just so rich with imagination, adventure, and fun, and every issue was just packed with enough ideas that would spawn whole series now. We really wanted to capture something in that vein. And even *Tom Strong*/Alan Moore stuff, the fun adventure stuff—kids could read it and adults could read it, and it wasn't dumbed down but it was just accessible and fun and big.

That's really what *The Terrifics* is an attempt at: to take some underused DC characters and put them together into this wacky family feel and have them have just big fun adventures with lots of heart. It's Plastic Man, Metamorpho, Mr. Terrific—who's just a really cool character—and then we have new character, Phantom Girl, who's mysteriously connected to the Phantom Girl from the Legion [of Superheroes], but I don't want to spoil the connection yet. It's those four characters bonded together by things that occur in the first issue, and we go from there and just have big fun adventures full of heart. Tom Strong is going to be in the book, which is really cool because that was one of the touchstones I was looking at when we came up with the idea. Tom and his family will guest appear in one big arc. What else? I don't know if there is anything else I can tease about that book.

Ivan Reis is drawing the first arc and then Doc Shaner is drawing the second arc. And they're going to rotate from there. You get these two different feels, both of which capture different sides of what we're doing. It's real fun.

*Inferior Five* is like a passion project for Dan DiDio, me, and Keith Giffen. There's a meta level to this book for me where Keith is one of my heroes. I grew up in the '80s, and Keith was the main man at DC then. I was obsessed with everything he was doing as a kid. His *Justice League* run, his *Legion* stuff, *Ambush Bug*, *Lobo*, everything, these were my bibles as a kid. I would sit and copy Keith's drawings and stuff. The chance for me now to write for Keith to draw is so cool; it's awesome. And the weird meta thing is that the concept of the book is these five kids in small town in the DC universe of the 1980s. It's like *Twin Peaks* or *It* or something but the backdrop, the world is the world of DC comics from 1987. Every comic that DC was publishing in 1987 is the backdrop of this world.

The ironic thing is I was the one reading those comics in 1987 and Keith was probably the one making most of them. And now we're doing this weird project set in that universe. We're doing a Marvel style where we just broke down a script yesterday. We'll just be on the phone on just throw ideas around and won't even write an outline. Keith, we just have a conversation and then Keith goes and draws the book and Keith tends to draw something totally different than everything we talked about anyway, in a good way. And then it comes back to me and I have to try to make sense of it. It's really fun. And then some of the added aspect of that is I'm finally to draw some stuff in the DC universe too because every issue will have a five-page backup story that I'm writing and drawing that will feature weird characters from 1987 DC, primarily the Peacemaker. Those backup stories will eventually connect to our main *Inferior Five* story. It is a crazy book, but it was a lot of fun and Keith's art has never looked better. It's really cool.

**Salvatore:** Is that ongoing or is that a miniseries?

**Lemire:** We'll see. I don't know what expectations anyone has for this book 'cause it's so wild.

Keith and I both said we'll do it as long we're having fun doing it and as long as it's selling. I guess we'll see what happens. I know we have a story planned that's probably around twelve issues and if the book's successful it can go longer. We'll see how it goes.

And then the other book that I'm real excited about is I have another Image book launching in March with Andrea Sorrentino, who I did *Green Arrow* and *Old Man Logan* with. It's a supernatural horror book called *Gideon Falls* that Andrea is drawing right now. I've written the first arc. It's going to be real crazy, a really fun book. That one's in March, too.

**Salvatore:** It's a good time to be a fan of Jeff Lemire comics.

**Lemire:** I appreciate you saying that. Certainly I'm living my dream. Honestly, I'm getting to do all of these crazy books with artists I love and do my own stuff, too. I never dreamed this could happen. I just wake up every day so grateful to be able to do what I do. All these people supporting my work I have to thank for that. Thanks.

# From the Land of the Impossible:
# An Interview with Jeff Lemire

## JOEL T. LEWIS / 2018

*Nerds That Geek*, April 20, 2018. Reprinted by permission.

Let's remove all pretense for a moment. I was scared to meet Jeff Lemire last weekend at the Denver DiNK Convention. Back when my favorite author was Charles Dickens or Charlotte Bronte I never had to worry about what I would say if I had the chance to meet them. Death has a funny way of preventing those kinds of conversations. But after reading his work, Lemire leapt to the top of my list. His compassion, the poignance of his work, and the seemingly inexhaustible stream of new and diverse projects hit me all at once and I had to think about it. What do you say to your hero? To a man who's made you laugh and cry and made you happy there behind the printed words of a single issue that could've been read or written by anybody.

But even then, the thought was merely cathartic fantasy. Sure, it was possible that I could meet him at a signing and have that brief moment of awkward chitchat, with me telling him how much his work meant to me, and him making polite small talk as he signed the issues I sheepishly pushed towards him. But the intimate conversation, the mild interrogation, the fevered gushing that I was planning wasn't possible. It would never happen.

But it happened, dear readers. I got to interview the man. I got to sit a foot away from a man whose work spoke to me, shattered me, and put me back together through the thin glossy pages of a comic book and ask him whatever I wanted. He was cool, he was kind, and he was very generous, both with his time, and with the answers he gave me. Here's what I asked him and what he said to me. I hope you enjoy it.

**Joel T. Lewis:** One of the things I really like about your artwork specifically is your character's facial expressions. They're very expressive and I was wondering when you start a project with a new character is that where you start?

**Jeff Lemire:** Yeah, it's always faces. It's the thing I like to draw the most. Usually with a new project it usually starts in my sketchbook and there'll be a character like Sweet Tooth or something, and you create a little character and you don't really know what it is and it might start reoccurring in your sketchbook and you start to build a story around them. My artistic style is very unique I think and kind of idiosyncratic and I have strengths and weaknesses. So I kind of play to my strengths and one thing I try to do is communicate a lot of emotion with my characters and their faces. So I think it's one of my skills so I kind of build around that.

**Lewis:** For sure, it definitely comes across. That's awesome. I notice a lot of trinkets in your work.

**Lemire:** Oh, really?

**Lewis:** Well, there's the stopwatch, or the pocket watch in *Underwater Welder*, and the vintage radios in *Royal City*. So, I have a collection of little things like that and I was wondering if you did too, if that's where that comes from?

**Lemire:** No, I'm not much of a collector at all. The only thing I really collect is books.

**Lewis:** Same here.

**Lemire:** But cool little objects like that can tell a story, too. It's not just characters. There's something about those old radios that just evoked a time and a story that's kind of supernatural to me, you know? I don't know why. Or that stopwatch. Those just cool sort of old things that have a story themselves, they can be really interesting. You can kind of fall in love with drawing certain little objects, different things that for some weird reason stick around.

**Lewis:** Very cool. Awesome. So I'm a massive Moon Knight Fan.

**Lemire:** Oh, cool.

**Lewis:** So I've got to take a second to say your run was spectacular. It meant a lot to me. Issue 9 is my favorite comic of all time.

**Lemire:** Which one's that?

**Lewis:** That's where he reconciles with his other personalities and kind of lets them go.

**Lemire:** Oh, yeah, I like that one, too. Where he hugs the one guy.

**Lewis:** Yeah, it was really cool to see you treat a character I care about so much with such seriousness and compassion. That was really cool.

**Lemire:** Thanks.

**Lewis:** So the question I had was: when you're coming into a character that's been established and they have this kind of nuanced history, how do you balance your vision for the character's arc and the history that's come before?

**Lemire:** Well, usually that history's really inspiring, and inspires new stories for me. So if I'm working on an existing character from Marvel or DC or something I haven't created myself, the first thing I'll do is collect everything on that character. Every run, every story, every comic I can get my hands on, and I'll just read everything and as I'm reading, I get story ideas like, "Oh, this is a cool idea, but what if it went further with this idea or that." So, with that stuff you take advantage of the fact that it has this history that you can use. Especially with Moon Knight, I mean, I made his whole history kind of part of the story. Sometimes it works better with certain characters with the idea that you have. Like the Moon Knight idea that I had, that stuff just lent itself to pulling from those different eras and characters. So when you can, that stuff's a gold mine to use. Even with Black Hammer, those are my own characters but I'm obviously drawing from eighty years of superhero comic book history. Why not use it when you know it's there? Like I was never a huge Moon Knight fan, but I was a big Bill Sienkiewicz fan so I always respected and kind of liked that version of the character. So I started there and then I found other things along the way that I liked. You know for a character that hasn't really had an ongoing series regularly over the years there have been some really good stories. The Sienkiewicz, [Doug] Moench stuff is obviously classic, it's amazing and the Bendis stuff was really interesting, I thought, and especially the Warren Ellis stuff was a great jumping off point for me. He really kind of repositioned things. You use all that stuff and you build off of it as much as you can, but, I mean, if you can't bring your own idea, your own point of view to it then there's no point in doing those things.

**Lewis:** I noticed that you did that too with *Old Man Logan* with the Past Lives run—that was cool that you kind of paid homage to all those tragedies in Logan's life.

**Lemire:** Yeah, you try to evoke the feeling of the stuff that everyone loves without just retelling those same stories and you can. It doesn't always work but when it does it can be fun.

**Lewis:** Was it always your intention to have several different artists for the different perspectives of *Moon Knight*?

**Lemire:** No. [*laughs*] Greg [Smallwood] just kind of got behind schedule. But again, it's one of those things where the story lends itself perfectly to that so just embrace it. Yeah, but it really worked out. Greg's pretty versatile himself. He can kind of do different styles but it was kind of seamless with what we were doing, so I kind of got lucky there.

**Lewis:** Yeah, you got Francesco Francavilla on there, which was awesome.

**Lemire:** Yeah, and Wilfredo Torres.

**Lewis:** And James Stokoe.

**Lemire:** Yeah, we got really cool people on there.

**Lewis:** So, speaking of collaborations, I love *A.D.: After Death*. That was such a cool synergy of writing and your artwork. I was wondering how you worked with Scott Snyder and how that writing process was.

**Lemire:** Yeah, it was really unique and I had never drawn anything before that someone else had written. I had done a couple of short stories that Damon Lindelof had written but those were just ten pages so it's not like a huge commitment, but I'd never done something big like this that I hadn't written myself. I'd written for other artists but never drawn for other writers so it was really intimidating and we kind of felt it out as we went along. I think Scott really trusted the fact that I also am a writer and visually I know how to tell a story. It kind of just evolved as we went, but what it ended up being was Scott would spend the majority of his time working on the prose sections because those were pretty labor-intensive for him and while he was doing that I would do the comics sections. And we really didn't have a script for those. We would just have conversations where this happens and that happens and I would just start thumbnailing it and drawing the comics. And when there were dialogue scenes I would just try to leave room for dialogue and then draw characters talking and hopefully get it sort of right and then he would go back and letter the stuff afterwards. And if in those dialogues I needed to tweak a facial expression or an emotion to match something he'd come up with, I would do that, but for the most part we kind of made it work. So it was sort of a unique collaboration.

**Lewis:** Yeah, it's such a unique book from those prose sections and then you have panels and panels with no dialogue. It was really playful. I loved it a lot. You've gotten to work with a lot of great artists, great writers—Andrea Sorrentino is outstanding, *Gideon Falls* is really good, Smallwood on *Moon Knight*—so I was wondering if there was somebody in the industry you haven't gotten a chance to work with past or present, living or dead, who that would be?

**Lemire:** Oh, boy, so many. I don't know. There's so many amazing artists it's hard; oh, God, there's so many! One guy that I've always felt like I really wish I had done more with was Rafael Albuquerque. We did a few *Animal Mans* together at the end of my run and we really clicked. I felt like we really had something, so I felt like he and I had like a similar sensibility kind of like the same way Dustin [Nguyen] and I had a similar sensibility. I feel like he and I could do something special together, but our schedules have never worked out so he's someone I'd like to do something with someday. But, I mean, there's dozens of artists just working today—I'm drawing a blank, of course, but there's so many talented people out there.

**Lewis:** I know it's early stages, but you were talking about a collaboration with Matt Kindt—do you know if you would draw, or if he would draw?

**Lemire:** No, we were both talking about that this morning. I think we decided we're just going to write it together and we know what artist we want to work with. Because we both have so many projects already lined up that we're drawing, we know that if we waited it might never happen and we want it to happen.

**Lewis:** Another question I had specifically about your work is, you have a lot of characters under water. There's a lot of submerged kind of cold moments.

**Lemire:** It's like a definite motif.

**Lewis:** Yeah, so I was wondering what inspires that?

**Lemire:** I don't know. It's just subconscious. I just love being underwater. I always have since I was a kid. There's just something so peaceful about it. Whenever I can, I love being in the ocean. So I've always had this weird connection to that, and, I don't know, symbolically I think water is so rich. It can mean so many things—life, death, rebirth—and I love drawing it. It's just a weird motif that I'm drawn to. I try not to overthink it. Because when you start overanalyzing stuff sometimes it can go away. But yeah, it's definitely a motif in a lot of my work. Surprisingly not a lot of people have pointed that out. I mean, it's in *Royal City*, *Underwater Welder* especially, it's all over that stuff.

**Lewis:** That was something about *A.D.: After Death* that I noticed: that even though it was Scott writing, he talks about the ice over water and it always being there. So it felt like you were writing it too in that sense.

**Lemire:** Yeah, I never thought of that but yeah it's definitely something very symbolic and I think it probably started with the *Welder*. But even in *Essex County* there were scenes where the old man would walk out into the water and sink below. So I've always been kind of drawn to that.

**Lewis:** So, you're going to be on *Sentry* soon.

**Lemire:** Oh, yeah.

**Lewis:** Which is really exciting for me as I'm a big fan of the Jae Lee stuff and Paul Jenkins. It's kind of like you're cherry-picking all of my favorite characters; it's really cool. Do you know when that process will start?

**Lemire:** I think the series starts in June. I've written four of them, and I know Kim [Jacinto], the artist, is finishing up the first issue so it's coming along.

**Lewis:** I think I was reading something you were talking about him [Sentry] in contrast to Moon Knight, about kind of the cerebral nature of their madness.

**Lemire:** Yeah, well, they're both characters that suffer from mental illness, but I didn't want to just redo the Moon Knight story, because it's a different character, it's a different illness, different way of seeing the world, different history. But I think there is a little bit of a link between the two in the way that I'm approaching it. But I want to tell a Sentry story that's a Sentry story the way the Moon Knight story had to be a Moon Knight story.

**Lewis:** Do you know if it's going to be ongoing, or is it going to be fourteen-ish issues or?

**Lemire:** I'm not sure. I don't know how long my run will be on that to be honest with you. I'm so busy right now so I'm definitely signed on to the first arc, and then we'll see from there where it goes.

**Lewis:** So I just have some rapid fire ones here to close out: What if any comics are you currently reading?

**Lemire:** My favorite kind of ongoing book is *Paper Girls*. I love Cliff [Chiang]'s art so much. There's a lot in that series I just find very entertaining and I like that a lot. Nate Powell has a new graphic novel coming out called *Come Again*, which, it's not out yet, but I got to read an advance copy and that was fantastic. I always read Matt [Kindt]'s stuff. He's always doing great stuff. Of the more mainstream-y superhero stuff I don't read a lot to be honest, but I try to keep up on Jason Aaron's stuff because I really like Jason's writing a lot.

**Lewis:** *Mighty Thor*'s been outstanding.

**Lemire:** Yeah, his superhero stuff and his creator-owned stuff is always so strong, he's just such a great writer. I follow more creators around. Those are the ones that pop in my head of the stuff that I'm into right now.

**Lewis:** If there's a single issue or series that you're most proud to have written what would that be?

**Lemire:** That I haven't drawn myself? Yeah, that's tough. I sometimes look at that stuff and sometimes it's hit and miss. Some things work better than others. I don't know if I could pick one, but I think the ones that I'm most proud of would be *Green Arrow* with Andrea [Sorrentino], *Animal Man*, *Moon Knight*, and my *Bloodshot* for Valiant. Those are probably the ones that pop up. I mean, that's not counting any of my created stuff. Obviously, *Black Hammer* and *Descender* are much more dear to my heart than any of that stuff. I'm just thinking of the more freelance work I've done, it would be those runs.

**Lewis:** So same question, but with drawing.

**Lemire:** That's tough, too. To me they're all like documents of where I was as a person when I was doing them so they're all special to me in different ways. You can't pick one, but *Essex County* was sort of like the first project where I found an audience, where I found a voice as a writer. So it's always going to be special to me. *Sweet Tooth*'s always going to be special to me because that was the longest project I ever did. It's like four years of writing, of drawing those characters everyday so they're always dear to my heart. And it's usually whatever I'm working on now is like the thing I'm most engaged in so that's like my favorite. Yeah, it's hard to pick between that stuff.

**Lewis:** What's the strangest request for a commission that you're ever gotten?

**Lemire:** Oh, God. [*laughs*] I don't do a lot of commissions anymore. I haven't done them in about ten years, but I used to get some weird ones. It's just weird where my art style is so specific and you'll get people who will ask you for something that clearly like plays against all my strengths. If you can ask me for all the things, why would you want, like, whatever, Donna Troy? I'm not going to do a good beautiful woman. Sometimes you get some pretty weird, infamously weird commission requests that all artists get from these certain people all the time that are like these weird kinky things. So there's some strange ones.

**Lewis:** And just the last one: if someone was new to comics and wanted a starting point, what would you recommend?

**Lemire:** The two entry points for all my work—always, over and over—I always say are *Sweet Tooth* and *Essex County*. I guess one of those. Those would be my starting points for my stuff.

# Lemire & Sorrentino Share Secrets of the Future of *Gideon Falls*

## MEG DOWNEY / 2018

*CBR*, July 12, 2018. Reprinted by permission.

Jeff Lemire and Andrea Sorrentino's creator-owned horror comic, *Gideon Falls* made the news last week with the announcement of a live-action TV adaptation with production company, Hivemind—but making the jump from page to screen isn't the only things looming on the book's horizon. Starting in the fall, *Gideon Falls* will be entering its second story arc as the mysteries surrounding the ominous town continue to deepen.

Described as "an atmospheric thriller colliding rural mystery and urban horror," *Gideon Falls* is the story of a town called—you guessed it—Gideon Falls, and the Black Barn, a surreal and haunting building that seems to have a connection to three, seemingly unrelated people in disturbing ways. From terrifying visions of malevolent monsters and real life murder investigations to ominous clues hidden in the town's trash, nothing in Gideon Falls is ever as it seems.

*CBR* sat down with Lemire and Sorrentino to discuss the story's future both in the comics and the upcoming adaptation, as well as take an exclusive look at the art for the upcoming issues #7, #8, and #9.

**Meg Downey:** The first thing that really drew me to *Gideon Falls* as a story was the idea that it's about the whole town and this event, if you could call it that, that's spilling out across all these different people and places. It feels expansive in a way that I think typical horror tends to avoid for that feeling of narrative claustrophobia—but on that same token, I have to imagine that the level of worldbuilding and juggling you both have to do is pretty tricky. What made you decide on taking that zoomed out approach?

**Jeff Lemire:** I don't know that I ever thought about it in that way—if I had I may have intimidated myself. This is really just how the story came out organically for me. It was always a book about community. We have Father Fred arriving in Gideon Falls and trying to find his place in this community after years of being transient. And we also have Norton who lives in the very opposite of this community. He lives a life of relative anonymity in a large city, but he is also being pulled towards Gideon Falls and the people there. So I always knew it would be a large cast, and to me that works even better because it really helps show the scope of the Black Barn's reach on the world.

**Andrea Sorrentino:** I think it could be interesting to add that the very first title Jeff came with for this story was "The Black Barn." Then the mystery and the backstory around it kept expanding as Jeff delved more and more into the story. The cast and the world around it grew bigger, and it became clear that it was not only around the Black Barn itself anymore but about a whole community. It's like, in the end, Gideon Falls becomes a living character itself, and it sounded just obvious to name the series after it.

**Downey:** In keeping with that worldbuilding, by the sound of things the next arc is going to be tackling some of Gideon Falls's past. Can you tease a little of what we should expect come the fall?

**Lemire:** We do start to delve into the past of Gideon Falls and the Black Barn. This rich history was only teased in arc one, in Doc Sutton's house with all his clippings and his work with The Ploughmen. But we will now start to actually see some of that history unfold firsthand. And we will also learn more about the more immediate past, and the back stories of both Fred and Norton.

**Sorrentino:** We'll definitely see a lot more of the past. As Jeff said, there're a lot of things we only teased in arc one about the rich history of Gideon Falls. I've just recently drawn some pages set in a Gideon Falls of 1900 for the second arc that shows the origins of the horror, how everything started. I think it will be very interesting for readers. Many of the answers they're looking for are in arc two.

**Downey:** I'm pretty obsessed with the dueling narratives that have been happening in the comic so far, and all the weird ways you've both managed to draw connections between the main characters despite the fact that, so far, they're only connected obliquely by their run ins with the Black Barn. Is that multifaceted style going to continue on in the next arc as well or can we expect to start seeing Father Fred and Norton's worlds collide?

**Lemire:** It will indeed continue and get even more complex as we start layering different timelines as well. So the book will be a bit of a challenging read, a puzzle of sorts. But, to me, that's what makes it so fun to construct, and hopefully to read as well.

**Downey:** With the first four issues, the major threat is most obviously the Black Barn, but there's a heavy implication that the real thing we should be scared of is who or whatever is inside it, rather than just the barn itself. What can you tell me about that terrifying grinning man?

**Lemire:** I can tell you nothing! And who says what is inside the barn and the barn itself are two different things? Issue #6 is a wild one, and some of this will begin to be revealed.

**Sorrentino:** Yes, we can't really say anything about him at this point, but I think that what's interesting about the guy is that his role changed a bit during the development of the story, as Jeff added more and more pieces to the puzzle. I think it will show how much thought and design Jeff has put in the whole mystery surrounding the Black Barn and how everything has its role in the big plan.

**Downey:** As things in Gideon Falls start to get more and more tense, Andrea, your artwork and page layouts really start to get experimental and psychedelic in ways that are really beautiful and engaging—have you given any thought about how you'd like to see those surrealist art elements translated into live-action for the TV show?

**Sorrentino:** Actually, I've always loved to get experimental with my layouts. I've done a lot of this in my previous work at Marvel or DC, but, with *Gideon Falls*, I wanted to make it a crescendo, starting a bit calmer than usual and then going crazier and crazier with layouts as the mystery and the craziness in the story began to unfold. I think it will be a rewarding experience for the readers once you get to the end of the first arc, much more than if I'd start to get crazy from the beginning. Issue #6 has some kind of things I've never done before—I can't wait for readers to put their eyes on it.

And about working with Hivemind for the TV series, I'm eager to see what they'll come up with. Both Jeff and I are very involved in the project, and we trust they'll do something wonderful with our little child.

**Downey:** In crafting both the book itself and the onscreen adaptation, have there been any major horror or thriller touchstones either of you have looked at for inspiration? Do either of you have a favorite horror story, show, or film you want to try and pay homage to?

**Sorrentino:** I've always drawn inspiration from all kind of media, especially movies and TV. I think that when you mix things from different worlds, you can really come out with something different and unique. And I've always loved horror, probably even more than any other genres. For my favorite

*Gideon Falls* #2, page 22. Credit: Andrea Sorrentino and Jeff Lemire.

horror pieces, I'd probably say *Alien* and the short tale, "The Color Out of Space," by H. P. Lovecraft. I love the way he describes the indescribable; it has always immediately set my mind in motion to imagine ways to convey his impossible descriptions into real visuals.

**Lemire:** For me the biggest touchstone has always been *Twin Peaks*. It is my favorite piece of art, film, TV, and has been since I was thirteen. So this is really my love letter to *Twin Peaks*. But that doesn't mean I am trying to copy or ape *Twin Peaks*—we want to create our own world here. Aside from Lynch and *Peaks*, the biggest influences on Gideon Falls for me are H. P. Lovecraft, *Jacob's Ladder*, *The Shining*, and *IT*.

**Downey:** In building the story as a comic, Jeff, has your script and outline stayed pretty crystallized through the process or are you approaching it more organically? Is *Gideon Falls* as it is now the same *Gideon Falls* it was at the start?

**Lemire:** It is really changing a lot as I go, probably more so than with any of my past projects. The book is really organic and layered, and I am always adding new pieces. Andrea's art stimulates this, too, because he gets so experimental, it pushes me in new directions. I have an idea of the ending, but everything else is shifting and growing as we go.

**Sorrentino:** That's a tricky question. In some ways it is, but it's also not. I think everything will be clear by the end of the first arc.

**Downey:** Finally, building off that, has the story shifted at all with the show now in the works? Are you hoping both versions of the story converge and diverge to keep each incarnation unique or are you hoping for a little more faith to the source material?

**Lemire:** It's too early to tell. Our partners at Hivemind love the comic, and I know they will honor what we are doing in their adaptation. But my focus remains the comic and telling the best story we can in the comics medium. This just gives them more to work with.

**Sorrentino:** I think what's important is that the comic remains faithful to itself. We don't want it to turn into a movie/TV series script now that we know about the TV series. It would only make things unnatural and forced. Both Jeff and I are working on this series in order to make it a good comic, and, as Jeff said, I think this will also give the TV series some much more solid foundation to work and expand on.

# Jeff Lemire Opens Up about *Black Hammer,* Writing Superheroes, and Trying New Things

**ALEX DUEBEN / 2019**

*The Beat*, July 9, 2019. Reprinted by permission.

Some of us will always associate Jeff Lemire with his award-winning trilogy *Essex County*, but in the years since he finished that project, Lemire has been an incredibly prolific creator. He wrote and drew most of the entire run of *Sweet Tooth*, his Vertigo series which ran for forty issues. He's written and drawn comics and graphic novels like *The Nobody, Underwater Welder, Trillium, Roughneck,* and *Royal City.*

As a writer, Lemire has worked for multiple companies, writing *Justice League* and *X-Men, Bloodshot* and *Animal Man, Old Man Logan,* and *Green Arrow,* and many more. He's also written a long line of award-winning creator-owned comics for other artists including *Descender, Gideon Falls,* and *Plutona.*

One series that has really taken off, and has managed to be a deeply personal series for Lemire even as it's a superhero story, of a sort, is *Black Hammer.* The series drawn by Dean Ormston launched at Dark Horse in 2016. In between the main series, Lemire has written a number of spinoffs including *Sherlock Frankenstein and the Legion of Evil, Cthu-Louise,* and *Doctor Star and the Kingdom of Lost Tomorrows* with different artists. He's also tackled the future of the universe in *The Quantum Age* and let Ray Fawkes and Matt Kindt tell stories in *Black Hammer '45.*

This summer, Lemire wraps up *Black Hammer: Age of Doom* with issue #12, though as Lemire made clear in an interview with *The Beat*, this issue is far from the end of the saga or these characters. In addition, the series is crossing over with the *Justice League*, and Dark Horse is releasing *The World of Black Hammer Encyclopedia.* Lemire also has a new series with artist Mike Deodato, *Berserker Unbound.*

**Alex Dueben:** I'm curious, what are the superhero comics you really liked when you were younger? Or, what are the ones that have stayed with you?

**Jeff Lemire:** For me it really started with DC. I was nine years old in 1985, and that was a hugely influential period for me. Both *Crisis on Infinite Earths* and DC's original *Who's Who* started that year and they hit me hard. I became obsessed with the scope and scale of the DC universe then and all the various Earths. I also really fell in love with Wolfman and Perez and *The New Teen Titans*. Giffen and Levitz's *Legion* was also a big one.

I bought anything I could find. We didn't have comic book stores, just newsstands, so I would really buy anything I could and I couldn't be picky about it. I bought a lot of Marvel stuff then too, but it was really the DC stuff that hit and that I continued to collect as I got older. As the late '80s hit and DC started publishing a lot more experimental stuff (from *Dark Knight*, *Swamp Thing*, etc.). I was the perfect age for all that stuff to make a big impact.

So, basically anything and everything DC published between '84 and '91 was my sweet spot. I was between the age of eight and fifteen then. Formative years, for sure. In terms of Marvel stuff, I was really into the Mark Gruenwald *Captain America* and the *Iron Man* stuff in that period as well.

But really DC's *Who's Who* was my bible. I knew that thing inside out. Still do.

**Dueben:** You wrote in the back of the first *Black Hammer* collection about how you had started writing this idea when you were finishing *Essex County* back in 2007–8. Back then, did you have this entire story laid out in your mind, story beats—beginning, middle, end?

**Lemire:** Not at the same scope it ended up being. I had the initial setup and most of the main cast and I had a very loose idea of where it might end, but it was never fully developed beyond character designs and histories and initial ideas. And many of those changed when I returned to it in 2014. The character of Lucy Weber, for example, was not a part of that early incarnation, and for me she was the key that unlocked the whole story. She is the heart of the whole universe now.

I can't fully remember how I thought it would end back then, but I know I have sketch books and notebooks with stuff in them somewhere.

**Dueben:** Is that how you like to work and think about story? You need all of it in your mind—even if it may change? Or does that vary from project to project?

**Lemire:** I used to always need to know my ending. For example, I always knew how *Sweet Tooth* would end. But that was mostly because I didn't anticipate that book being able to last beyond eight or ten issues, so I needed to have an ending in mind to make it feel like a complete story when it got cancelled. Then it ended up succeeding and I kept that ending but was able to expand the journey to get to that point for forty issues.

Now, I generally have a direction and loose ending idea, but keep it much looser and take it one arc at a time, finding the story as I go. This keeps things fresh and keeps me a bit more engaged long term. If you know everything that's going to happen, it's hard to keep excitement going on a longer series like *Descender* or *Gideon Falls*. You need to create a process where you can still find new things and follow new ideas and directions that excite you. But I am a very structured person, so even if things change, I do start with a structure and plan, but it always evolves.

**Dueben:** How did your perspective on superhero comics change between when you first thought of the idea and when you started writing *Black Hammer*? How do you think it would have been different if you had started it back then?

**Lemire:** Back when I started, I never anticipated getting a chance to actually do any "real" superhero books for Marvel or DC. So this was just my personal fun little love letter to superheroes done in my own style. And then when I returned to it in 2014, I had been writing heavily for DC and Marvel for about five or six years. I still loved the characters but was exhausted by the deadlines and the restrictions that can be placed on you when doing work-for-hire. This was like total freedom to go back and do it all by myself, without any concern for what the other writers were doing, what the editors wanted, etc. Utter free reign. It was a blast, and it still feels that way.

**Dueben:** As you were writing and thinking about *Black Hammer*, what was the challenge as far as crafting these characters and finding ways to make them archetypal in some ways but also not derivative? Because I think that is one of the challenges when it comes to crafting new superheroes and new universes like you've done here.

**Lemire:** Honestly, I never thought much about that. I just went for it and created most of these characters in 2008 thinking they would probably never be seen by anyone else or live beyond my sketchbook. So I just took flavors from all the different eras of superhero comics. More than trying to imitate any one character, I wanted each character to embody a specific era or archetype, and then put my own little personal spin on it.

Golden Gail and Abe were both Golden Age heroes. Barbalien was like the Bronze Age sword-and-sandal heroes meets a more sci-fi Bronze Age concept. Colonel Weird is obviously Silver Age sci-fi and Dragonfly was '80s or '90s proto-Vertigo horror. Black Hammer is a '70s blaxploitation character, etc.

I didn't worry about them being derivative, because I knew as I started writing them in actual, rendered scenes they would all have their own life and character.

**Dueben:** Having read *Black Hammer*, I have to ask: are you a fan of *The Prisoner*?

**Lemire:** It is a show I have always wanted to get into, but have yet to watch. I will one day. I know enough about it to understand why you are asking that in relation to *Black Hammer* though. Honestly, the biggest influence on *Black Hammer* is *Lost*. That may surprise some people, but it's true. I love *Lost* to death.

**Dueben:** So at what point did you ask your editors—or did they ask you—I want to write a spinoff? And what's the process of figuring out what to do and how to make it markedly different from the main series—and the other spinoffs?

**Lemire:** It came out of necessity. I didn't plan on it, or plan on expanding. Dean Ormston had some health issues and it slowed him down a bit, so we needed to have a fill-in issue to keep the schedule going. I wanted to make sure Dean drew all of the chapters of the main farm story, so I had to come up with something separate from that to use as a fill-in for David Rubín. So, I wrote the issue where Lucy Weber finds her Dad's "Hall of Hammers," I believe that was issue 12. And as soon as I wrote that and saw how David rendered it I realized I could do more stories set in this world and the doors just flew open then. I did *Sherlock Frankenstein*, then *Doctor Star*, and then there was no turning back. The universe started growing and growing and all I see now is potential.

There is and was no master plan. It all just grew organically out of that initial need to do a fill-in.

**Dueben:** I wanted to ask about *Doctor Star*. Like a lot of people, I smiled when the character first popped up—I loved James Robinson's *Starman* like I have loved few comics—but the miniseries was a really beautiful, quiet, self-contained comic, and I just wonder if you could talk about putting together this story.

**Lemire:** It started as a love letter to James and *Starman*, but became one of the most personal and autobiographical stories I have ever done. I don't want to get to deep into my personal life, so I will leave it at that. But I wrote all four issues in a week and it was one of the most emotional creative experiences I ever had. I am happy that it seems to have really resonated with people.

If you are truly feeling the things you are worrying about and drawing, then the emotions you feel go into the work and people can sense that. I honestly believe that.

**Dueben:** You are now crossing over with the *Justice League*. How did that happen?

**Lemire:** I have no idea. Ha! Honestly, I think someone at DC approached someone at Dark Horse originally. I was as shocked as anyone. But, as I stated earlier in this interview, my love of the DC Universe runs deep and far back, so I couldn't pass it up. I still love DC. Doing freelance work can have its challenges, but I still have a lot of friends at DC, and I love the characters and universe. I am actually writing three other DC projects at the moment.

This was just too much fun to pass up and hopefully it helps bring a few new readers to the *Black Hammer* Universe too!

**Dueben:** So we've mostly been talking about the main series and the past, but with artist Wilfredo Torres, you made *The Quantum Age*. What is it?

**Lemire:** It was a chance to jump ahead one hundred years into the future of the Black Hammer universe and see how our present-day characters and their legacies will echo into a new age and new generation. Obviously, this is something both DC and Marvel have done a lot too, with *Legion* and other properties. But for me it was about seeing the legacy of *Black Hammer* carried forward like a torch.

**Dueben:** You have the character of Colonel Weird who has seen how everything will turn out and so you have this set plan. At least that's what such a character suggests. So do you have this plan about how *Black Hammer* and *The Quantum Age* will work out and how everything fits together?

**Lemire:** Absolutely. We see how Weird's fate connects in *The Quantum Age*, and that just opens more stories for him and the universe. But there is a plan now on how it all ties together. I have charts and maps and timelines. It's a lot of fun to do that sort of worldbuilding. We have a *Black Hammer Encyclopedia* coming out soon that will reveal some of this stuff and hint at future stories and connections.

**Dueben:** We've seen the superhero comics do a pretty inconsistent but mostly poor job of dealing with legacy characters and time and change. In these books you're collectively covering roughly 200 years. What's key for you in making sure that it feels like this epic multigenerational story, where each book and each time period are different, but resonate and connect? And it's not just a different iteration of what we've already seen?

**Lemire:** First, I am creating all this stuff myself, there are not fifty titles a month and fifty different creative teams that you need to wrangle and get to work together. So, it is a lot easier for me to keep a consistent feeling and energy. And the second factor is that I am not having to reconcile fifty or eighty years of history with new contemporary ideas and stories. I can pick or choose what I show and the history I reveal retroactively.

But it really comes down to only telling a story if I *really* fall in love with it and really want to tell it. It has to add or offer something new. I am not just pumping out new books for the sake of expansion, or to fill any quota. If I want to do one new series a year or six, it's all up to me and I get to be very selective.

**Dueben:** I keep thinking about that initial idea you talked about for *Black Hammer*—that it's about a farm and a small town and this found family (accidental family?) and their dynamics. I feel like that is so key to how you think about and build story, starting from that regardless of the genre or anything else.

**Lemire:** I really feel the story has to have a heart and an emotional core. If it doesn't, I lose interest and it feels shallow. It all starts there for me, with emotion, and those are the kinds of ideas that stick and that I end up doing. I have had ideas for *Black Hammer* stories or characters that were fun or felt "cool" to me, but just had no heart or no core emotional spark that I could hook into, so I dropped them. Going back to your previous question, each new *Black Hammer* series needs an emotional core that I can then take superhero tropes and use them as metaphor to explore.

**Dueben:** One consistent member of the team throughout all the spinoffs has been colorist Dave Stewart. He is brilliant, as we've seen for years, but what role has he played in helping to define the world and help set the tone and approach for each book and all the artists?

**Lemire:** It is hard to overstate Dave's contribution. He is brilliant and he has created a consistency across all the various books that help them feel cohesive and part of the same world. Dave is a vital ingredient in what makes *Black Hammer* work.

**Dueben:** Since I have you, I do want to ask about the new completely unrelated book you have coming out from Dark Horse with Mike Deodato, *Berserker Unbound*. This starts out as a barbarian/sword-and-sorcery comic— which Deodato draws beautifully—and then there's a twist. What interested you in writing a sword-and-sorcery character, and what are you trying to do with the story and the setting?

**Lemire:** First, I had never done a sword-and-sorcery book. I like trying new things. Second, and most importantly, this is what Mike really wanted to draw so I took it as a challenge to do a barbarian book that has a lot of heart and a really strong human story at its core.

**Dueben:** Do you see a difference in your mind between the work that you write and draw yourself, and the work that you write for other artists? For you, what is it that connects *Lost Dogs* and *Essex County* and *The Nobody* and *Roughneck* and *Underwater Welder* and *Royal City*?

**Lemire:** Generally, the stuff I write for others, I develop with that artist I mind. So, I developed *Descender* specifically for Dustin; likewise, *Gideon Falls* for Andrea. My imagination tends to go in other directions that it may not if I was drawing something myself because I am thinking of things that they (Dustin, Andrea, Dean, etc. ) would excel at. Likewise, when I develop something I am going to draw, I know that I am going to draw it as I am fishing for new ideas. So, I tend to develop a certain type of story that suits my strengths as an artist and the things I like to draw.

Now, there are certain themes and ideas that I am just naturally drawn to as a storyteller, so a lot of things pop up in all my work, the stuff I am drawing and the stuff others are. There are certain reoccurring things in all my stuff. But the stuff I draw myself usually tends to be less genre-specific, a little more grounded in the "real" world. Though there are exceptions to that, like *Sweet Tooth* and *Trillium*, so who knows.

Originally, I planned on drawing *Black Hammer*. Which may be why it feels a bit closer to some of the stuff I have drawn myself. It's hard for me to analyze my own stuff though. I feel like all the stuff I do now is very personal even if I am not drawing it. A big part of that is that I mainly do creator-owned stuff now. And when I do work-for-hire, I have to feel really connected to it and know I can put myself into it. There have been more than a few work-for-hire things that I have walked away from over the last few years because I knew I couldn't put enough of myself into them.

**Dueben:** *Black Hammer: Age of Doom* #12 comes out in July, which ends this volume, and I think it's pretty clear for readers that things will change afterwards and that this is the end of something. People who are reading the trades, know that something big is coming. Just as things changed when the first *Black Hammer* series ended.

**Lemire:** The world of *Black Hammer* has grown into something much bigger than I could ever have dreamed. It is now a world full of potential and new stories. It is with that in mind that the "farm story"—what many consider to be the core story—will end with *Black Hammer: Age of Doom* #12. This is the ending I always intended for these heroes, and this story, and I am incredibly grateful to all the retailers and readers who have supported *Black Hammer* and allowed Dean Ormston, Dave Stewart, Todd Klein, and I to tell the story we wanted to tell on our own terms, exactly how we wanted to tell it.

But that is not the end of *Black Hammer*. It is simply the end of what we can consider "Chapter One."

In the coming months, we will announce a number of new *Black Hammer* comics, some featuring familiar characters we've come to love, and others starring brand new heroes. Dean Ormston and I are already hard at work on our follow-up to *Age of Doom*—on "Chapter Two"—featuring Lucy Weber as the all-new Black Hammer! And we're excited to share where the world goes next with all of you.

**Dueben:** I don't want you to spoil anything, but could you talk a little in broad strokes about what comes next in this universe. More *Quantum Age* and stories about the century that separates them? More spinoffs like *Cthu-Louise* and *Doctor Star* that are more tangential? Do you want to let other people play in this sandbox, like Ray Fawkes and Matt Kindt have been doing with *Black Hammer '45*? Do you want to draw some of them? What are you thinking about right now?

**Lemire:** I am open to any and all things. I currently have five new *Black Hammer* series in the works and they are all very different from one another and from what has already been published. I will continue to write most of this stuff, and will only allow other writers in for very specific reasons. Matt and Ray came in because they are two of my best friends, and I knew it would be fun to do a *Black Hammer* story with them.

I have one other series that I knew was not my story to tell. It speaks of a perspective that is not mine, and I wanted a writer who could bring an authentic voice and life experiences to it. I have been mentoring a brilliant young writer named Tate Brombal. He helped me with the *Black Hammer Encyclopedia*, and we became friends while working on the *Essex County* TV show. Tate had a story he wanted to tell that used a certain *Black Hammer* character to speak to his experiences as a gay man. I think it will really be something special, and I am proud to have created a universe where this new, up-and-coming writer could tell a story that was deeply personal to him. So, if other opportunities like this present themselves, I am very open to that as well.

Honestly, there is no master plan. I am so busy now that I have to fall in love with the story and really want to do it. So, it really is just taking each new piece as it comes to me and continuing to have fun, work with great artists, and tell stories that I am passionate about and I truly enjoy telling.

# Jeff Lemire & Michael Walsh on
*Black Hammer/Justice League*

## COLLIER JENNINGS / 2019

*But Why Tho?*, July 24, 2019. Reprinted by permission.

Comic book crossovers tend to follow a standard formula: a cataclysmic event or an alliance between villains draws two characters from different universes together, they fight for a bit, then put aside their differences and join forces to save the world. *Black Hammer/Justice League,* a joint effort between DC Comics and Dark Horse Comics, is looking to subvert those tropes. I spoke to writer Jeff Lemire and artist Michael Walsh about how the story came to be and the joy of making crossovers.

**Collier Jennings:** How exactly did this project come about?

**Jeff Lemire:** I've been doing the *Black Hammer* books at Dark Horse for about three years and kind of built out a universe of my own. And I guess at some point Dark Horse and DC were discussing potential crossover properties they could do. I think this one came up as a pretty natural fit of taking the *Black Hammer* characters and mixing them up with all the DC characters that I loved growing up. And as soon as I heard about it, I obviously embraced the idea because it was a lot of fun and hopefully it'll bring a lot of readers to *Black Hammer.* And I got the chance to work with Michael [Walsh] which is great. It was just good fortune and good timing.

**Michael Walsh:** I was approached after the project was already underway. They were looking for an artist to draw this book, and Jeff had already written a few scripts, and they asked me if I would be interested and I came on board. Ever since it's just been a dream job!

**Jennings:** Comic book crossovers have certain tropes they adhere to: heroes meet, misunderstanding, they punch the crap out of each other, then punch the crap out of the villains. How does *Black Hammer/Justice League* differ from other crossovers?

**Lemire:** We kind of inverted it so that the heroes don't actually meet for a while. They switch places instead and get caught in each other's universes. They don't actually encounter each other until the very end of the story and I won't say what happens there. We kind of took that trope and basically put it upside down.

**Jennings:** [Addressed to Walsh] Do you have a favorite character you like to draw?

**Walsh:** Probably Colonel Weird. [He] is the one I'm having the most fun with from the *Black Hammer* universe. He's a blast to draw, and I get to do a lot of weird particle effects on him and draw him upside down most of the time.

**Jennings:** [Addressed to Lemire] You're no stranger to the DC Universe: you wrote *Green Arrow* for a while. What was it like writing characters such as Superman, Batman, and Wonder Woman?

**Lemire:** It's cool! I did a lot of writing over at DC for four or five years, but the most significant work I did there was on the secondary and third-tier characters, which I excel at. To be honest, I prefer those when I'm doing longer runs because you get more freedom with the characters. I never really had the chance to do the big guns, the big iconic characters, so this is a fun way to scratch that itch but also to do something kind of unique and to mix them up with my own creations. It was fun to write some Batman scenes and some Superman scenes because I hadn't done much of that yet.

**Jennings:** If you could both describe this series in one word, what would it be?

**Lemire:** I'd say fun; I think any superhero crossover has to be fun to read. If I'm not having fun writing it and Michael's not having fun drawing it, it's not going to be fun to read. So I just tried to give him stuff that was super-fun to draw and that I enjoyed writing, and I tried to embrace everything that's fun about these big crossovers and the tropes of them. Just embrace it and have as much fun with it as you can, but also put kind of a twist of it so it's not the same thing you read in the past and that there's something special and unique about it as well.

**Walsh:** I probably would have said the same word! I guess I'll just say "exciting." There's a lot of exciting action, there's a lot of exciting character moments, there's a lot of exciting interactions between characters you would never expect to meet.

**Jennings:** What would you say to a new reader to convince them to pick up this series?

**Lemire:** I think if you haven't read any *Black Hammer* books, this is a great introduction. You don't need to have read the previous books to kind of understand what's going on. It's a good intro to that universe. If you're already familiar with the DC characters, I think this is a way to see them in a completely new light—we put them in a situation that is really unfamiliar to them and to the readers and you see them react to that and it brings us something new with them.

**Walsh:** Yeah, I think fish-out-of-water stories are always interesting because they tell you something about the characters that you may not have seen before or may not have known before or an aspect of their personality that hasn't been depicted. It's cool to see these characters that you know and love in unfamiliar territory.

# Jeff Lemire Talks *Family Tree* and Living "Beyond the Dream"

MATT O'KEEFE / 2019

*The Beat*, September 17, 2019. Reprinted by permission.

Jeff Lemire has long been one of my favorite cartoonists, and he's one of the few fast enough and talented enough to balance writing and drawing his own comics while also writing series for other artists. Lemire excels at working with artists of all different styles, but I was especially excited to see him work with Phil Hester. They both illustrate rougher, gritty worlds, and I was interested in how they'd pair together. Turns out, they pair extremely well! After reading the first issue, I was thrilled to interview Jeff Lemire about his series, where Nature seems to take Earth back from the humans.

**Matt O'Keefe:** What made Phil Hester someone you were excited to make comics with?

**Jeff Lemire:** I have been a big fan of Phil's for a while. I read his run on *Swamp Thing* with Morrison and Millar back in the day, and from that point on, I was a fan. More recently, it was his work on *Shipwreck* with Warren Ellis that really hit me. It was so bold and evocative, and I had been working in the ideas for *Family Tree* when that book launched, so I really started to think about Phil's art a lot when I was writing.

**O'Keefe:** Did partnering with Phil affect the plans you already had for the series?

**Lemire:** I knew Phil was the artist as I started on the scripts, so I was writing with him in mind. The character of Judd especially was a "Phil Hester" character in my mind. I saw one of Phil's faces when I was writing Judd for sure.

**O'Keefe:** Phil's art shares some sensibilities with yours, having a similar roughness to it. How does writing a comic for someone with a similar art style compare to writing for an artist with a very different style?

**Lemire:** It's interesting that you say that. Honestly, I don't see the similarities. Phil's work is all about shadow and shape. My art is all about thin line work with rough blacks spotted on it. It's quite different to me. I guess there is a similarity in that we both have a very distinct style. At any rate, these things are subjective, so if you see a similarity between Phil and I, I will take it; that's good company.

I can't say that writing for different artists really changes the way I script or write the issues, no more than an artist would change their style when drawing for a different writer. The subject matter I choose to write about, or the overall story and idea is definitely shaped by who I am working with though. So that's more in choosing the right collaborators for the project. Once we get rolling, I write the way I write.

**O'Keefe:** You hired Will Dennis as the editor of *Family Tree*. What does he bring to the project?

**Lemire:** Will has been working on all my Image projects with me for the last couple of years. It got to the point that I had three or four Image books going and I just couldn't keep up with everything, and still have the time I need to write the actual books.

I met Will back when I was working at DC and Vertigo, of course. He was a staple at Vertigo when I was doing *Sweet Tooth*, and we hit it off right away, even though he never directly edited any of my projects back then.

I love Will; he's a great guy and a great editor. He's really smart, and he and I have very similar tastes in story, art, and comics. He knows when to step in, and when I need help with something, and when to back off and let the creators create.

He was also instrumental in helping to assemble the rest of the creative team around Phil and I, and in the design and look of the book as well. Will and letterer Steve Wands are the anchors for sure.

**O'Keefe:** Do you pace horror comics differently from stories set in other genres?

**Lemire:** Not really. The trick with working in any genre is not to treat it like that genre. If you do, you just fall into tropes and patterns and the familiar. And horror, in particular, needs to feel unfamiliar and uncomfortable if it is really going to resonate. I generally approach all of my genre books the same way, as emotionally driven character pieces. And any genre element, whether its horror, or superheroes, or whatever, needs to service that, not the other way around.

**O'Keefe:** Similar to *Animal Man*, this is a horror story centered around family. What appeals to you about that dynamic?

**Lemire:** Almost everything I do is centered around a family. It's just a dynamic I am really drawn to. The things that can tear a family apart, and the bonds that keep people together despite extraordinary circumstances. The parent/child dynamic is also very appealing to me as a father myself. I try not to overthink why I keep going back to particular subjects and themes, I don't want to ruin it by analyzing it. I think any artist is drawn to the same ideas, imagery, and themes.

**O'Keefe:** As of the first issue, the narrator can still be any member of the Hayes family. What made you decide to leave the narrator's identity ambiguous?

**Lemire:** Mystery is a great way to drive a story. In this case, that narration really tied the book together and it will start to really tease and hint at things to come in the book in a fun way. But, it being a mystery, I can't say much more.

**O'Keefe:** You've worked for a number of different publishers, but now mostly make comics for Image and Dark Horse. What makes them good homes for your work?

**Lemire:** Freedom. Freedom to create and be myself. It really comes down to that. Both publishers are very supportive of my projects, and there is a comfort level now as well, after five years of working with each.

**O'Keefe:** When deciding on a publisher, what makes some projects appealing to create at Dark Horse and others at Image?

**Lemire:** That really comes down to history. I had originally pitched *Black Hammer* to Diana Schutz at Dark Horse back in 2008, when I was thinking of doing it myself as my follow up to *Essex County*. Dark Horse loved it and wanted to do it, but I also got *Sweet Tooth* greenlit at that time. I decided to draw *Sweet Tooth* at Vertigo, but years later, when it came time to get some creator-owned books rolling, I felt that it was only right to take *Black Hammer* to Dark Horse, since they were so supportive back in 2008 when I was a relative nobody in the comics world.

So, I decided to do the *Black Hammer* stuff at Dark Horse, and all my other creator-owned projects at Image. The exception was the recent *Berserker Unbound* project at Dark Horse, but that was a very specific project that Mike Deodato and I felt fit really nicely at Dark Horse.

Moving forward, for the foreseeable future anyway, I see all my creator-owned books being through Image and the *Black Hammer* stuff at Dark Horse. It's a nice balance that is working well.

**O'Keefe:** You've stepped away from Big Two comics, except for your work on *The Terrifics*. What makes that title worth continuing to write?

**Lemire:** I am actually not writing that one anymore. The great Gene Luen Yang has been writing *The Terrifics* for a while now. I do have a few DC books in the hopper, the two Black Label books, *The Question: The Deaths of Vic Sage*, with Denys Cowan and Bill Seinkiewicz, and *The Joker: Killer Smile*, with Andrea Sorrentino. I am also continuing to work on *The Inferior Five* with one of my comics heroes, Keith Giffen.

But the two Black Label books are fully written at this point and off my plate, so aside from *Inferior Five*, I am finished with work-for-hire for the foreseeable future. Right now my creator-owned books; *Ascender*, *Gideon Falls*, *Family Tree*, and *Black Hammer* are keeping me more than busy. I am also drawing a new graphic novel for 2021, probably for Image, and showrunning and writing the *Essex County* TV show, which will start filming here in Canada in April, and the *Black Hammer* adaptation for Legendary. So, I don't see any more DC or Marvel work in my immediate future.

**O'Keefe:** You seem to be in a groove right now, releasing great comics with a devoted readership. Do you feel like you have exactly the career you want in comics, or is that an evermoving target?

**Lemire:** This is it. This is beyond the dream. All I ever wanted was to make comics on my own terms. I am finally at a point where my creator-owned stuff is successful enough that I can do the projects I want, on my own terms, and I don't need to do any Marvel or DC stuff to supplement my income. I get to wake up every day and make my own comics, in my own worlds, with a group of incredibly talented collaborators and creative partners.

Anything else at this point is just a bonus. This is exactly the career I wanted. I feel incredibly lucky, and grateful to all the retailers, readers, and librarians that make it possible.

# DC in the 80s Interviews Jeff Lemire about *Inferior 5*, Peacemaker, and His Love of *DC in the 80s*

**MARK BELKIN / 2019**

*DC in the 80s*, September 18, 2019. Reprinted by permission.

We at *DC in the 80s* absolutely love Jeff Lemire and his amazing work he's been putting out since 2007, starting with the award-winning *Essex County*, the phenomenal Vertigo series *Sweet Tooth* (which you should go read *right now*), his work on *Green Arrow, Animal Man, Trillium, The Terrifics*, and all the way to his amazing ode to comic books, *Black Hammer*.

When we read he was going to be working with Keith Giffen on an *Inferior 5* comic, with a Peacemaker back up, *we needed* to interview him. Then we learned he would be working on a *Question* series with Denys Cowan, and we died a little bit. Mark Belkin reached out to Jeff, and he agreed to give us some free time for a *DC in the 80s* interview!

**Mark Belkin:** What was the first comic book, any publisher, that made you realize you had a love for comics?

**Jeff Lemire:** The first comics I remember getting were the DC Digests from the local grocery store where I grew up in rural Ontario. They were reprints of Silver Age DC stuff; I remember lots of Curt Swan Superman, *Adventure Comics*, and I also remember the digest that reprinted the Paul Levitz/Joe Staton '70s JSA stuff, which really knocked me over because it had *so* many heroes in it and the Earth-2 heroes, which seemed so weird and mysterious because they were alternate versions of heroes I knew. They hinted at this bigger universe and history behind all these stories I'd been reading and that hooked me.

I would have been pretty young, probably five or six years old, I guess. And I was drawing pictures from those books for as long as I can remember.

**Belkin:** What was your first DC comic that you bought or were given?

**Lemire:** Same answer as above. My grandmother used to buy me one of those digests when I went grocery shopping with her and my mom. So this must have been before I was in school.

**Belkin:** *Crisis on Infinite Earths* got me into comics. When did you read it? What are some of your memories of reading *Crisis*? Did anything stand out?

**Lemire:** That was the *big one* for me. *Crisis* and *Who's Who*. That was what put me completely over the top as a DC fanatic. Just the sheer scope of the DC Universe, all those different worlds and all those different characters. I poured over *Crisis* and *Who's Who*. I was literally obsessed with them. I read *Crisis* so many times. I even remember reading it backwards once, just to change it up.

And *Who's Who* was huge, too. Not only getting to know all the characters but all the different artists too, and getting to know their styles and who I liked and who I didn't. They were the big bang for me.

**Belkin:** How did you feel after the first time you read *Watchmen*?

**Lemire:** I probably didn't read Watchmen until I was a bit older. I was ten when *Watchmen* and *Dark Knight Returns* came out, so I was a bit young for them. But I was aware of them. And I was aware that they were "important" books that were more grown up. I probably read them when I was twelve or thirteen and they blew my mind.

But I probably didn't really appreciate them until I was in my teens and really started to see the full potential of comics and comic book storytelling.

**Belkin:** What Alan Moore issues or storylines from the *Swamp Thing* did you like the most? Did any of them mean anything to you? Did you read the title when Rick Veitch took over?

**Lemire:** I didn't get into those until I was a teenager. The first wave of Vertigo stuff hit in 1993 when I was sixteen or so. I had already been reading *Hellblazer* before it officially became Vertigo, and then I got into all of those books. They came at the perfect time in my life when I was getting a bit sick of the more mainstream superhero stuff, especially the '90s Image stuff. And when Vertigo launched it made me go back and seek out the Moore Swampys, which I knew were sort of the precursor to this stuff I was loving.

I think I got an early trade paperback of American Gothic storyline and the issues with Doctor Fate, Deadman, and Phantom Stranger were incredible. I fell in love with that run and I still consider it my favorite comic of all-time today. It has everything that I love about comics.

I actually missed the Veitch stuff, but was reading the Nancy Collins run, the initial Vertigo run. I loved those Vess covers. And I remember reading the first few Morrison/Millar/Hester issues, too.

**Belkin:** Was Grant Morrison's *Animal Man* a favorite? If you did read it, was Coyote Gospel something that affected you? Is Animal Man as a father something that defines his narrative?

**Lemire:** I read the Delano stuff first, which I think you can see in my own *Animal Man* stuff. The Delano/Pugh issues were still coming out when I got into *Animal Man* and I didn't have the Morrison stuff. I *loved* the Delano/Pugh stuff and it was a real joy to reread when I became the writer of *Animal Man* in 2011. And then I lobbied to get Steve Pugh on the book as my artist, too. Dream come true.

**Belkin:** Have you ever been offered Doom Patrol? Your commission of the original four was my computer background for a year, and I would love to see you do a miniseries. If Dan Didio said, "Give me a pitch," what would you tell him? Just for fun. Would you want to explore the original four, or use other elements?

**Lemire:** Doom Patrol would have been my dream gig at DC, but it was never available. But to be 100 percent honest, I think the tone of any Doom Patrol story I would have done is very close to what I ended up creating with *Black Hammer*. *Black Hammer* was my chance to do an epic about outcast superheroes. So it all worked out.

**Belkin:** It's 1985, and Len Wein asks you to do some *Who's Who* pages. What character pages do you tell him you would like to do?

**Lemire:** Ha! I wish! Boy, that is a tough one because there are *so* many characters I would love to draw. Let's see, off the top of my head: Deadman, Anti-Monitor, Swampy, Unknown Soldier, Mister Miracle, Blue Beetle.

**Belkin:** What are some of your favorite writers and artists that worked for DC in the 1980s?

**Lemire:** It all started and ended with Wolfman and Perez for me. *Crisis* and *Teen Titans* were my everything. But I also *loved* Levitz and Giffen's *Legion*. And ironically and wonderfully, my very first DC writer's summit I was positioned at the table between Giffen and Levitz! I could not believe it. I was so nervous.

I also got to meet Marv and George once and Marv told me that my work at DC was some of the only stuff he still read. That was incredible.

**Belkin:** I have a museum dedicated to commissions of Solomon Grundy, and love showing the ones drawn by David Lloyd or Michael T. Gilbert. You have some great commissions from the likes of Carmine Infantino and Tim

Truman. What is your favorite character to get commissions of, and if you could get a drawing from any four artists, living or dead, who would they be?

**Lemire:** I am lucky enough to have my dream list: Hawkman by Joe Kubert, Flash by Carmine Infantino, Earth-2 Superman by Perez and Ordway (I own a page from *Crisis* #11) and Swampy by Bissette.

**Belkin:** Did you have any good memories of Joe Staton on *Green Lantern*? I have always felt you and Joe Staton would create an interesting book together.

**Lemire:** The Staton *GL* was one of my favorite runs. I adored it. The very first commission I ever asked for from an artist was a Hal Jordan from Joe Staton at MOCCA in 2008. I would have loved to have worked with Joe. I would die to see his version of *Black Hammer* characters. Speaking of this, I think I will reach out and ask him!

A Beetle/Booster book with Staton would be pretty fun to write.

**Belkin:** Did you have any *Super Powers* figures? Did you watch *Super Friends* or *Super Powers*?

**Lemire:** I did. I still have my original ones. My son plays with them now and I watched both shows religiously. My play with the superpowers figures was really intense. I had ongoing serialized stories that I would create using my figures that spanned months. Thinking back now, this play was clearly my early versions of creating my own stories, I just didn't really think about it until now.

**Belkin:** What were some of your other favorite titles or storylines from DC in the 1980s? Is there any that you reread today? Any that have gotten you through a hard time?

**Lemire:** There are *so* many. The one's I reread again every few years are:

—Giffen's *5-Year Later Legion*
—Wolfman/Perez *Titans*, especially Terror of Trigon and Judas Contract
—Truman's *Hawkworld*
—Giffen/Demattais *JLI* [*Justice League International*]
—Alan Moore's *Swamp Thing*.
—The Great Darkness Saga

But so many others, too. Practically anything published by DC between about '84–91 is right in my wheelhouse.

**Belkin:** I'm excited for your Peacemaker backups. Your question illustrations are some of my favorite anything that I've ever seen on the internet, and I am *beyond* excited for your upcoming series. What did you think of the O'Neill/Cowan run on *Question*? Will it be an influence on your series?

**Lemire:** I love that run so damn much. When I got to write *Green Arrow*, I knew I wanted to take the book into a darker more serious direction and it was the O'Neill/Cowan *Questions* that I read and used as my template. I even got Denys to do a couple stores with me. His covers on the run are some of my all-time favorites. So now, the chance to return to *The Question* with him and Bill is unbelievable. What a dream come true!

**Belkin:** Since *Peacemaker* will be set in 1988, will we see your versions of Cadmus, Suicide Squad, and Checkmate?

**Lemire:** Yes. Literally *all* of those characters are in the first three chapters. Also Rocket Red, Captain Atom, and KGBeast!

**Belkin:** Will The Comedian be influential in your Peacemaker story?

**Lemire:** Not really. I did do one fun homage to The Comedian in a panel, but that was it. I'm more focused on DC continuity of '88 rather than *The Watchmen* versions.

**Belkin:** Will the Paul Kuppenberg "haunted by everyone in the mask" character be the crux of what you would like to do?

**Lemire:** A bit, I sort of use the setup of this character from '88 and then take it in a pretty weird and wild direction all my own. Keith was also involved in this. He actually did a Peacemaker story for *Action Comics Weekly* back in '88 that was never published and I took some of his ideas as my starting point, too. He sent me a page of original art from that story as a gift when we started working on the book.

**Belkin:** Obviously you write people hurting so amazingly well, will you be exploring his mental illness, his father's suicide, and his father's crimes?

**Lemire:** Yes, yes, and yes!

**Belkin:** Finally, if you could choose to write/draw any series in the 1980s, time-traveling and working for Dick Giordano in 1986, what would it be?

**Lemire:** Oh, wow. That is tough, too. I would probably want to do my own version of a character that wasn't really being done regularly back then. Like a nice long Deadman series or maybe Doctor Fate. But if I could write *any* DC characters, Hourman and Doctor Midnight would be pretty cool, too.

**Belkin:** Thanks again, Jeff. Once again, your work means a lot to me, and I look forward to introducing *Sweet Tooth* to my daughter someday. It gets my vote as the most heartfelt long form story I have ever read. Thanks for writing it.

**Lemire:** Thank you. This is the most fun I have ever had with an interview. Why can't they all be about DC in the '80s?

# Jeff Lemire and Phil Hester Talk *Family Tree* and Its "Pre-Apocalypse"

## L. D. NOLAN / 2019

*CBR*, October 26, 2019. Reprinted by permission.

Writer Jeff Lemire (*Animal Man, Black Hammer*) and artist Phil Hester (*Green Arrow, Shipwreck*) are two comics powerhouses. Lemire and Hester have worked for such publishers as Marvel, DC Comics, Dark Horse Comics and more, receiving a lot of praise for their work in the process. The two are now teaming up for a new ongoing horror series from Image Comics: *Family Tree*. The story of that upcoming book follows Loretta Hayes and her two children, Joshua and Meg, as the lattermost of the three starts to transform into a tree. On their quest to save Meg's life, they'll be joined by the family's eccentric—possibly insane—grandfather on a quest to Meg's life. *Family Tree* explores a lot of different themes—such as family, fear, and more—in its first issue, while also embracing body horror in its depiction of Meg slowly losing her human form, drawing comparisons to the work of David Cronenberg and Junji Ito's *Uzumaki* in the process.

*CBR* talked with Lemire and Hester over the phone about *Family Tree*. In the interview, the creative team talked about some of the story choices, influences on the book, writing "preapocalyptic" fiction and much more.

**L. D. Nolan:** In the early pages of *Family Tree*, you choose to reveal that this is really just the opening salvo of this particular apocalypse. Why did you guys make the choice to reveal that this was only the beginning?

**Jeff Lemire:** I thought it was a great way to tease the larger stakes of the story and give it an epic, almost mythic feel as a backdrop to what is a very specific story about one family. To show that, while the story will focus on this one family, it has greater implications to the world at large. Also, the apocalypse teased in the opening may or may not come to pass, that will be part of the mystery moving forward.

**Nolan:** You've chosen to set the beginning of the end of the world on a very particular date: March 14, 1997. Why that date?

**Lemire:** The onset of technology, specifically cell phones, would make certain details and aspects of the story that I want to tell very difficult. I know that's not a very specific answer, but I don't want to spoil what's coming. In general, I find that cell phones and the internet don't fit well into a lot of my stories. I'm not sure why that is, maybe I like how much more disconnected characters can feel without them.

**Nolan:** *Family Tree* is billed as an ongoing series. Do you guys have any definitive end in mind or length you see the series running?

**Lemire:** I do have an ending in mind, but the journey to get there may stretch or change as we go. As with all things we need to see how people respond to the book, and if the audience is there, we would love to tell a big sprawling story for sure. But I always need to know my end point, and *Family Tree* is no different. It is going in a very specific direction and the greater mythology and mystery has been all worked out in advance.

**Nolan:** Phil, on Twitter the other day you said there would be no variants for *Family Tree* and "everyone gets the same damn comic." Can I get you guys to talk a bit more about your opinions on variant covers?

**Lemire:** I don't mind them, personally. I love seeing other artists interpret our characters. But for *Family Tree* we really wanted to focus on Phil and his vision for this book and make it a very singular thing.

**Phil Hester:** Well, I was just having a little fun. I certainly don't have any negative feelings about variant covers. We used them on my last Image book, *Mythic*. They were a lot of fun and goosed sales a bit. They can be a useful tool. That said, I know a lot of retailers are weary of chasing order thresholds to get rare variants. I was expressing a little solidarity with their fatigue.

**Nolan:** What books and media did you look to for inspiration and reference when you were creating *Family Tree*? Junji Ito's *Uzumaki* and the works of Cronenberg have been mentioned in relation to the book.

**Lemire:** Funnily enough, I have never read any *Uzumaki*, and I have only really watched Cronenberg's later period films where he had stopped doing so much horror. But I can certainly see why these would be referenced here. Honestly, Alan Moore's *Swamp Thing* was the biggest inspiration as was my own time writing *Animal Man*. I really loved writing the mix of horror and family dynamic in that story and missed it, so I started building my own story where I could explore that a bit more.

**Hester:** I certainly like those creators, but wouldn't consider them a direct influence on what I'm trying to do with *Family Tree*. Throughout my career, I've straddled the two worlds of indie books and superhero comics, favoring the dark and angular side of my style for those edgier projects and the cleaner, streamlined look for mainstream gigs. *FT* definitely falls into that darker side of things, so I naturally lean toward my grittier drawing influences like José Muñoz, Jorge Zaffino, Alberto Breccia, even Jeff Lemire! The storytelling decisions themselves are still 100 percent Hester, for better or worse.

**Nolan:** Jeff, this isn't the first time you've worked with apocalyptic settings. You've done, for example, *Sweet Tooth*. What appeals to you about telling stories of humanity's struggles with its last days?

**Lemire:** I don't really see this one as an "apocalyptic" book. While we tease a certain type of world ending in the first issue, it may not turn out the way it first seems. There is a bigger mystery here and these visions of the end of the world are part of that.

Having said that, I always loved postapocalyptic stuff. I love the heightened stakes of these worlds and the extremes people can go to, so it is a fun setting for sure. If anything *Family Tree* is more a reflection of the uncertainty of the world we currently live in, and the fears I have as a parent trying to keep that away from my own family. So I think this is a "preapocalyptic" story not a post.

**Nolan:** Phil, you do a lot of work on horror comics. In what ways is *Family Tree* different from other books you've done?

**Hester:** I threw out my straight edge. All the themes of the book revolve around life, death, decay, rebirth, nature run amok, human frailty. Those all seemed to call for a more spontaneous line, something itchy. I want the drawings to have a life of their own, a life that seems to be growing out of control like cancer or weeds. Rendering everything with spidery lines and miasmic blacks puts me in the mind of an open grave, for good or ill. I mean, it's this yawning pit of blackness and oblivion, but it's still the earth itself, the source of new life.

I always strive for some economy in my drawing, but if I pared this book down to Toth-like cleanliness it would become sterile and cold. To get technical, I tried to make sure I was always holding my pencil near the end, far from the point. I wanted to cede a little control and bring in some—if not outright automatic mark-making—idiosyncratic, less controlled drawing decisions.

I wanted lines to almost take their own course in this book, to indicate that life itself takes its own unpredictable turns. Like nature itself, I wanted the pretty things to have some ugliness just under the surface, and the ugly things to have a kind of intractable, divine grace. That all sounds kind of

insufferable, but I've been doing this over thirty years, and am always search-
ing for some new methods to keep things fresh and engaging for me as an
artist. I hope the reader sees those aesthetic decisions the same way.

**Nolan:** Eric Gapstur and Ryan Cody are also working on this book with you
guys. What about them makes them ideal for this project?

**Hester:** I've been working with both guys for quite a while now, especially
Eric. When Ande Parks, my usual longtime inker, stepped away from everyday
inking to focus on writing, I needed a new partner. Thankfully, I'd known Eric
since he was a student and knew he had the chops to step into Ande's place. I
think Eric brings more affinity for the dead line (meaning a line without illus-
trative line weight variations or florid brushstrokes) than most other inkers
would. This book is meant to look creaky and brittle. Eric's deft enough to put
aside his own rather warm and expressive drawing style to give me back the
spindly pen lines and bottomless black spaces required by the title.

Ryan, also an ace illustrator in his own right, approaches these pages with
the full knowledge of exactly what they need to function as a whole, not merely
to replicate natural light or color. He lets the drawing do the talking. I couldn't
be happier with his muted palettes and judicious restraint in modeling. This
book has a lot of nightmarish qualities, and Ryan knows how to evoke that sensibility with diffused light and nonliteral color choices. Pretty amazing.

**Nolan:** What's the most challenging part of working on this book for both
of you?

**Lemire:** Working with Phil. He is a total diva.

But seriously, just balancing the mystery and giving the book a great mo-
mentum without revealing too much too soon. But these are fun challenges.

**Hester:** Trying to stay out of old habits. Like I said, I've been doing this for
thirty years. I have tried and true methods for almost every situation. But for
this book, I want everything to be spontaneous and fresh. That means, coun-
terintuitively, contemplating each page for a lot longer than normal before beginning the drawing. Of course, I dash through the thumbnails pretty quickly,
as usual. But in the case of *FT*, I back off before drawing and let the pages stew
for a bit. Invariably, I will find another angle or layout that's more rewarding
than my initial, "good enough" solution. We'll see if this two-stage process sur-
vives once deadlines get tighter.

Also, Jeff's scripts are a challenge in themselves. Not that they're difficult to
translate to images, but that they convey a subtlety, especially in dialogue, that I
am always struggling to match with my character's acting. There's true poetry in
Jeff's story; it's my job to turn it into a song. I'm not that confident in my voice,
but I'll be out there sweating blood on the stage, giving it everything I've got.

# Jeff Lemire Delves into the Psychological Horror of *Killer Smile*

SAM STONE / 2019

*CBR*, October 30, 2019. Reprinted by permission.

DC has steadily increased its library of more mature, creatively unrestrained titles since the debut last year of DC Black Label. Now, acclaimed creator Jeff Lemire is launching two miniseries through the imprint, beginning today with *Joker: Killer Smile*. Reuniting Lemire with longtime collaborator Andrea Sorrentino, the three-issue miniseries delves deep into psychological horror as the Joker's latest psychiatrist in Arkham Asylum begins losing his sanity in a mental game of cat-and-mouse with the Clown Prince of Crime.

In an interview with *CBR*, Lemire discussed the timeless appeal of Batman's archnemesis, his ongoing partnership with Sorrentino, and building a grittier, more horror-tinged vision of Gotham City.

**Sam Stone:** Jeff, the Joker is perhaps at his apex of visibility today thanks to the successful solo film. What do you think makes him such a captivating, charismatic villain, both creatively and as a fan?

**Jeff Lemire:** Well, I think visually he is an incredible looking character. So iconic. He mixes the familiar (clown) with the horrific. And psychologically, he represents what we could all become if we crossed a line, and that is scary as well. Like Batman, he is not a superpowered, or supernatural threat. He is real. He is human. I think all of these things add up.

**Stone:** With that said, what did you and Andrea want to add or change as you both established your own approach to the character?

**Lemire:** I think we wanted to present a very grounded and very realistic version of both Gotham and the Joker. This will not be the heightened, gothic architecture that we sometimes see in Gotham. It will be a very spartan, very realistic looking city. And the Joker's design reflects this as well. He looks like a real man.

We also wanted to play around with the idea of the suburbs of Gotham. The people who live just outside of the city and commute in every day. I haven't seen a lot of that in the past. And in this case, it's a man who spends his days in Arkham, interacting with madness incarnate and then goes home to the suburbs and his family and tries to leave that behind.

**Stone:** You've worked with Andrea steadily since your *Green Arrow* run; what makes him such a natural collaborative partner and what made him right for this story?

**Lemire:** We just captured lightning in a bottle when we started working together. There was just this natural chemistry between us that showed up on the pages. I think we both like to experiment, and we push and allow the other to do that fully. That brings out the best in both of us.

Andrea's style leans towards the darker aspects of the human condition, so seeing him draw Joker and Gotham was a natural fit. It was his idea to pursue this project, he initiated it.

**Stone:** Describe Ben, the protagonist of the miniseries and our POV character into the Joker's twisted mind games.

**Lemire:** Ben is very smart and very confident. He thinks he can succeed where everyone else has failed with the Joker, and his hubris is his greatest weakness. And the second you expose a weakness to Joker, you've already lost.

This is very much a story about an inner battle for Ben's soul. On one side you have Joker, on the other his family.

**Stone:** Ben is a family man and a father. Much of your previous work (*Underwater Welder, Animal Man, Sweet Tooth*) involves the dynamic between fathers and sons. What makes that emotional angle continually intriguing to you as a storyteller?

**Lemire:** I try not to dwell too much on that, because we are getting into personal territory and I want to let the work speak for itself. For whatever reason these dynamics have always pulled me, and in this case, I think having a son of my own really influenced the book. The idea of the Joker's madness infiltrating a family was terrifying to me.

**Stone:** This is the first of two DC Black Label miniseries you've been writing. How has the experience been, especially in comparison to your previous work in the main DC Universe?

**Lemire:** It's been wonderful. We've had almost complete creative freedom and support. I've worked with both [editors] Chris Conroy and Mark Doyle in the past, and they have always been great to work for. The extended length of the Black Label books really allows for me to dive in deep and not be so restricted by the twenty-two-page format, which is very nice.

**Stone:** What can readers expect across *Joker: Killer Smile* and the descent into madness you and Andrea have in store for them?

**Lemire:** I will say that the end of this story will not be what people are expecting. This is a very different Joker story than what has been done in recent comics or films. I think where this goes, and what comes next will be genuinely surprising.

# ADDITIONAL RESOURCES

## INTERVIEWS

Alamah, Nadia. "Jeff Lemire Talks New *Black Hammer* Spinoff, *Sherlock Frankenstein and the Legion of Evil*." *Comicsverse*, August 1, 2017.

Boruta, Martin. "An Interview with *Black Hammer* Creator, Jeff Lemire." *First Comics News*, February 6, 2017.

The Dean. "AICN Comics Q&@: The Dean Interviews *Animal Man*, *Justice League Dark*, *Sweet Tooth*, *Lost Dogs* Writer Jeff Lemire." *Ain't It Cool News*, February 21, 2012.

Delhauer, Matt. "Jeff Lemire Talks Descender & Shares Exclusive Spotify Playlist." *Nerdist*, March 4, 2015.

Friend, David. "Jeff Lemire on Intersections of *Roughneck*, Work with Gord Downie on *Secret Path*." *InfoNews*, April 27, 2017.

"Jeff Lemire Breaks Down *Royal City*." *Image Comics*, February 2, 2017.

Johnson, Ross. "Jeff Lemire Talks His Diverse, Genre-Defying New Books: *Descender*, *Royal City*, and *A.D.: After Death*." *The B&N Sci-Fi and Fantasy Blog*, June 14, 2017.

Kistler, Alan. "Jeff Lemire on *Justice League United* and Its New Cree Superhero, Equinox." *The Mary Sue*, April 3, 2014.

Manning, Shaun. "Lemire on *Essex County* & New Vertigo Work." *Comic Book Resources*, July 7, 2009.

Matz, Kyle. "'My Love Letter to Frank Miller': Jeff Lemire and Tonči Zonjić Discuss *Skulldigger and Skeleton Boy*." *Adventures in Poor Taste*, November 26, 2019.

McConnell, Robin. "Jeff Lemire." *Inkstuds Radio*, September 10, 2009.

McGillis, Ian. "From Essex County to Rangoon: Jeff Lemire and Guy Delisle." *Montreal Gazette*, December 12, 2009.

McMillan, Graeme. "Writer Jeff Lemire on Moving from Image Comics' *Descender* to *Ascender*." *Hollywood Reporter*, July 25, 2018.

McVay, David. "Behind the Panels One-Shot—The Jeff Lemire Interview." *Behind the Panels*, February 6, 2013.

Monje, Pedro. "Interview with Jeff Lemire Talking about *Descender*." *Zona Negativa*, February 19, 2016.

Neilson-Adams, Craig. "Jeff Lemire Talks *Black Hammer*." *Big Comic Page*, June 27, 2016.

"The New 52 Interviews: Animal Man." Miguel Perez. *IGN*, September 9, 2011.

Optimus Douche. "AICN Comics Q&@: Optimus Douche Chats with Sweet Tooth's Jeff Lemire." *Ain't It Cool News*, July 1, 2010.

O'Shea, Tim. "Talking Comics with Tim: Jeff Lemire." *Comic Book Resources*, July 19, 2010.

Riseman, Abraham. "Jeff Lemire Is the Hardest-Working Man in Comics." *Vulture*, December 22, 2017.

Santori, Matt. "Jeff Lemire Gets Inside Green Arrow and the Outsiders." *Comicosity*, June 18, 2013.

Seitz, Dan. "*Descender* Writer Jeff Lemire Talks Science Fiction and Robot Wars." *Uproxx*, September 9, 2015.

Weil, Stephen. "Exploring *Trillium*: An Interview with Jeff Lemire." *Tor.com*, August 7, 2013.

Wilson, Matt D. "Jeff Lemire Aims for a More Relatable Ollie in *Green Arrow*." *Comics Alliance*, January 9, 2013.

Wilson, Matt D. "The Last Love Story Ever Told: Jeff Lemire on *Trillium*." *MTV Geek*, August 7, 2013.

Young, Shaun. "Of Sweet Tooths and Superboys: Chatting with Jeff Lemire." *Comic Book Daily*, May 18, 2010.

# INDEX

# ABOUT THE EDITOR

Credit: Gene Kannenberg, Jr.

**Dale Jacobs** is the author of *Graphic Encounters: Comics and the Sponsorship of Multimodal Literacy* (Bloomsbury Academic, 2013) and, with Heidi LM Jacobs, *100 Miles of Baseball: 50 Games, One Summer* (Biblioasis, 2021). His essays on comics have appeared in *English Journal, College Composition and Communication, Biography, ImageText, Journal of Comics and Culture, Canadian Review of Comparative Literature, Studies in Comics,* and *Journal of Teaching Writing.* With Jay Dolmage, he has published chapters on comics and disability in *The Future of Text and Image: Collected Essays on Literary and Visual Conjunctures* and *Disability in Comic Books and Graphic Narratives.* He is the editor of *The Myles Horton Reader* (University of Tennessee Press, 2003) and the coeditor (with Laura Micciche) of *A Way to Move: Rhetorics of Emotion and Composition Studies* (Boynton Cook/Heinemann, 2003). His academic/creative nonfiction book, *The 1976 Project: On Comics and Grief,* is forthcoming from Wilfred Laurier University Press.

CPSIA information can be obtained
at www.ICGtesting.com
Printed in the USA
BVHW081706220322
631905BV00001B/2